What We Can
and Can't Afford

ALSO BY W.D. EHRHART
AND FROM McFARLAND

*Passing Time: Memoir of a Vietnam Veteran
Against the War,* rev. ed. (2023)

Busted: A Vietnam Veteran in Nixon's America (2021)

Thank You for Your Service: Collected Poems (2019)

*Dead on a High Hill: Essays on War, Literature
and Living, 2002–2012* (2012)

*In the Shadow of Vietnam:
Essays, 1977–1991* (2011 [1991])

*The Madness of It All: Essays on War, Literature
and American Life* (2002)

*Passing Time: Memoir of a Vietnam Veteran
Against the War* (1989)

Vietnam–Perkasie: A Combat Marine Memoir (1983)

AND ABOUT W.D. EHRHART AND FROM McFARLAND

The Last Time I Dreamed About the War,
Jean-Jacques Malo, editor (2014)

W.D. Ehrhart in Conversation, Jean-Jacques Malo, editor (2017)

What We Can and Can't Afford

Essays on Vietnam, Patriotism and American Life

W.D. EHRHART

McFarland & Company, Inc., Publishers
Jefferson, North Carolina

ISBN (print) 978-1-4766-9220-3
ISBN (ebook) 978-1-4766-4989-4

LIBRARY OF CONGRESS AND BRITISH LIBRARY
CATALOGUING DATA ARE AVAILABLE

Library of Congress Control Number 2023009299

© 2023 W.D. Ehrhart. All rights reserved

No part of this book may be reproduced or transmitted in any form or by any means, electronic or mechanical, including photocopying or recording, or by any information storage and retrieval system, without permission in writing from the publisher.

Front cover image: *left to right* Mike Gillen, U.S. Merchant Marine; Frank Corcoran, U.S. Marine Corps; Bill Ehrhart, U.S. Marine Corps; John Grant, U.S. Army—all are members of Philadelphia Area Thompson Bradley Veterans for Peace Chapter 31 at the Smedley Butler Bench on the campus of Butler's alma mater, the Haverford School for Boys (photograph courtesy of Michael Gillen).

Printed in the United States of America

*McFarland & Company, Inc., Publishers
Box 611, Jefferson, North Carolina 28640
www.mcfarlandpub.com*

For the women in my life:
my mother, my wife,
and my daughter

Table of Contents

Preface   1

1. Paul Fussell: A Remembrance   3
2. "Turning Thirty/Sixty"   9
3. Thank You for Your Service   14
4. With All My Heart, Dan   16
5. What We Can and Can't Afford   18
6. What Daddy Did in the War: "Casey" Kehs Remembers World War II   20
7. The Arrogance—and Emptiness—of Power   36
8. Remarks in Honor of the Media FBI Burglars   38
9. Where the Dangers Lie   40
10. Con Thien and Dancin' Jack   43
11. Me and Veterans of Foreign Wars   48
12. The American War in Vietnam: Lessons Learned and Not Learned, University of Tokyo, June 30, 2015   50
13. When the Chickens Came Home to Roost: The Vietnam War and the 60s Generation   61
14. Samuel Johnson Was Right   69
15. Remarks at the Horsham Air Guard Station   72
16. In Memory of Horace Coleman   76
17. A True Spat-Upon Soldier Story   78
18. God, Jesus, and the Vietnam War   80
19. The Tail Wagging the Dog   84

Table of Contents

20. America's Modern Military: Who Serves and Who Doesn't	87
21. From Pennridge to Vietnam: What I Knew and Didn't Know	92
22. "A Band of Brothers": Senior Dinner Remarks	99
23. A Foolproof Solution to Gun Violence in the U.S.	102
24. *Earth Songs II:* A Review	105
25. Chiseled in Stone by God's Hand?	109
26. Veterans Day vs. Armistice Day	112
27. Bernie Sanders: Extreme Radical Socialist	113
28. Captain Crozier Deserves a Medal	116
29. Tom McGrath: A Political Poet	119
30. A Letter to My Daughter: Election 2020	122
31. Racism: As American as Apple Pie	125
32. Trump and the Military: Is Anyone Really Surprised?	128
33. Why I'm Not Voting for Donald Trump	130
34. The Democratic Party Has One Last Chance	133
35. Insurrection: Are We Really Surprised?	136
36. Is This Who We Are?	140
37. Will You Settle for Returning to Politics as Usual?	142
38. Welcome to the Shooting Gallery	146
39. "We Forced Them to Be Brutal to Us"	149
40. It's Time to Dump the Filibuster	152
41. Afghanistan: The Graveyard of Empires	155
42. Afghanistan: Vietnam Redux	158
43. Afghanistan: Who's Responsible?	161
44. Sanitizing American History	164
45. Re-thinking American History	167
46. More Fun Facts About American History	170
47. It's a Big Universe Out There	173

Table of Contents

48. Do You Believe in Unicorns?	176
49. You Want to Serve Your Country?	179
50. A New Birth of Freedom	182
51. This Is Democracy?	186
52. Who Needs Diversity, Equity, or Inclusion?	189
53. Does This Mean War?	192
54. Propaganda 101: The Art of Creative Lying	195
55. What Is a Bayonet? Or, Who Wins and Who Loses?	198
56. Going Green, Or: Poetic Justice	201
57. Smedley Darlington Butler: From Consummate Imperialist to Strident Anti-Imperialist	204
58. In Praise of 21st Century Luddism	212
59. Woe Is Me!	215
60. A Farewell to Arms?	218
61. The Way Things Are	222
62. Let's Talk About Original Intent	225
63. The New Normal	228
64. Trumpster Nation	231
65. Why I Like to Watch Bike Racing	234
Military History of W.D. Ehrhart	237
About the Author	239
Index	241

Preface

It seems that I accumulate enough essays to publish a new collection once a decade. The first came out in 1991, the second in 2002, the third in 2012, and now this one, all of them published by McFarland & Company, to whom and for whom I am more grateful than I can say.

Indeed, it was Robbie Franklin who first put me onto the idea of an essay collection. I had just made my second postwar trip to Vietnam, and he suggested I write a book about it. But I'd already written a book about my 1985 trip, *Going Back: An Ex-Marine Returns to Vietnam*, so another such book felt too much like *Son of Frankenstein* or *Star Trek II: the Wrath of Khan*.

However, I'd written four essays about that second trip, so I suggested to Robbie that I combine those four with an assortment of other essays I'd written, and he liked the idea. Thus: *In the Shadow of Vietnam: Essays 1977–1991*. This was followed by *The Madness of It All: Essays on War, Literature and American Life* and *Dead on a High Hill: Essays on War, Literature and Living, 2002–2012*. And now, this fourth collection.

My niche with McFarland has always been the Vietnam War, and to paraphrase Oscar Wilde, "the only thing worse than having a niche is not having a niche." I have long since come to accept that whatever modest reputation I have as a writer is directly connected to that war. Better that than no reputation at all.

But while my encounter with the American War in Vietnam permanently changed the course of my life, and I have been living and dealing with the consequences ever since, there really is much more to my life than that. Even in that first essay collection, I wrote about Black South African poets in the apartheid era, the Reagan Wars in Central America, and the then-burning issue of flag-burning. In the subsequent collections, along with writing connected directly or indirectly to the Vietnam War, I wrote about everything from health care, income taxes, tugboats, and drawbridges to party politics, corporate advertising, high school teaching, and wildlife conservation.

Preface

A number of the essays in volumes two and three resulted from the research I did on American poetry from the Korean War, and from which I produced a 362-page dissertation and earned a doctorate at the ripe old age of 52. When I would tell people what I was working on, not a few of them responded with something like, "Are you still stuck on that war thing?"

But working on the Korean War was like being on holiday. After so many years immersed in a war that had so personally and permanently impacted my own life, I had no connection at all to the Korean War. It was over before I turned five years old. I have only one dim memory of it, and that memory may actually postdate the war. As the saying goes, I had no skin in the game.

I will, of course, never escape my encounter with the Vietnam War, and this new collection reflects that reality. A handful of the essays deal directly with that war, and a few others touch on it indirectly. But the topics I write about here are many and varied.

If you are familiar with my previous collections, you may also notice that this collection contains many more essays than the previous three, most of which are also fairly short, the length of a newspaper opinion piece, because that's what they are.

In 2014, I became a regular contributor to Dick Price and Sharon Kyle's websites, *LA Progressive* and *Hollywood Progressive*, and shortly thereafter I also began contributing regularly to Steve Fowles' bi-weekly newspaper, *The New Hampshire Gazette*. These very gracious people and their platforms have given me the opportunity to write about a wide variety of topics and issues and have afforded me the opportunity to keep my head from exploding in the face of the increasingly ugly circumstances we are living with today in our nation and the world.

Indeed, to close off this collection just two months before the November 2022 midterm elections—which will have come and gone by the time this book is published—feels like walking out of a movie before it is over or closing a book before reading the last chapter. But I have the feeling that if I hang on for another six months, or even another six years, I will find myself in the same situation with a story that is not yet concluded.

So that's why this volume ends where and when it does. Whether or not I'll last another decade and publish Essay Collection #5 remains to be seen. I wouldn't hold my breath if I were you, but you never know.

Bill Ehrhart
Bryn Mawr, Pennsylvania
October 1, 2022

1

Paul Fussell

A Remembrance

(*Connections*, June 2012; WLA #24, 2012;
Vox Populi May 31, 2020)

Not surprisingly, virtually every publication in the English-speaking world from the *New York Times* and Britain's *The Guardian* to the *Scranton Times Tribune* and the *Kennebec Journal* took note of the death of Paul Fussell back in 2012. Beginning with the 1975 publication of his landmark study *The Great War and Modern Memory*, which earned him both the National Book Award and the National Book Critics Circle Award, he rapidly became a towering figure on the cultural landscape of modern American life.

One need only head for the computer and search for "Paul Fussell obituaries" to see the magnitude of his influence and to read about the particulars of his life from his privileged upbringing as the son of a prominent lawyer to his near-fatal wounding in Europe during World War II to his career as scholar, professor, and social critic. Most of the obituaries describe him as grouchy, curmudgeonly, caustic, or acerbic. He himself attributed his attitude to his experiences in the war, which left him permanently, in his own words, "a pissed-off infantryman."

My first encounter with Fussell—or, more accurately, with Fussell's writing—came in the fall of 1970, during my second year of college, before he had become famous. I was taking a course with the poet Daniel Hoffman in which the assigned text was Fussell's *Poetic Meter and Poetic Form*, a book which was then rapidly on its way to becoming for the writing of poetry what William Strunk and E.B. White's *The Elements of Style* became for the writing of prose. Forty-two years later, I still have that copy of *Poetic Meter and Poetic Form*, heavily underlined,

What We Can and Can't Afford

annotated, dog-eared, and always close at hand.

I don't remember when I first began to hear about *The Great War and Modern Memory*, but I kept hearing and seeing deferential references to it for years before I finally got around to reading it. Long before I had finished it, however, I found myself berating myself for not having read it sooner. Aside from the sheer brilliance of the thinking and writing Fussell demonstrates, his analysis of Robert Graves's memoir *Goodbye to All That* lifted from my shoulders a powerful burden of guilt I had been carrying regarding my own memoir of the Vietnam War. How accurate does memoir have to be? Fussell's answer: Memory is fallible, but the truth is not; tell the truth.

Paul Fussell (photo courtesy of John Grant).

Well, I may be slow, but I learn from my mistakes, so when Fussell published his 1989 study of World War II, *Wartime: Understanding and Behavior in the Second World War*, I read it immediately. Iconoclastic and irreverent, *Wartime* destroys all pretense that World War II was a good war, let alone "*the* Good War," and for his audacity and cheek, Fussell took no small amount of guff from the owners of the oxen he had gored.

For me personally, however, the book had a profound impact. It taught me that while there are significant differences between the war I fought and the war he fought, what we share is much greater than what separates us.

But that does not convey what I mean. I had grown up in the shadow of World War II, that great crusade my father's generation had so bravely fought and so decisively won, only to find myself adrift in the rice fields and moral aimlessness of the war in Vietnam, and finally

1. Paul Fussell

forever diminished by it. Worse still, the generation of the Second World War implicitly—and sometimes explicitly—told us soldiers of the Vietnam War that the My Lai Massacre, and the years of nightmares and cold sweats, and all the other baggage we brought home from Asia were only reflections of our own weaknesses of character, our own failures of will.

Now, for the first time in my life, someone of the generation Tom Brokaw would later call "the Greatest Generation" (a label Fussell, incidentally, ridiculed) was telling me, "No, kid, it's not you. It isn't your fault. This is what war is. This is what war does. What happened to you is what happened to us." It was as if a conspiracy of silence had finally been broken. *Wartime* changed my entire way of thinking about war, my entire way of looking at generational differences and at the generation that raised me and my generation. That is what I mean when I talk about the profound impact Fussell's book had on me.

Only a few times in my life has something I have read crucially and immediately changed my way of thinking about something important to me, and all but one of those times has been occasioned by Fussell (the other was a chapter in Paul Lyons's 1994 book *Class of '66*). A prime example is his essay "Thank God for the Atom Bomb," which forced me to reverse long-held beliefs I had had about the dropping of the atomic bomb on Nagasaki.

It was about this time that I first met Fussell, who was then teaching at the University of Pennsylvania, at a gathering of authors at Robin's Bookstore in Philadelphia (now Moonstone Arts Center). He subsequently read several of my memoirs and wrote me a most generous letter that launched a friendship I felt—and still feel—honored to have shared. Adding another layer of delight to the relationship, his second wife, Harriette Behringer, became a great fan of Svitanya, the women's Eastern European vocal ensemble my wife and daughter helped found, even hiring the group to sing at Paul's 80th birthday party.

Fussell was a curious combination of political and social progressiveness coupled with arch cultural conservatism. He was scathingly critical of cant, hypocrisy, greed, stupidity, and the Powers That Be (be they in academia or business or politics). As he wrote in *Doing Battle: The Making of a Skeptic*, "I came to see the similarity between *infantrymen* and *labor*, and to develop some social-justice convictions quite at odds with my upbringing." But he demanded that all things artistic pay visible homage to tradition.

A great advocate of the likes of Siegfried Sassoon and Isaac

What We Can and Can't Afford

Rosenberg from the Great War, of Lincoln Kirsten and Keith Douglas from World War II, he made no secret of his low opinion of Vietnam War poetry. "But Bill," he once told me with genuine exasperation, "You can't *scan* it!" He included only three poems from the Vietnam War in his massive *Norton Anthology of Modern War*, one of which was written by the World War II veteran Hayden Carruth.

I could live with that, however, because most of what he thought and said and wrote was so spot-on that it took your breath away. Or at least it did mine. In his books, you will find page after page of what I mean. Here are a few samples:

From *Class: A Guide through the American Status System*: "To achieve even greater ugliness, the prole will sometimes wear his cap back to front. This places the strap in full view transecting the wearer's forehead, as if pride in the one-size-fits-all gadget were motivating him to display the cap's 'technology' and his own command of it."

From *Uniforms: Why We Are What We Wear*: "Comprehensive as the re-enactors' ambitions to achieve absolute authenticity are, they neglect certain details, like the writhing of the wounded, their attempts to thrust back into their abdomens their protruding intestines, and their weeping and calling on Mother."

From *Thank God for the Atom Bomb and Other Essays*: "If around division headquarters some of the people [J. Glenn] Gray talked to felt ashamed [of the U.S. use of atomic bombs], down in the rifle companies no one did, despite Gray's assertions."

From *Wartime*: "In war it is not just the weak soldiers, or the sensitive ones, or the highly imaginative or cowardly ones, who will break down. Inevitably, all will break down if in combat long enough."

From *The Boys' Crusade: The American Infantry in Northwestern Europe, 1944–1945*: "While drawing up tables of organization and elementary guides to tactics, [higher echelons] appear to have neglected a sufficient study of actual human behavior."

From *Doing Battle*: "How could I help equating the college administration [where Fussell was teaching] with the military staff I'd been hating for years? Both seemed to me to consist of parasites, sequestered safely in offices and orderly rooms while others performed the real strenuous work in the field."

While Fussell wrote on a wide variety of subjects over his long life—ranging from Augustan humanism, Samuel Johnson, and Kingsley Amis to the 2nd Amendment, the Indianapolis 500, and travel in between-the-wars Europe—war, the irony of war, the suffering and

1. Paul Fussell

Paul Fussell and Bill Ehrhart (seated) speaking at Friends Center after a 2006 showing of *Voices in Wartime* sponsored by Veterans for Peace Philadelphia Chapter 31 (photo courtesy of John Grant).

lunacy and permanent damage of war, the unfairness of war, lay at the heart of his writing and of his being. He never outgrew the 20-year-old infantry officer lying badly wounded next to his dead platoon sergeant.

The last few times I saw Paul, he was looking very old indeed, and he walked with a visible limp that had not been there when I'd first met him. The limp was the result of his encounter with German artillery those long years ago, Harriette told me, but age had exacerbated the pain and

What We Can and Can't Afford

made him less able to ignore it. He never mentioned it himself, of course, which was no surprise, given that he had once written, "Even the coarsest conception of honor requires that when hurt, one keep it to oneself."

It had been several years since I'd heard from either of them, so it came as a surprise when I saw that he had died in Oregon, where he and Harriette had been living for the past several years. I was even a little hurt that they had not let me know they were moving. But then Dan Hoffman, the man who had first introduced me to Paul's writing and who had been a much closer friend than I had been, told me that the news of Paul's whereabouts in his last years had come as a surprise to him, too. Paul and Harriette seem to have kept the move largely to themselves and their immediate family.

I'll never know, of course, but I suspect that as Paul's health deteriorated, he chose to remove himself quietly from public life and others' sympathy, even that of his friends, living out his belief about "even the coarsest conception of honor." As with his assessment of Vietnam War poetry, I'm not sure I agree with him about what honor requires. My own experience has taught me that hiding the hurt can often do more damage than the initial hurt itself, and I wonder if he would have been so grouchy, curmudgeonly, caustic, or acerbic if he had confronted earlier in his life the hurt his war had done him.

On the other hand, if he had done so, perhaps we would not now have the wonderful, diverse, often hilarious, often profound, always provocative body of work that Fussell leaves behind. I, for one, am grateful to have known him, and even more grateful for the body of work that has so enriched my life. The world is a livelier place for his having been here, and an emptier place for his absence.

2

"Turning Thirty/Sixty"

Senior Dinner Talk
The Haverford School
June 7, 2012

Most of you know that I came of age in the sixties. Many of the members of my generation—including me—took it as an article of faith that you couldn't trust anyone over 30. We had some good reasons to believe that, too. Robert McNamara was over 30. Henry Kissinger was over 30. And Lyndon Johnson. Richard Nixon and George Wallace and Phyllis Schlafly and J. Edgar Hoover. Anita Bryant. The people who gave us the Vietnam War and racial segregation and sexism and homophobia were all over thirty.

When I was young, this did not present any sort of philosophical or existential dilemma. But eventually the years caught up with me, and the summer before I turned 30, I realized that I was in trouble. What was I going to do? I would no longer be able to trust myself. I would have to rent a safe deposit box to keep my wallet in to make sure I didn't steal it from me. I would no longer be able to believe anything I said. This was, indeed, a major life crisis.

I spent most of that summer in a quandary, turning it over and over in my head, trying to sort it all out. And while I've oversimplified the situation a bit, it really was a serious situation. Indeed, it was a kind of mystery. Thirty seemed very old. How had I gotten so old? I didn't feel old. I didn't think old. I was still just a kid. Where had the time gone? A few weeks before my 30th birthday that September, late one sleepless night, I ended up writing this poem, titled, appropriately enough, "Turning Thirty":

> It isn't that I fear
> growing older—such things as fear,
> reluctance or desire
> play no part at all

What We Can and Can't Afford

    except as light and shadow sweep a hillside
    on a Sunday afternoon,
    astonishing the eye but passing on
    at sunset with the land
    still unchanged: the same rocks,
    the same trees, tall grass gently drifting—
    merely that I do not understand
    how my age has come to me
    or what it means.

    It's almost like some small
    forest creature one might find
    outside the door some frosty autumn morning,
    tired, lame, uncomprehending,
    almost calm.
    You want to stroke its fur,
    pick it up, mend the leg and send it
    scampering away—but something
    in its eyes says, "No,
    this is how I live, and how I die."
    And so, a little sad, you let it be.
    Later when you look,
    the thing is gone.

    And just like that these
    thirty years have come and gone,
    and I do not understand at all
    why I see a man
    inside the mirror when a small
    boy still lives inside this body
    wondering
    what causes laughter, why
    nations go to war, who paints the startling
    colors of the rainbow on a gray vaulted sky,
    and when I will be old enough
    to know.

    Three decades later, you will find another poem in another book of mine that bears certain similarities to "Turning Thirty." It's called—surprise, surprise—"Turning Sixty":

    It isn't that I fear
    growing older—such things as fear,
    reluctance or desire
    play no part at all
    except as light and shadow sweep a hillside
    on a Sunday afternoon,

2. "Turning Thirty/Sixty"

astonishing the eye but passing on
at sunset with the land
still unchanged: the same rocks,
the same trees, tall grass gently drifting—
merely that I do not understand
how my age has come to me
or what it means.

It's almost like some small
forest creature one might find
outside the door some frosty autumn morning,
tired, lame, uncomprehending,
almost calm.
You want to stroke its fur,
pick it up, mend the leg and send it
scampering away—but something
in its eyes says, "No,
this is how I live, and how I die."
And so, a little sad, you let it be.
Later when you look,
the thing is gone.

And just like that these
sixty years have come and gone,
and I do not understand at all
why I see a gray-haired man
inside the mirror when a small
boy still lives inside this body
wondering
what causes laughter, why
nations go to war, who paints the startling
colors of the rainbow on a gray vaulted sky,
and when I will be old enough
to know.

"Hey, wait a minute," I can hear you thinking. "What kind of a rip-off is that, anyway? It's the same damned poem. You just changed a couple of words." And you're right, of course. It *is* the same poem. But that's not because I'm trying to pull a fast one or have finally reached a point where I can no longer come up with something new to say. It's because, though the years keep piling on, I'm still asking myself the same questions, still trying to figure out where the time went, and how I got here. When I was your age, I thought 30 was old. Now 30, for me, is more than half a lifetime ago. Now I really *am* old. And I still don't have any answers to the questions that matter most.

What We Can and Can't Afford

When you are young, the world is a confusing and complicated and mysterious place. You are confronted with all sorts of questions: Who am I? What will I become? What do I believe? How will I make my way? Which way do I go? Where do I belong? How does it all work? Why is it so difficult?

But when you are young, you imagine that at some point up ahead—when you go off to college, when you've launched a career, when you've found your life's partner, somewhere out there in the years in front of you, when you "grow up," when you become an adult—you will find the answers. It will all get easier. Life will begin to make sense.

Well, I've got some bad news for you: It doesn't and it won't. That's the point of these two poems. Or rather, this one poem that I re-read thirty years after I'd first written it and realized that not much had changed. I still feel like a kid. I still can't figure out where all those years went. I'm still struggling to find the answers, and mostly failing. It all makes no more sense to me now than it did when I was graduating from high school only a couple of years after Columbus set sail for China.

How's that for a rousing send-off as you prepare to leave the Haverford School and step off into your future? What a message for the newly minted graduates! It won't get any easier. You won't find the answers. You will be as befuddled and lost when you are old and gray as you are now. Life isn't a puzzle you can solve. It's not a riddle you can figure out. It's not a mathematical word problem. It is illogical, irrational, nonsensical, frightening, often cruel and brutish, cold and unforgiving, and almost never fair. And that's the truth.

But it is also beautiful, wondrous, awesome, joyful, loving (ask Travis about that one). It is endlessly fascinating and rewarding, and that, too, is the truth. Just because you can't find the answers doesn't mean you should stop looking for them. When you stop looking for answers, you start to grow cobwebs in your brain. When you stop looking for answers, a part of your soul dies. When you stop looking for answers, you might as well climb into your coffin and pull the lid shut because there's not much left to look forward to except the funeral. And if and when you think you've found the answers, think again because you are either delusional or dangerously arrogant, and you only need to read the great tragedians like Sophocles and Shakespeare to know how that's likely to end.

Life really is a confusing and complicated and mysterious place, and there's not much you can do about it. But the good news is that you are already equipped to handle it. You have already learned what you

2. "Turning Thirty/Sixty"

need to know: that there are people around you who love you and care about you and will be there to support you, no matter what lies ahead. Look around at the friends you've already made. Think about the parents and siblings and teachers and coaches and mentors who believe in you. And you are only beginning; as you go forward, there will be others. Many, many others. Embrace them. Lean on them. Take them along on your journey. Be there for them when they need you.

And remember that back when I believed that you couldn't trust anyone over 30, I forgot that Bayard Rustin, the gay black genius behind the 1963 March on Washington, was over 30. That Viola Liuzzo, the white housewife and mother who gave her life for black civil rights, was over 30. That John Sirica, the judge who wouldn't take no for an answer from the Watergate burglars, was over 30. That the courageous Vietnam War journalist Gloria Emerson was over 30. That Jimmy McAdoo, my college swimming coach and the most marvelous mentor a young man could ever wish for, was way over 30. Heck, I'm way over 30 now myself, and I've never once stolen my wallet from me.

So take it from me when I say that the answers don't really matter. It is only the questions that count. As I wrote a few years ago in another poem, "Question it all. Question everything." So long as you are asking questions, you are not just wasting oxygen while you wait to stiffen up; you are truly alive and open to possibility.

Thank you for asking me to speak to you tonight. I've had a great four years with you. I love you. Have a nice life and try to leave the world a better place than it was when you got here.

3

Thank You for Your Service

(*Thanh Nien News*, August 24, 2012;
VVA Milwaukee Chapter #324, February 2013)

Over the past decade or so, it's become quite the fashion, when people learn that I once served in the Marines, to say to me, "Thank you for your service." I'm sure they mean well, but I wish they would take just a moment to reflect on what they are saying.

I went halfway around the world to a place called Vietnam, where I killed, maimed, brutalized and made miserable a people who had never done me or my country any harm, nor ever would or could.

I served proud, arrogant, and ultimately ignorant politicians and statesmen who thought they could mold the world into whatever shape they believed it should have. But it was hardly service in the interest of my country or the majority of Americans, let alone in the interest of the majority of the Vietnamese, who wanted little else than for me to stop killing them and go back where I came from.

Do those well-meaning folks who thank me for my service really want to thank me for that? I surely hope not. It is not service I am proud of.

Back in the 1980s and 1990s, the stock genuflection to Vietnam War veterans was "Welcome Home." But what makes anyone think I've ever come home? Because I got out of Vietnam with all ten fingers and all ten toes? Because I vote and pay my taxes? Because I keep my shoelaces tied and don't drool? It's hard to feel at home in a country that learned so little from such a destructive and ruinous debacle.

And now I see that the Pentagon has launched a decade-long Vietnam War Commemoration to "thank and honor veterans of the Vietnam War." There's even a website that says, "A Grateful Nation Thanks and Honors You."

3. Thank You for Your Service

Hey, I could use some decent affordable healthcare, or even just a free tank of gas for my car. But what am I supposed to do with that website? Eat it? Take it to the bank? Meanwhile, consider the "service" I performed while in uniform. My nation is grateful for that?

And now "the other one percent" who fill the ranks of our so-called "volunteer" military today is carrying the entire blood burden of our latest wars, getting sent to Iraq and Afghanistan over and over again, while the rest of us go about our lives as if nothing at all out of the ordinary is going on.

What the military seems to have learned from the Vietnam War is: get rid of the draft and you get rid of domestic opposition to foreign interventions. So far, it's working.

But the cost is steadily mounting. Suicides among active-duty military and recent veterans have reached epidemic proportions. The Veterans Administration has a backlog of over 800,000 claims for medical disability. And substantial allegations have been made that the VA and the Department of Defense are falsely diagnosing veterans and soldiers with pre-existing "personality disorders" prior to their military service so that these veterans can be denied benefits for Post-Traumatic Stress Disorder, though the military was happy enough to sign them up when they first enlisted. Thank you for your service, indeed.

Frankly, I suspect that this whole Vietnam War Commemoration is less about a grateful nation thanking and honoring us Vietnam War veterans than it is about a frightened and nervous government trying to gloss over the follies and consequences of military adventurism so that the next generation of young Americans remains willing to place their trust in the hands of people who clearly believe that those they send to fight our wars are expendable (rhetoric not withstanding; actions speak louder than words).

Instead of thanking our servicemen and women for their service, perhaps we ought to be asking less service from them and more service from ourselves.

4

With All My Heart, Dan

(*Per Contra* #27, 2013)

I first encountered Dan Hoffman in the early fall of 1970 at the outset of my sophomore year at Swarthmore College. By then, Dan was teaching at Penn, but he lived in the town of Swarthmore, near the campus, and he was offering a poetry workshop that semester to Swarthmore students. I'd never heard of Daniel Hoffman, but fancying myself a poet (at least in the deepest recesses of my secret heart), I signed up, and every week an earnest group of us young writers would meet in Dan's living room to discuss our poems. (We didn't call him "Dan," of course; he was Professor Hoffman.)

About midway through the semester, I was browsing in the college bookstore one day when I came upon a book of poems called *Broken Laws* by none other than Daniel Hoffman. I was startled. Moreover, as I read through the poems, I discovered that they were good! The man who was leading my workshop was not just another college professor, but a real live, genuine published poet. Talk about ignorant. But I was young. And it really fired my ambitions to know that a real poet—the first I'd ever known—was actually taking my poetry seriously.

Well after the semester ended, I found a notice clipped from the *New York Times Book Review* soliciting poems by Vietnam War veterans for a possible anthology along with a note from Dan suggesting that I submit something. I did. A year later, *Winning Hearts and Minds: War Poems by Vietnam Veterans* was published to more critical acclaim than most poetry books ever get.

I had eight poems in the book, some of them so bad that I've never included them in any of my own books, but holding that book in my hands, seeing my name in print, knowing that people were reading what I had written—man, that was it. The hook was set. I knew what I wanted to do with my life, and that is what I have done. A lot of people have

4. With All My Heart, Dan

helped me along the way, but it was Dan Hoffman who first gave me the courage and self-confidence to believe I could really be a poet.

Over the years since, Dan has been a recurring presence in my life. He was one of only a very few people to review Jan Barry's and my anthology *Demilitarized Zones: Veterans After Vietnam* in a mainstream publication (the old *Philadelphia Evening Bulletin*). He recommended me for the creative writing program at the University of Illinois at Chicago Circle a few years later. He allowed me to reprint his poem "A Special Train" in *Carrying the Darkness: The Poetry of the Vietnam War*. And every year in my U.S. History classes, when we study the European conquest of North America, my students read sections of Dan's marvelous poem *Brotherly Love*.

My fondest memory of Dan is the night he and his daughter gave a reading together of his wife's posthumously published poetry. How painful it must have been for him to let Liz go after all their long and loving years together. How hard that evening must have been for him. But the evening was so full of grace and dignity, so powerful a testament to the uncrushable durability of love, so imbued with poetry, that I came away both awestruck and exhilarated.

Dan, for the poet you are, for the man you are, for the friend and mentor and example you have been to me over all these years, I thank you with all my heart.

5

What We Can and Can't Afford

Summary of opening remarks to the
Lancaster Interchurch Peace Witness Conference
Sunday, January 25, 2015

According to the Pennsylvania Department of Transportation, the state has 577 bridges that are structurally deficient or fracture critical. Due to lack of funds to keep up with repairs, PennDOT expects this number to increase by 100 bridges annually.

Nationally, there are 86,413 structurally deficient or fracture critical bridges.

The Association of American Medical Colleges predicts that by 2020, the shortage of doctors in the U.S. will reach 90,000, including 45,000 patient-care physicians. According to *Health Affairs*, the nation faces a shortage of 250,000 nurses by 2025.

According to the American Association of Colleges of Nursing, U.S. nursing schools turned away 79,659 qualified applicants from baccalaureate and graduate nursing programs in 2012 due to insufficient number of faculty, clinical sites, classroom space, clinical preceptors, and budget constraints.

According to the National Foundation for Trauma Care, less than 10 percent of U.S. hospitals have trauma centers.

The U.S. Department of Education received $141 billion in fiscal year 2014. In the same year, the same amount of U.S. taxpayers' money was given to the top 12 Defense Department contractors.

In 2013, the 100th Defense Department contractor, World Airways, received over $557 million. The top Defense Department contractor, Lockheed Martin, received $44.1 billion. That's *billion*, not million.

The U.S. Navy currently has 14 ballistic missile submarines at a

5. What We Can and Can't Afford

cost of $4.9 billion each, 4 guided missile subs, also at $4.9 billion each, 11 fast attack submarines at $2.6 billion each (with 5 more under construction), and 45 attack submarines at $900 million each.

The most recent of the U.S. Navy's 10 aircraft carriers, commissioned in 2009, cost $6.2 billion. The first of a new class of carriers is expected to be commissioned in 2016 at a cost of $17.5 billion.

The U.S. Army currently fields over 9,000 Abrams main battle tanks at a cost of $4.3 million each. Our current fleet of Predator drone aircraft stands at 259, costing $4.03 million each. Our newer, bigger Reaper drones, of which 104 have been built so far, cost $28 million each. Since 9/11/01, the U.S. has fired over 15,000 Hellfire missiles at a cost of $70,000 each.

A very well-equipped elementary school playground would cost about the same as a single Hellfire missile. Two more modest playgrounds could be built for one Hellfire.

Our society does not have the money to provide updated infrastructure, decent education, or adequate healthcare, but we've got plenty of money for submarines, aircraft carriers, tanks, drones, and a host of other military hardware that added up to $711 billion in 2011 alone. This is more than the total amount of military spending by the next 14 countries combined.

6

What Daddy Did in the War

"Casey" Kehs Remembers World War II

Edited & introduced by William D. Ehrhart, Ph.D.
(*Krieg und Literatur/War and Literature*, vol. XX, 2014)

In 1942, 21-year-old Walter Lamar Kehs had a good job at the U.S. Gauge factory in Sellersville, Pennsylvania, and could probably have gone through the entire Second World War in safety and comfort as a civilian. Instead, he chose to volunteer for service, became a bomber pilot, and eventually ended up assigned to the 766th Bomber Squadron, 461st Bombardment Group ("The Liberaiders"), 49th Bomber Wing, 15th U.S. Army Air Force, stationed in Italy.

His daughters remember being allowed every now and then to go up to their attic and look through the box of military paraphernalia their father had kept from the war: medals, insignia, uniforms, a flight suit, and other souvenirs. In all the long years after the war, however, their father never talked to them about his experiences.

But in the mid–1990s, one day he picked up a tape recorder and began talking. He had already been diagnosed with medullary thyroid cancer, and an operation had caused nerve damage to his vocal cords that leaves the voice on the tape gravelly and rasping. There are frequent long pauses between the short phrases as Kehs catches his breath. What follows is the transcript of his recording.*

* * *

---

* As nearly as possible, I have tried to retain Kehs' phrasing and pacing, inserting commas where he pauses for breath. I have also tried to do minimal editing only for the purposes of clarity or to eliminate repetition.

6. What Daddy Did in the War

This recording is being made to answer the question, "What did you do in the war, Daddy?" Just in case someone should ask. This will be the rambling reminiscence of some of my service experiences of fifty years ago.

To start with, in the summer of 1942, many of my friends were being drafted. And while I was working in the defense plant machine shop,* I may or may not have gotten a deferment, but another fellow and I took off one day in the fall and went to Allentown [Pennsylvania] to take the test for the aviation cadet program. I passed, he didn't. I then took my physical, passed that, and was sworn into the reserves. They told me I would get called in about three months and have approximately three weeks, two to three weeks' notice before going into active duty.

Well, on Friday, January 29 [1943], while at work, I received a phone call from my Mom telling me a letter was there from the War Department. I had her open it, and she said it said I was to report to the courthouse in Philadelphia on Saturday, January 30, 9:00 a.m., the next day! Now starts my two and three-quarter years of active duty in the U.S. Army Air Forces. This, for a 21-year-old whose only overnight visit, night trip, was my senior trip [during high school] to Washington, D.C.

My first stop was Miami Beach for basic training. From there, to North Carolina State College in Raleigh, where I took aeronautical engineering, got credit for two semesters of college in three months. From there to Montgomery, Alabama, where I was classified for pilot training.

To Ocala, Florida, for primary training, then to Bainbridge, Georgia, for additional training, and then Albany, Georgia, for advanced twin-engine training, where I graduated and got my wings and bars [2nd lieutenant].

This was followed by a fifteen-day furlough at home, my first trip home in fifteen months. From there I went to Fort Myers, Florida, for training in the B-17. This is when my Dad had a stroke. I came home on emergency furlough, went back to Fort Myers, and then was sent to Holyoke, Massachusetts, where I was assigned to a B-24 crew. A plane I had never seen, knew nothing about. The crew went to Charleston, South Carolina, for training, then from there to Mitchell Field, Long Island, where we received an over-a-million-dollar airplane. And we had

---

* U.S. Gauge in Sellersville, PA.

What We Can and Can't Afford

Standing L-R: Miller, William J. (P); Kehs, Walter L. (CP); Di Rienz, John A., Jr. (N); Tynan, Gene (B). Front Row L-R: Battelle, Richard K. (RO/G); Jones, Lowell E. (RO/G); Clark, Laverne R. (E/G); Frontera, Joseph (E/G); Radziminski, Edwin F. (G). Grosz, Otto L., Jr. (G) is missing from the above picture, as is his replacement, Richard McKnight (photo courtesy of Walter Kehs's daughters).

exactly eighteen hours of flying time [on this type of aircraft]. We had to check out the plane to see that everything was all right. And then, in about a week, we took off for Bangor, Maine, and on to Gander, Newfoundland, the Azores, Marrakech [Morocco], Tunis [Tunisia], and finally Italy.

I flew 53 combat missions plus countless training missions and several aborted missions. My war, I always said, was an 8-to-5 war. I never slept without a roof over my head. I always had a cot, a bed, sheets, or a sleeping bag. Most of the time, I had a sit-down meal. On the days my crew was scheduled to fly, rather the night before, we would know because it would be scheduled on the big board in operations, the crew numbers that were scheduled to fly. We normally would not know where we were going or how long or anything else. But we would go to bed

6. What Daddy Did in the War

early that night because the next morning we would get awake, be wakened, usually about five a.m., get dressed, have breakfast.

Usually on those days, breakfast included anything you wanted, and as much as you wanted. After breakfast, we would go to the operations center on the flight line for the briefing. There we would find out where we were going, how long a mission, what altitude to fly, what enemy opposition to expect, the weather, and all the details. The missions themselves would last six, generally six to ten hours with the average running about seven or eight. That was actual airtime. We would usually take off between 7:00 and 8:00 in the morning, drop our bombs around noontime, and be back at the base between 3:00 and 5:00.

Following return to base, we would turn in our equipment, go to a debriefing where we would tell the intelligence people everything that happened in the mission, turn in our reports on the plane's performance, and then when that was finished, we'd head back to the squadron area, where those who wanted it would be given a government-issued drink. This usually was a shot of whiskey with a chaser. Now if you had one or two fellows on the crew that did not drink alcohol, they would get theirs anyway, and give it to one of the other crewmembers. Well, when you hadn't had anything to eat for that period of time, and you got a double belt, that warmed you up. And from there, we'd go have supper, and we were through for the day.

Our missions were flown over Italy, Yugoslavia, Hungary, Czechoslovakia, Austria, and, of course, Germany. Some, a few, were rather uneventful.

1st Lieutenant Kehs in flight suit, Torretta Field, Italy, 1945 (photo courtesy of Walter Kehs's daughters).

What We Can and Can't Afford

We'd just take off, fly to the target, drop our bombs, come back, land, and that was it. Of course, there were not too many of these.

One of the first missions that I have much of a memory of, probably about the 3rd one, we were flying somewhere in northern Italy, and it was what we called a milk run—no enemy opposition—clear day, went down the target, dropped our bombs, and we rallied off the target, the entire formation to the right, but Miller, our pilot, kept going straight with the rest of the formation rallied sort of to the right. Now fortunately, we were on the extreme left side of the formation, so no one else was over that way.

I glanced over at Miller. I saw his head hanging, and it looked like he was out cold. I grabbed the controls, turned, and joined the rest of the formation. Called on the intercom for the engineer, Joe Frontera, and it turns out that Miller's oxygen supply had become unhooked, and at 24,000 feet, it takes about two minutes with a moderate exertion to become unconscious. Joe hooked him back up, and in a short while he was back flying the plane, and he never could remember anything about the incident.

Another mission, possibly about our 5th, to, I believe it's to Regensburg, Germany, we were flying to the target, and over to our left was another group of bombers. Now the group is made up of four squadrons. Each squadron contained, on a normal effort, seven planes. We were flying to the target, and we could look over there, about two miles away, at this other group being attacked by fighters, and quite a few of our bombers were shot down. We just had a bird's-eye view; the fighters didn't bother us. By the time I got over there [to Italy], the German fighter force was reduced to the point they could not attack and defend everything, so they were selective. We didn't know how they figured who to select; it was just one of those things. But it made you stop and think.

The next mission I remember was to Linz, Austria. Linz is an industrial city between Vienna and Munich, still in Austria. Many factories, oil refineries, and marshaling yards. We were going up there with a maximum effort. That means all the [serviceable] planes the group had were there. Our plane was flying in the number four position, which is directly behind the lead plane in our squadron. Our squadron was directly behind the lead squadron of the group. The fighter opposition was nil, but the anti-aircraft fire was very heavy. We said of that type, you can just about get out and walk on it. Going down to the target, from the initial point, which is the point where you start the bomb run, you usually flew straight to the target for about two minutes. About

6. What Daddy Did in the War

thirty seconds from bombs away, anti-aircraft fire began exploding rapidly, right around the plane directly in front of us, piloted by a fella from New Orleans with the name of O'Neill, an Irishman from New Orleans.

There were some bursts right around O'Neill's plane, and then there was a terrific explosion as he was hit, evidently right in the bomb bay.

There was this big ball, orange ball, of fire and, of course, in less than a second, we were in that ball of fire, too. And it sounded like rocks, and hail, everything, was bouncing off our airplane. From the concussion of the explosion, our plane went straight up in the air.

Now a B-24, if it falls over on its back, the wings have a habit of coming off. We went straight up, and somehow or another, instead of falling over to the back, we fell to the side and wound up reasonably intact, but going straight down. Our air speed indicator only went up to 325, and the needle was against the 325 mark. Miller and I both fought to get the thing under control, and we did at around 6,000 feet. Six thousand feet, and we had been at 24,000 feet. And we still had our bombs.

Thankfully, since the flight was so heavy, the turret gunners were pulled out of the turrets until we crossed the target. Our front turret was bashed in from the debris and force of the explosion. We pulled out of our dive; it was over the city at 6,000 feet. The only problem was, we were going back the way we came. You could look down and see on the ground the anti-aircraft guns shooting up at us. Not necessarily at us, but at all the bombers, and you could look up and see the bombers dropping their bombs, and we were in between. Well, we turned off and got out of there safely. Only we were on the other side of the Alps headed back by ourselves, which is not a good situation.

We headed south towards Yugoslavia, where the Alps aren't as high, because one engine was running very rough and losing oil, and we had to shut it off and feather it. We were running on three engines. In the distance, we saw another plane, and it got close enough, we checked it out. It was a B-17, also flying on three engines. Now for every flight, every day, we had a code signal where the radioman could flash it with a light-gun to another plane in a situation like that. So, without breaking regular radio silence, we could tell if he was friendly or not. So, Rick [Battelle] gave him the signal of the day, and he, someone on that plane, gave the correct response on his light to us, and then, we answered him correctly, so we closed into each other and became a two-ship formation of cripples.

What We Can and Can't Afford

And another part of our procedure was for fighter escort in emergencies. There was a special code to call fighters for emergency. And for location, all you had to do was give a reference from point A or point B or point C on the map, and so many kilometers from there, and the heading. This our radioman did. We got the proper response and a signal. I don't know if it was five minutes or what, but not long anyway, before you knew it, there were two beautiful-looking P-51s with black and yellow checkered tails coming sliding towards us.

I say sliding because anywhere in enemy territory, or what we knew as the bomb line, any airplane, fighter particularly, that pointed its nose toward you, you didn't care what type plane it was. Whether it had the stars and stripes on and was flying six American flags. If it pointed its pistons at you, you shot at him. These two slid in close to us, one on each side, and we heard, "Relax, white boys, we'll get you home." These planes were part of the first Negro fighter squadron in the Air Force [then still the U.S. Army Air Force]. They started out at Tuskegee Institute, and they were good. They stayed with us back almost to the Adriatic when we got a short message over the radio, "Sorry, we're going to have to leave you or else we'll have to walk home. Fuel is running low." But we were pretty well out of the woods by then. And we flew down the Adriatic a little further. The B-17 left us to go to its own base, then we flew into our airbase, landed, taxied into the parking area, and that was that for that day.

Incidentally, that was O'Neill's 33rd mission. At that time, thirty-five were needed to return to the States. There we were with about six missions under our belts. That gave you, gave us some food for thought. Actually, along those lines, the prevailing attitude among the flight crews was the first approximate third of your required missions, maybe a little less, you were really afraid, but you flew 'em. After that, approximately the middle third, maybe the eighth or tenth mission to the eighteenth or twentieth, you thought: well, I'll do what I can, and do my job as good as I can, and the rest is pretty near just fate, things you have no control over. After that, for the last third of your missions, you mostly thought, "Hey, I might make this after all." So, you start getting very cautious, overly cautious, which wasn't good either.

Our crew was made up of a veritable United Nations. The pilot was Bill Miller; of course, I was the co-pilot. Gene Tynan, a real shanty Irishman, was our bombardier; John Di Rienze was the navigator. Joe Frontera the engineer, who incidentally still had relatives in Italy. The radioman was Rick Battelle; nose turret gunner was Lowell Jones; top

6. What Daddy Did in the War

turret gunner Ray Clark; tail gunner Ed Radziminski, and the ball turret gunner was Otto Grosz. Grosz spelled with a Z.

Now this to tell you about Grosz. I don't even remember where the mission was to. It might have been Vienna, but first a word about the turrets in the B-24. In order to get in and out of any of the gunnery turrets, they have to be in a certain position. Nose and ball turrets, the guns have to be pointed straight ahead. The ball turret, the guns had to be pointed straight down and the ball turret retracted. They had to be in alignment or the door to them will not open. Now the gunner can maneuver his turret into position from inside the turret, or it can be hand-cranked into position from inside the plane by another crewmember.

The joker in the ointment is that for the ball turret gunner, the turret had to be retracted to a certain position before the door would even open. Once the ball turret gunner got in, he could not retract or lower the turret. In other words, he got in, and then was lowered by another crewmember. And the crewmembers could not wear a parachute inside the turret. As a matter of fact, none of us wore a parachute while we were flying a combat mission. You could not do your job with it. We all had chest chutes, and all you had to do was pick up your chute. There were two rings on a strap across your chest that you snapped; you could do it in one motion. The two snaps on the parachute would snap into the rings on a chest harness. There was a place for the ball turret gunner's chute, like a slat, right next to the turret where it was lowered, so that when, if he had to get out, it would be as handy as possible.

Now, during this particular mission, when Grosz got into his turret, he evidently did not have his chute positioned right, and from the rough air or anti-aircraft fire bouncing the plane, his chute dropped down, fell on top of the ball turret, and when he rotated the ball turret, his chute got tangled, and popped into the gear mechanism, so he could not rotate the ball.

Normally, we got the crewmembers out of their turrets for the minute or two of the bomb run, and they just stood by and got ready to get back in. Well, Grosz called on the intercom, he couldn't move his turret. This was before the bomb run. It was locked, and the waist gunners went to check, and they could not raise it either. So he was sort of stuck in there. It was a little bit of the case, except in a more serious nature, of me getting the Allentown paper jammed in my snow blower. The guys cut and tore the parachute, and finally pulled it out of the works of the ball turret, but it took about two hours. During which time we flew the

What We Can and Can't Afford

bomb run, dropped our bombs, and were headed home. And believe me, the ball turret is a place no one wants to be if it is still lowered when the plane lands. But the boys got the mechanism cleared, raised the turret to its up position, and got it rotated, and they got him out.

That took care of that, but on the next mission, which incidentally I have no idea where it was, nothing stands out except the engineer came up to me when it's time, and he said, "Grosz won't get in his turret." Well, he was sitting back there next to his turret with his chute on, and he said, "I don't give a damn what you do, I'm not gettin' in there again." Which he didn't.

The mission itself was uneventful. We came back, but we had a problem on our hands. It was resolved in this manner: there was no court-martial, no disciplinary action other than, through the flight surgeon and some other people, Grosz was declared certified unfit for aerial flight, and he was taken off our crew. He was given a clerk's job, and shortly thereafter, was transferred out of the group. I have no idea what happened to him after that.

We picked up a spare ball turret gunner by the name of McKnight, and he flew the rest of our missions. We went over there with ten people. We came back with ten, but with this exception: the tenth was a different person. No one in the crew ever got a scratch due to enemy action. The only thing I ever heard was a bump on the head when somebody didn't duck enough going through some low bridge on the plane.

I think at about this time [the arrival of McKnight], we were sent for a week to the Isle of Capri for R&R. That's rest and rehabilitation. It's a very historic and beautiful isle, and we enjoyed ourselves. Of course, how much rest we got was debatable. Between combat missions, we often flew training flights. Yes, training never ceased. We also flew other crews to and from rest camps for R&R, both down to Naples for the Isle of Capri and to Rome. This was a very desirable diversion because we would fly them down in the morning, spend the rest of the day in Naples, and in the evening return with some other personnel. The same thing would happen in Rome. Also, planes had to be flown, or retested, whenever engines were replaced or other equipment, such as new navigation aids, was installed. New crews had to be familiarized with the area.

But back to the more vivid memories, and what was probably the most vivid, and still is, was Christmas in 1944. As I said, the night before a mission, they would post the crew numbers of those crews who were flying the combat missions the next day. However, Gene Tynan,

6. What Daddy Did in the War

our bombardier (who, shall I say, was very friendly?), had his nose into a lot of things. What I'm getting at is, on Christmas Eve our crew was scheduled. Our crew number was on the board; we were flying the next morning. Gene, being our armament officer, had become acquainted with the group armament officer and other key personnel on the base. And as such, he could find out what bomb load they were loading for the next day. He also could find out what the fuel capacity was for the mission.

Now for this mission the next day, which was Christmas Day, he found out that they were installing extra capacity tanks in the bomb bays of our 24s. This meant we were going a long, long way. We wouldn't be carrying as many bombs. We also found out the bomb load because the bomb bay was partially taken up with fuel. One of the few targets which necessitated these procedures was a huge oil refinery known as Blackhammer.* This was in suburban Berlin, possibly to Berlin about as far away as Marcus Hook or Chester would be from Philadelphia.

This news upset me greatly. I don't know why, but I had a premonition that if I flew on this mission, I would not come back. I never had this feeling before, and I never felt anything like it for another fifty years. This was one time, I guess you could say, I got some religion over there. I did not want to go to Blackhammer for feeling I would not come back. I thought, wouldn't it be terrible for the folks back home to hear that on Christmas Day our plane went down? Well, the next morning, after being awakened very early, having our breakfast, going down to group headquarters for briefing, we found out our mission was scheduled for Blackhammer, Germany, just as I had thought it would. But then, being busy, things to do, I got onto it and pushed my feelings aside.

We took off for the mission with a very overloaded plane. The bad weather was very iffy. However, they told us that by the time we got across to the Adriatic and up to northern Italy, we should break into the clear; over the Adriatic, we would be above the clouds and be able to assemble in formation. We took off, because climbing through the clouds before assembly, the interval between take-offs was increased from thirty seconds to two minutes. We started up through the clouds, and in the clouds, it began to snow very hard. Climbing through this sea of white, we were supposed to break through the clouds around seven or eight thousand feet. We did, but not until around twelve thousand

---

* Blechhammer, but the American airmen called it "Blackhammer."

What We Can and Can't Afford

feet. When we looked around, above the clouds, there was not another plane in sight. So, we began heading north up the Adriatic, still climbing and on the lookout when Joe, the engineer, came up and tapped me on the shoulder, and he says, "Can you come back here? I want to show you something." I went back, and in the bomb bay, the main power cable going from the front to the back of the plane had come loose from one of the terminals. And this cable was swinging back and forth.

And at each end of the swing, the one end was the metal body of the plane, a spark would jump several inches from the end of the cable. On the other end of the swing, it would go over the front of one of the bombs, about four inches away from the fuse detonator; it would come on some of the swings within a few inches of the bomb, and the spark would jump across. Then, as altitude increased, the electrical resistance of the air decreases. So, as we were climbing, the distances this spark would jump would become greater, and we did not know what would happen if the cable swung in a little bit different arc, and came more to the front of the bombs. So, we tore an intercom cable about three feet long off the side of the plane. A loop was made, and this electrical cable was secured with the intercom cable and tied down so it could no longer swing. However, when I returned to the cockpit, Miller says, "What the hell is going on? Half of the instruments are out." We knew we could no longer continue the mission. So we turned around, headed back south.

One of the prime rules over there was, under no circumstances, were bombs to be brought back to the field. It was not a good procedure to try and land with a bomb bay full of bombs. The bomb bay doors were opened, and the bombs were dropped in the Adriatic Sea. We began the slow descent through clouds and the snow. We did not break out of the clouds until about five hundred feet above the sea, and it was snowing very hard. We flew south to about where we figured we were getting close to our area off the coast of Italy, but what we found out, we could not transmit on the radio.

There was one special radio that we could receive on. Rick [the radio operator] came up and told us all the airfields in southern Italy were closed except in the extreme southern tip. So, we headed down there. While heading down there, we decided that with some of our instruments out, we would have a devil of a time getting into a strange field, even if the weather was much better down there. So, we turned around again, and started heading north, and decided we were familiar enough with the area around our field. By flying along the coast, we found the river that led in between the hills, and we flew up this, just

6. What Daddy Did in the War

above this riverbed, for about six minutes and John [the navigator] says, "Ok, now climbing, turn to the right, and then let down, and that should take us right over our field in about three minutes." It did!

However, our field consisted of two runways, both going in the same direction parallel to each other. We crossed them at 90 degrees. We flew past, made a circle, came back, and still weren't lined up. Did it again, came back, and this time we were lined up on the runway and landed safely. We were the only plane in our squadron of seven planes that came back to its own field on Christmas Day. The rest were scattered, having landed mostly in airfields in northern Italy because of the weather. Meanwhile, we took care of what was necessary, and returned to our squadron area just in time for Christmas dinner and turkey. And while eating, it suddenly dawned on me, I didn't fly to Blackhammer that day, and I never did. We found out later that this mission had been recalled due to the inability, because of the weather, of getting a proper formation together. However, we never heard the recall message.

During January and February, the weather was lousy over Italy. I don't think we ever had a temperature lower than in the 20s. It didn't freeze that often, but we got damp weather. Wet snow, large, wet flakes, maybe several inches, and a lot of mud. Because of stand-downs, because of the weather, and the fact that new crews were arriving daily between the months of January and February, our flying turns did not come around nearly as often. I believe, during the month of February, we only flew one mission. By we, I mean our crew. However, in March, there was one to Vienna that comes to mind.

The mission itself was not exceptionally out of the ordinary. I think we attacked the marshaling yards. Our main targets were rail marshaling yards, oil refineries, critical factories, and airfields. The mission to Vienna, what I remember the most, was coming back we received several anti-aircraft flak hits in the right wing. After leaving the target, we noticed gasoline was leaking out of one of the wing tanks. We could tell it was gasoline because it looks different than oil, and we had no smoke.

I must say a little something about the fuel system in the B-24. The normal fuel configuration, there was one main wing tank in the wing behind each engine. There was also an auxiliary tank for each engine. Now the fuel could be, by using the fuel pumps, auxiliary fuel pumps, properly, gasoline could be pumped from any one tank to any one of the four engines. Because of this ability, we immediately, the engineer, Joe Frontera, began pumping the remaining gas out of the leaking tank into the tank next to it. He also shut off fuel from going from that tank to any of the other engines, and that engine, which was normally fed by that tank, was fed by the tank next to it.

This went smoothly, and we continued on our way in formation with all four engines running. But having lost considerable fuel from the one tank, now in flying back over the mountains in northern Yugoslavia, since the one remaining main tank on the right side was feeding gasoline to the two engines on the right side, that tank became nearly empty, and the tanks on the other side, in the left wing, still had a considerable quantity of fuel left. This made the plane considerably heavier on the one side than the other. So, Joe was instructed to transfer fuel from the left-wing tanks into the one good main tank on the right wing. He proceeded to do this, and the next thing we knew, all four engines spitted and sputtered, one after the other, and stopped.

Needless to say, we began rapidly losing altitude, and the formation pulled ahead of us as we dropped out. The boys in the back of the plane called on the intercom, "What's goin on? It's so quiet. We're going down. Shall we bail out?"

They were instructed, "No. Get ready to bail out. Snap your chutes on. Open the escape hatches, but do not, under any circumstances, leave the airplane before the alarm bell goes off. We're trying to get the engines restarted, and we will stay with the plane down to five or six thousand feet."

At about seven thousand feet, we got one of 'em sputtering and then started. That slowed our descent. Now at five thousand feet, we got a second one started, and then we held our own. In a few moments, we brought the other two back online. And word was passed along to close the escape hatches and relax. By this time we were coming out over the Adriatic, and it was just a matter of flying home.

Something had gone wrong in the transferring of the fuel which cut off the fuel to all the engines. But the problem was corrected. We flew the rest of the way back to the base with no problems except we were wondering whether we could trust the fuel gauges because they were sure down to the bottom. The big "E" was coming up on all of them. We landed without incident, but in taxiing back to our parking area, all engines stopped again. We were completely out of gas, called on the radio, and had to be towed the rest of the way in.

Shortly thereafter, in the spring of '45, we again went on a week of rest and recuperation. But this time, to Rome. Stayed for a week in a very fancy hotel, which was taken over by the military, as was everything over there. Saw most of the sights of Rome. Our bombardier, Gene

6. What Daddy Did in the War

Tynan and my good friend on the crew, was a Catholic, he took me along to St. Peter's in Vatican City. It was very interesting. We naturally took in all the sights of Rome, all the old ruins, the coliseum, the forum, and it was all quite interesting.

One of the last missions I remember was to Prague. Actually, not to the city of Prague, but to an airfield in the vicinity, where the Germans were training pilots in jets. They had the first operational jet planes at the end of the war.* They didn't have many of them, their range was limited, but their speed and maneuverability could fly rings around anything we had.

On May 5, 1945, while flying a simulated flight in a Link Trainer [flight simulator], in a lab, I suddenly heard over the radio from the instructor who was running the simulator that I might as well come out of the thing. They just got word, just heard over the radio that the Germans had surrendered. This was a day before you people [in the States] knew anything about it. We had quite a celebration.

Two days later began a series of three flights, which I consider among the most satisfying I had over there. Our Air Force, not just the heavies, but the medium and light bombers, did such a good job in southern Austria and up in the Alps. All the bridges were knocked out. There were several big prisoner of war camps up there, and they had no way of supplying them. So we flew three missions up there, where we'd fly up the valley and low over the POW camps, dropped the supplies. The first mission we did, we flew real low, and dropped these specially packaged supplies out without parachutes. We could see the people down on the ground very clearly. We were only a couple hundred feet off the ground. But they were so anxious to get supplies, they couldn't wait until everything was clear. They ran out to get the packages while these were still coming down. The next two missions, supply missions, these supplies were dropped by parachute so we wouldn't hurt anybody on the ground.

Within a couple of weeks, after the war, all the flight crews flew back to the U.S. Our crew went back to Tunis, flew across the Sahara Desert to Dakar [Senegal], then across the South Atlantic to Natal, Brazil. From Brazil, we started for Puerto Rico. But by the time we got three-quarters of the way there, we heard over the radio that the airfield in Puerto Rico was closed because of bad weather. We did not have

---

* The Messerschmitt 262

What We Can and Can't Afford

enough fuel to return to Natal, so we landed at some emergency strip along the Amazon River. It was quite an interesting short field take off to get out of there, but, from there, we reached Puerto Rico, and then to Charleston, South Carolina. From there, I took a plane trip to Fort Dix, New Jersey, where I came home for a 30-day furlough. That's when I got married, in June of '45 [to Kathryn Godshall].

After our furloughs, the crew reported to Drew Field in Tampa, Florida. It turned out we were not supposed to be in Tampa, another army "snafu."* We were supposed to be in Sioux Falls, South Dakota. The officers in our crew found out, mainly through Gene, that private transportation could be authorized. That means, instead of going by train like the rest of the group, when private transportation is authorized, if you have a vehicle, you can use that to go and they would pay us, each, ten cents a mile, and give us the necessary gas rationing coupons. We were only required to make two hundred miles a day. Since it was two thousand miles, this means we would have ten days to get there, to Sioux Falls, South Dakota. We got coupons, gas coupons, for two thousand miles of gas. Only problem was, we had no car, so we went out, scoured used car lots, and bought a 1928 Chevy. The title transfer was no problem, more like a folding picture postcard. You just tore off the bottom, and mailed it in.

We had drivers' transportation authorized, and set out, deciding that since we had ten days, we could go to Sioux Falls by way of Pennsylvania and nearby places where the other fellas were from. Gene was from Connecticut, Miller from western Pennsylvania. We started out late at night, the night before the big group was leaving, got about forty miles, and one of our tires blew out. We changed that, continued on our way, went about another ten miles, another tire blew out. These tires looked real good, but they were rotten.

Just up the road from where the second tire blew out, there was a combination gas station-garage-diner. So, we proceeded up there, and we wind up selling this old car to the proprietor there for four bus tickets to Jacksonville. In Jacksonville, we got the train, since we were traveling on orders, for Philadelphia and points north. I got off the train at 30th Street Station, took a cab to 20 Beverly Avenue.† I knew where the key was. I opened the door, went in, went upstairs, crawled in bed with my wife, and woke her up. She didn't know I was coming.

---

* Situation Normal: All Fouled Up.
† In East Lansdowne, Pennsylvania, where Kathryn was living with her parents.

6. What Daddy Did in the War

After a very pleasant four or five days at home, I met Gene at the 30th Street Station [Philadelphia]; he came down from Connecticut, and we both proceeded to Sioux Falls, South Dakota, where I was reclassified as eligible for discharge, and sent to Brownsville, Texas. After about five weeks down there, doing nothing but swimming in the Gulf and loafing around the canteen, I got sent to Indiantown Gap, Pennsylvania, for discharge.

* * *

Kehs was discharged in October 1945 with the rank of 1st lieutenant. His decorations included the Air Medal w/Oak Leaf Cluster, the Army Meritorious Unit Citation w/Oak Leaf Cluster, the Army Good Conduct Medal, the American Defense Service Medal, and the European–African–Middle Eastern Campaign Medal w/4 Stars. Presumably, he also received the World War II Victory Medal, though his children have no record of that.

After his discharge, he returned to his hometown of Sellersville, Pennsylvania, where he took a job at Schulmerich Electronics for several years before going back to the U.S. Gauge as a machinist and lathe operator until his retirement in 1986. He and Kathryn's marriage produced three daughters and lasted over half a century until his death from the cancer in 1997.*

---

* The girls—Beverly, Judie, and Janice—were schoolmates of mine and my brothers at Pennridge High School in Perkasie, Pennsylvania, in the 1960s and 1970s. Judie married Dave Much, whom I've known since my family first moved to Perkasie in 1955. During a visit with Dave and Judie in 2011, Judie mentioned her father's recordings, which caught my interest immediately. I am profoundly grateful to Bev, Judie, and Janice for allowing me access to this material. My thanks also to Betsy Gehlot for doing the initial transcription of Kehs' recordings.

7

The Arrogance— and Emptiness—of Power

(*LA Progressive*, June 21, 2014;
VVAW Veteran, Fall 2014)

As I watch events unfolding in Iraq over the last weeks, I find myself wondering if Iraq War veterans are feeling the way I felt in March and April of 1975 when the fiction that was South Vietnam collapsed like a house of cards.

Eight years earlier, I had arrived in Vietnam as an 18-year-old Marine, convinced of the rightness of our cause, and eager to save the Vietnamese from the scourge of communism. I left Vietnam thirteen months later, wounded in body and spirit, struggling to process the reality that our Saigon allies were corrupt and incompetent, their soldiers largely unwilling or unable to fight, while my Viet Cong enemies were dedicated and relentless.

When, seven years after my return, the entire edifice crumbled in a matter of weeks, even after more than twenty years of U.S. support and a decade of massive U.S. military effort, I was neither surprised nor angry nor jubilant. I just felt empty. Utterly empty. Fifty-eight thousand dead Americans, some of them my friends. Millions of Vietnamese and Laotians and Cambodians. And for what?

Years later, Dean Rusk blamed our defeat on the failure of the American people to have the will to soldier on to victory. Peter Braestrup blamed it on the liberal media who, he argued in his book *The Big Story*, made the U.S. victory at Tet 1968 look like a U.S. defeat. The redoubtable Col. Harry Summers, Jr., (Ret.) argued that we never lost a single battle. Others blamed the antiwar movement or the meddling politicians who made the military "fight with one hand tied behind its back."

It never seems to have occurred to any of these very bright and

7. The Arrogance—and Emptiness—of Power

powerful people that Vietnam was not and never had been ours to win or lose. It never occurred to them that Vietnamese dedication, motivation, and determination—an ancient proclivity to resist the presence of armed foreigners in their midst—might have had something to do with the U.S. defeat. One might reasonably argue: not something, but everything.

Now, once again, we are witnessing the incompetence, corruption, and inability of a government we created and have supported for over a decade. And once again, according to a June 14, 2014, op-ed piece in the *Washington Post* written by a prominent counterinsurgency expert, "by declining to provide a long-term security assistance force to an Iraq not yet able to handle the fight itself, we pulled defeat from the jaws of victory."

He goes on to argue, "We are reaping the instability and increased threat to U.S. interests that *we [emphasis in the original]* have sown through the failure of our endgame in Iraq…. There is a clear lesson here for those contemplating a complete withdrawal of U.S. troops from Afghanistan."

It does not seem to occur to him or those who agree with him, as it did not occur to the politicians and generals who created and persisted in the disaster that was the Vietnam War, that Iraq was never ours to win or lose. Just as we could not train our Saigon allies to become self-sufficient in spite of massive U.S. aid and intervention, now we seem to have failed to create a viable and self-sufficient government in Baghdad—and it's all our fault because we pulled out too soon instead of having the moxie to stay the course.

It has nothing to do, according to this point of view, with the motivation, composition, determination (or lack of determination) of our allies and their opponents; it is all about us: US. U.S.

The Iraq War is not, of course, the Vietnam War. The differences are myriad. But there are two similarities, and these two trump all the differences: (1) in each case, U.S. policymakers tasked the military with achieving goals that were and are unattainable by force of arms; and (2) when you send scared and heavily armed kids into a hostile environment they have no hope of understanding or navigating, nothing good will result.

Oh, yes, there is one more similarity, and that is the arrogance of bright and powerful people who persist in imagining that American military might can accomplish whatever they desire, and in blaming their failures on anything and anyone but themselves.

8

Remarks in Honor of the Media FBI Burglars

Philly Veterans for Peace Chapter 31
Annual Dinner
June 20, 2014

"American Heroes"

There are few people more thoroughly odious in United States history than J. Edgar Hoover. A self-serving, egotistical, small-minded tyrant who created a subterranean empire based on terror, prejudice, hypocrisy, venality, and institutional evil, he was powerful enough to force even the most powerful public figures in and out of government to tremble in fear of him.

Woe unto those who fell afoul of his righteousness. He once said of the antiwar movement—that would be us, of course: "It is time we stopped coddling the hoodlums and the hippies who are causing so much trouble these days. Let us treat them like the vicious enemies of society that they really are."

One can imagine, then, Hoover's anger in March 1971 when he heard that one of his offices had been burglarized and its files stolen. Moreover, as days turned into weeks turned into months—and still none of these vicious enemies of society were in custody—Hoover's anger must steadily have morphed from rage to fury to blue-faced apoplexy.

One can also imagine old J. Edgar going to bed every night praying to God to deliver into his hands those who had dared to violate the sanctity of the FBI's temple and reveal the darkest and ugliest secrets of the priesthood. This outrage. This treason. This desecration.

I don't know about the rest of you, but it gives me great comfort and abiding joy to know that Hoover went to his grave never knowing

8. Remarks in Honor of the Media FBI Burglars

who had tied his knickers in a knot and gotten away with it. Clean away. Scott-free. Nary a whisper nor a fare-thee-well. Just vanished into the night never to be seen or heard from again.

Well, actually, the burglars—who called themselves the Citizens Commission to Investigate the FBI, but were really vicious enemies of society—were heard from again. Or at least the files they made off with began to show up in the public domain, exposing Hoover's FBI for what it was: an out-of-control agency engaged in unconstitutional domestic spying, political intimidation, racial discrimination, and thought-control.

One can only stand in awe of the people who had the courage, the audacity, the sheer moxie to attempt such a burglary, let alone the brains, skill, patience, and discipline to pull it off. Like most of you here, I have wondered for 43 years who were these people who were willing to face a lifetime in prison—for surely J. Edgar would have had no mercy—in order to reveal to the American people the truth. I have wanted to shake their hands and thank them and tell them that they are heroes and patriots.

Tonight, we have that opportunity. Of the seven vicious enemies of society who participated that night, William Davidon has since died and two have declined to reveal their identities, but three are here with us this evening: John and Bonnie Raines, and Keith Forsyth. I want you to take a good look at them: don't they look vicious?

But in all seriousness, I can hardly begin to tell the three of you how grateful I am to you, how in awe I am of your bravery and commitment to justice, how happy I am to be able to know and acknowledge who you are.

When people learn that I am a veteran, they will often say to me, "Thank you for your service." Most of the time, I just say, "You're welcome" because it would only upset or insult or baffle them if I said, "Do you really mean to thank me for going half-way around the world to kill, maim, and brutalize people who have never done me or my country any harm nor ever would or could?"

But tonight, maybe for the first time ever, we can use that phrase without apology or explanation or qualification. Bonnie, John, and Keith, thank you for your service to your country, to your fellow citizens, to justice, and to humanity.

PS: And thank you for sticking it to J. Edgar Hoover; I can think of few people who ever deserved it more.

9

Where the Dangers Lie

(*LA Progressive*, October 22, 2014)

The Islamic State in Iraq and Syria is violent, fanatical, barbaric, brutal, intolerant, and ... add whatever other adjectives you'd like to throw in. I won't argue that these characterizations are not true. But over the summer and into the fall, I have watched and listened with increasing dismay to the shifting sands of the U.S. approach to the situation.

Not so many months ago, we were assured that the U.S. would not get drawn into another war in the Middle East. But all through the summer and into the fall came an endless barrage of stories about Yazidis being raped and buried alive by ISIS, and the horrifying videos of Americans and other Europeans being savagely beheaded by ISIS, and the failures of the Iraqi and Kurdish militaries to stem the advance of ISIS.

The drumbeat for U.S. intervention among U.S. policymakers, lawmakers, and pundits began to grow louder and more insistent, and now the U.S. is regularly sending airstrikes and drone attacks against the ISIS forces. Airstrikes, but no more, we were assured. This minimal military involvement, however, does not seem to be working, says counterinsurgency expert John Nagl, who argues that we should put "boots on the ground" by embedding "teams of combat advisers with" Iraqi and Kurdish forces fighting ISIS.

A year ago most Americans had never even heard of ISIS, yet now the U.S. is once again militarily embroiled in a war in the Middle East. What if we send U.S. advisors and they prove to be ineffective, as they have proved to be over and over again ever since 1961—including in Iraq in the past decade? Will we then have no choice but to send in the Marines?

Of course, we're not doing this alone. Secretary of State John Kerry says that 40 nations have offered to join our coalition, though he adds,

9. Where the Dangers Lie

"It's not appropriate to start announcing" which nations will participate and what each will do. One remembers G.W. Bush's "Coalition of the Willing" that included such nations as Albania, Latvia, the Fiji Islands, and the Dominican Republic, and can only wonder which nations belong to our coalition this time.

Back in 1990, when Saddam Hussein accused the Kuwaitis of slant-drilling and stealing his oil, the U.S. ambassador to Iraq told Saddam that the U.S. "does not take sides in Arab-Arab disputes." What would you make of that if you were Saddam? Only after he acted on what appeared to any reasonable person to be a Green Light from the U.S. did the U.S. decide that putting the Emir of Kuwait back on his gold-plated toilet was a moral imperative.

We were told by a tearful young girl that Iraqi soldiers tore Kuwaiti babies from their incubators and threw the babies to the floor. Only much later did we learn that the "eyewitness" turns out to have been the Kuwaiti ambassador's daughter, who was coached in her testimony before Congress by the same public relations firm that had handled George H.W. Bush's 1988 election campaign. Her testimony could not be and has never been corroborated.

Meanwhile, the vaunted Iraqi Republican Guard turned out to be a bunch of rag-tag peasant draftees who were far more eager to run away than to fight Americans. American audiences were never shown the Highway of Death by the American media, but the rest of the world saw it. You want to talk bloodthirsty savagery? Google "Highway of Death" and see what you get.

And a year later, no less a person than George Will—no bleeding-heart liberal—admitted that the Kuwaitis had been doing exactly what Saddam had said they were doing: stealing Iraqi oil.

Before the U.S. started putting boots on the ground in the Middle East in August 1990, Iraq was a stable country. Syria was a stable country. Libya was a stable country. Not happy places, to be sure. But stable. And secular. Al Qaida didn't exist. ISIS didn't exist.

Almost a quarter of a century later, with the U.S. 5th Fleet headquartered in Bahrain, U.S. air bases in Saudi Arabia, and U.S. army bases in Kuwait, how is the Middle East doing? After eight years of U.S. boots on the ground in Iraq, how is Iraq doing? After thirteen years of U.S. boots on the ground in Afghanistan, how is Afghanistan doing? How is Libya doing after being liberated from Muammar Gaddafi with significant help from the U.S.? Have we neutralized al-Qaida? How can ISIS be so effective a fighting force with no air force, no navy, no

What We Can and Can't Afford

Pentagon, and no assistance from any major world power while those on whose behalf we want to expend American treasure and American blood can't defend themselves without our help?

For that matter, where did al-Qaida come from? Isn't al-Qaida the direct descendant of those Afghan mujahideen the U.S. so gleefully armed and funded against the Soviet Union back in the 1980s? Isn't ISIS a direct outgrowth of al-Qaida?

Do we never seem to notice the Iron Law of Unintended Consequences playing itself out over and over again? Do we not notice that the United States of America cannot make the world behave as we would wish?

I am not arguing that what is happening in the Middle East is anything other than a disaster for those who are living in the midst of it. I am not arguing that ISIS deserves a seat in the United Nations. But I am asking: how much more damage are we going to do in the process of trying to fix the damage we have already done? How many more enemies will we make trying to kill the ones we've already made? Will the Middle East be better off after we have intervened once again?

Finally, which is the greater threat to our national security? Al-Qaida or a crumbling infrastructure of highways, bridges, and tunnels, leaking municipal water systems, and an ancient electrical grid? ISIS or failing public schools, understaffed hospitals, and overcrowded prisons? Afghan Taliban or a national debt of nearly $18,000,000,000,000 and rising every day by $2,450,000,000? Islamist jihadis or a dysfunctional Congress gerrymandered beyond any possibility of compromise?

We cannot bend the world into the shape we desire through military might, or by any other means for that matter, and our attempts to do so have failed time and time again. Yet we seem to remain, as a people, as gullible as ever, once again stampeded into winless war by leaders so besotted by the hammer of American military might that they persist in seeing every problem in the world as a nail.

10

Con Thien and Dancin' Jack

(*We Gotta Get Outta This Place*:
The Soundtrack of the Vietnam War
Bradley & Werner, UMass Press 2015)

 I don't know where or why the Vietnam War got the nickname "the rock-n-roll war." That certainly wasn't my experience during my thirteen months with 1st Battalion, 1st Marine Regiment from early February 1967 to late February 1968. I never heard a broadcast of Armed Forces Radio, let alone watched Armed Forces TV, and the only USO show I ever saw starred Mrs. Miller, an overweight middle-aged housewife whose one claim to fame was an AM radio spoof of a hit by Petula Clark.
 My memories of music in Vietnam are so memorable precisely because they were so rare. I first heard the Doors' "Light My Fire" and the Iron Butterfly's "In-A-Gadda-Da-Vida," played on battery-powered portable turntables during down time in the battalion's command post southeast of Da Nang in the summer of 1967. I remember hearing Buffy Saint Marie singing "Codeine" and "Now that the Buffalo's Gone." And when we were up near Quang Tri in January 1968—it might have been New Year's Day—someone had a copy of the Beatles' *Sgt. Pepper* album, and played it over and over again until the batteries on his turntable wore out.
 The one exception to this paucity of music came during the weeks our battalion spent at Con Thien up on the demilitarized zone. Con Thien was a miserable lump of mud and barbed wire where there was little to do except sit inside the two sandbagged bunkers occupied by the battalion scouts and play cards or talk and just pass the time while waiting for the next barrage of incoming North Vietnamese artillery to arrive from the other side of the DMZ, which it did with nerve-wracking regularity. And when it did, we'd all double up inside

What We Can and Can't Afford

Corporal Ehrhart at Con Thien, November 1967 (author's photo).

our flak jackets and helmets, and put our fingers in our ears, and hold our breath, and shiver, and hope like hell none of the stuff landed in our neighborhood.

You didn't walk around outside any more than you absolutely had to. Getting caught in the open by incoming was both mentally harrowing and physically uncomfortable. The telltale whistle of the rounds didn't give you much warning, and the heavy knee-deep mud made it impossible to run for cover, so you'd just have to flop yourself down right where you were and try to bury your body in the mud like a pig wallowing down on the farm. Then you'd have to spend the next few hours trying to scrape the mud off your one pair of jungle utilities, and out of your nose and rifle.

10. Con Thien and Dancin' Jack

There weren't too many places to go anyway, except maybe to the helicopter landing pad to get the mail, when the weather was good enough to allow a chopper to land, or over to the supply dump to get a few more cases of C-rations. The one time we ran a company-sized patrol outside the wire, we got our asses kicked in an ambush the NVA had set up using mortars and landmines. And it was almost always raining. Who wants to walk around in the rain when you don't have to?

Nighttime was different. More relaxed. You could unclench your jaws and unwind your fists. The NVA didn't fire at night because the flashes would reveal the locations of their guns. Of course, there was always the possibility of getting hit with a ground assault some night, but our bunkers were far enough inside the perimeter wire that we would have plenty of time to say our prayers before some NVA soldier flipped a grenade through the opening. Nighttime actually got to be sort of fun, and I soon came to look forward to it through the long daylight hours of ducking and cringing. Here's why:

About the fourth or fifth night we were at Con Thien, several of the scouts from the other bunker came pouring into our bunker in a tangle of arms and legs and laughter. "Get on the Bullshit Band!" Mogerdy shouted, all excited, "They got tunes!"

"Get outta here, you assholes," said Wally, wrapping his arms protectively around his PRC-10 radio. "You're trackin' mud all over our goddamned house."

"Come on," said Mogerdy, "Turn on the radio. They're playin' music on the Bullshit Band. I kid you not. We were just listening to it in the S-3s' bunker. Somebody's playing music."

On military radios, there's a frequency way up near the top of the band that's left unassigned at all times, and is supposed to be used only in emergencies. It was regularly used, however, as an open conference line among enlisted men, and anybody with a spare radio and a little time to kill would get on the air and try to find somebody else from Podunk, Iowa, or Bumfart, Maine, or wherever. "Hey, hey, hey, this is Cool Albert from Detroit," you could hear on any given night. "Any Motor City Soul Brothers out there? Who knows a good joke?" Thus, the frequency acquired the nickname of the Bullshit Band.

After much cajoling, bribery, and threats, Wally finally consented to turn on his radio. Nothing but static. "Fuck you guys," he said.

"Put on the whip and run it outside," said Hoffy. "You can't get nothing in here with a tape antenna." Wally got out the ten-foot-long whip antenna, plugged it in, and stuck it out the open entrance of the

What We Can and Can't Afford

bunker. He fiddled with the radio. "Baby, baby, where did our love go?" Diana Ross and the Supremes were singing to us right through the radio's handset speaker, clearly audible in spite of the static.

"Hot damn!" shouted Morgan.

"Wha'd I tell ya!" said Mogerdy.

"Run next door and get Kenny and them, Rolly," said Wally. "Let's have a party." The song ended, and a voice came over the box:

"Diana Ross and the Su-Premes," said the voice. "Ain't they wonderful? Eat the apple and fuck the Corps; that's what I always say. And who am I? Why, I'm Dancin' Jack, your Armed Forces Bullshit Network DJ, comin' to you from somewhere deep in the heart of the heart of the country. Do I have any more requests out there, you jive motherfuckers?"

"You got 'Dancin' in the Streets'?" another voice broke in.

"All right! Martha and the Vandellas," said Dancin' Jack, "an excellent choice. Anybody out there in Radioland got 'Dancin' in the Streets'?"

"Yo!" came in a third voice. "I do."

"Well, spin it, comrade!" Another song began: "Callin' out around the world, there'll be dancin' in the streets...."

"How are they doing that?" asked Wally.

"Must be guys down around Dong Ha and Camp Carroll with turntables and tapedecks and stuff," said Mogerdy. "All you gotta do is put your headset up to the speakers and the airways fill with music."

The bunker got very crowded very quickly when several more scouts piled in from next door, but we all squeezed in together and pulled up our knees and made room because we only had the one PRC-10 assigned to the scouts. We smoked cigarettes, and laughed and listened, and sometimes we got real quiet—like when the Beatles were singing, "Yesterday, love was such an easy game to play; now it seems as though it's gone away"—and sometimes we all shouted along at the top of our lungs; "Gimme a ticket for an airplane!"

Con Thien was also the first and only place I smoked marijuana in Vietnam. Most of the time, it just didn't pay to be high because out where we were most of the time, if you were high, you were likely to end up in a body bag. But at Con Thien, as I said, the scout bunkers were well inside the wire. If we got hit by a ground attack, and the NVA got as far as the scout bunkers, we might as well be stoned out of our minds because we were all going to be dead anyway.

For a while, then, we had it pretty fine. Daytime was no fun, but we spent our nights getting stoned and listening to Dancin' Jack and the

10. Con Thien and Dancin' Jack

music, hour after hour after hour. When Otis Redding sat on the dock of the bay, I could really see the tide rolling away, and the kicks just kept getting harder to find for Paul Revere and the Raiders, and Mitch Ryder and the Detroit Wheels had us all daydreaming about getting the devil out of her blue dress. Whatever anybody wanted to hear out there in Radioland—which consisted, I assume, of the far northern I Corps from Gio Linh to the Rock Pile—somebody else seemed to have it: rock-n-roll, blues, jazz, soul, country.

Eventually, the no-sense-of-humor screw-the-enlisted-men military brass caught up with the whole operation and chased everyone off the air. I've no idea how they managed to do it. Maybe they used radio direction-finding equipment to track down the guys with the music and threatened to throw them in the brig. Maybe Adrian Cronauer got jealous of Dancin' Jack. Who the hell knows? Whatever happened, the Bullshit Band fell silent, and we spent our last nights at Con Thien sitting in our silent bunker, listening to the occasional air strike, or outgoing artillery, or the pop and hiss of illumination rounds.

But the music had been fun while it lasted—just about the only fun I ever remember having in Vietnam—and I can still hear the driving beat of the Rolling Stones thumping through the static, the whole bunker screaming in unison, "I can't get no! Satisfaction! No, no, no!"

11

Me and Veterans of Foreign Wars

(*VVAW Veteran*, Fall 2015)

About a month after I got to Vietnam (February 1967), I got a letter from my father saying that the local VFW chapter, Forrest-Post Lodge, wanted to make me a member and they would cover my membership fee as long as I was on active duty. I wrote back that it seemed kind of weird to make me a "veteran of a foreign war" while I was still in the war, and only recently in it at that. (My father was neither a member nor a veteran.) He wrote back saying that it didn't matter; they would make me a member immediately and pay my fee. I figured, what the hell, why not, at least I'd be able to get a beer when I got home (I would be 19 and the legal age was 21). And when I got home from Vietnam, I dutifully went to the VFW Post to be officially made a member.

I grew up in a small town in Pennsylvania. My father was a minister. The members of the VFW Post were the fathers of the kids I'd grown up with; I knew them and they knew me. It felt kind of weird sitting at the bar drinking beer with these men who were a generation older than me, and men I'd known most of my life; in one case, one of my teachers; some of them members of my father's church. Very weird. This was compounded by the fact that when I came home from Vietnam, I was an emotional and psychological wreck. On multiple levels, I had nothing to say to these guys, nothing to share with them. I don't remember the conversation at all; I only remember an intense feeling of discomfort.

And then the formal meeting began, and the first thing they did was swear me in as a member. I mean, they literally swore me in. I had to raise my right hand (I don't recall if there was a Bible involved or not) and solemnly swear to defend the Constitution of the United States against all enemies foreign and domestic. Seriously. I had to swear to

11. Me and Veterans of Foreign Wars

the exact same oath I'd taken when I had joined the Marines nearly two years earlier. I did not know this was coming. I remember thinking, "What the fuck is this? I thought I was joining my local VFW, not the National Home Defense Force. This is Perkasie, Pennsylvania, for chrissake!" As soon as that meeting was over, I beat it out of there. And I never went back. This was March 1968.

In retrospect, I realize that those men probably meant well, but we had about as much in common as a Maine lobster and the Man in the Moon. Within a few years, I got involved with Vietnam Veterans Against the War. I'm still involved with VVAW 45 years later.

12

The American War in Vietnam

*Lessons Learned and Not Learned,
University of Tokyo, June 30, 2015*

(*LA Progressive*, May 17, 2015; *Vietnam Full Disclosure*, May 20, 2016)

On Memorial Day 2012, standing in front of the Vietnam War Memorial in Washington, D.C., President Barack Obama gave a speech announcing the 50th Anniversary Commemoration of the Vietnam War. The entire speech is far too long to repeat here, but let me give you a few key passages:

> One of the most painful chapters in our history was Vietnam—most particularly how we treated our troops who served there. You were often blamed for a war you didn't start, when you should have been commended for serving your country with valor. You were sometimes blamed for the misdeeds of the few, when the honorable service of the many should have been praised. You came home and sometimes were denigrated, when you should have been celebrated. It was a national shame, a disgrace that should have never happened.
>
> And so a central part of this 50th anniversary will be to tell your story as it should have been told all along. It's another chance to set the record straight.
>
> Because history will honor your service, and your names will join a story of service that stretches back two centuries.
>
> Finally, we might begin to see the true legacy of Vietnam. Because of Vietnam and our veterans, we now use American power smarter, we honor our military more, we take care of our veterans better. Because of the hard lessons of Vietnam, because of you, America is even stronger than before.

These are only a few short excerpts from the president's speech, yet even this little bit is so riddled with errors, distortions, and outright falsehoods that it is hard to know just how and where to begin.

12. The American War in Vietnam

Let me start by telling you that I am a veteran of the American War in Vietnam. I was not drafted. I volunteered for the U.S. Marine Corps when I was 17 years old, went to Vietnam when I was 18 years old, and earned the rank of sergeant by the time I was 19 & ½ years old. I was wounded in combat, and eventually received the Good Conduct Medal and an Honorable Discharge.

I also joined the antiwar movement after I finished my time in the Marines, joining my fellow students—none of them military veterans—at Swarthmore College in various antiwar activities and becoming active in Vietnam Veterans Against the War. I know something about how soldiers and veterans were treated when we came home, so let me start there.

I returned to the United States from Vietnam in March 1968, passing through San Francisco Airport and Philadelphia Airport in full military uniform. I repeated the same trip in June 1969 when I returned from my last posting—in Japan, as it happens—before I was released from active duty. On neither occasion was I confronted by civilians out to denigrate and abuse me. No one called me "baby killer" or spit on me. When I later became active in the antiwar movement, I never once saw or heard any antiwar demonstrator blame the soldiers for the war, let alone act out verbally or physically toward soldiers or veterans.

As Vietnam War veteran Jerry Lembcke documents in his book *The Spitting Image*, the myth of the spat-upon veteran is exactly that: a myth. There is not a single documented contemporary account of such behavior. All of these stories begin to emerge only after 1975, only after the end of the war, when many veterans began to claim, "This happened to me back then." But memory is, at best, unreliable, and psychology readily demonstrates that people can convince themselves of things that never actually happened to them. For the most part, veterans came home to silence, returning not to grand victory parades and tickertape as their fathers had done after World War II, but one at a time to hometowns and cities that had hardly been touched by the events that had changed these veterans' lives forever. It was isolating and lonely and without closure. But that is not the same as being vilified and abused and blamed.

But powerful people saw in the veterans' pain and festering unhappiness an opportunity. It was an opportunity that Republican candidate for President Ronald Reagan seized upon in a campaign speech in September 1980 when he said, "It is time we recognized that ours was, in truth, a noble cause." In the post–Vietnam War, post–Watergate era,

What We Can and Can't Afford

both trust in the U.S. government and belief in the justice of American military might as an instrument of foreign policy were badly shaken. Morale and discipline in the armed forces, as documented by Colonel Robert J. Heinl, Jr., in "The Collapse of the Armed Forces," were at an all-time low, and very few young Americans were eager to serve in a discredited military. When the U.S. attempt to rescue American hostages being held in the U.S. embassy in Tehran by Iranian revolutionaries ended in humiliating disaster, the U.S. foreign policy elite became determined to restore the luster of American arms and the legitimacy of American military intervention.

This is the context in which Reagan gave his "noble cause" speech, and he was elected in a landslide victory by the millions of Americans who did not want to believe what they had witnessed and lived through during the Vietnam War: the world's most powerful nation pounding into rubble an agrarian people who plowed their fields with water buffalo and wanted nothing more than to be left alone. A war of aggression foisted upon the Vietnamese by arrogant men who thought they could bend the world into whatever shape they desired.

The "national shame, the disgrace," was the war itself, not the way returning veterans were treated. But this was a reality that few Americans, including many veterans of the war, could bring themselves to come to terms with. Haven't Americans always been on the side of right and justice? Doesn't the United States only fight wars as a last resort and only when forced to do so by aggressor nations led by evil leaders? How could a nation built upon "Give me liberty or give me death," "all men are created equal," and "of the people, by the people, for the people" have ended up waging a shameful, disgraceful war against a people who had done us no harm nor ever would or could?

So, when Reagan declared that "ours was, in truth, a noble cause," millions and millions of Americans eagerly embraced this vision of the American War in Vietnam. This was reinforced over the next decade by the dedication of the Vietnam War Memorial in Washington and hundreds of other similar memorials erected in state capitals, cities large and small, and local communities all over the U.S. along with "Welcome Home" parades belatedly honoring Vietnam veterans; by Hollywood movies such as *The Deer Hunter, Missing in Action, Born on the 4th of July*, and *Rambo*; the vilification of the antiwar movement as a bunch of dope-smoking hippie traitors; and the transformation of the American soldier from the instrument of a failed, unrealizable, even criminal foreign policy into an unappreciated and much-abused victim.

12. The American War in Vietnam

The first of the Welcome Home parades took place in New York City on May 7, 1985. I watched part of it on television, and later wrote this poem titled "Parade":

>Ten years after the last rooftop
>chopper out of Saigon.
>
>Ten, fifteen, twenty years
>too late for kids not twenty
>years old and dead in ricefields;
>brain-dead, soul-dead, half-dead
>in wheelchairs. Even the unmarked
>forever Absent Without Leave.
>
>You'd think that any self-respecting
>vet would give the middle finger
>to the folks who thought of it
>ten years and more too late—
>
>yet there they were: the sad
>survivors, balding, overweight
>and full of beer, weeping, grateful
>for their hour come round at last.
>
>I saw one man in camouflaged utilities;
>a boy, his son, dressed like dad;
>both proudly marching.
>
>How many wounded generations,
>touched with fire, have offered up
>their children to the gods of fire?
>Even now, new flames are burning,
>and the gods of fire call for more,
>and the new recruits keep coming.
>
>What fire will burn that small
>boy marching with his father?
>What parade will heal
>his father's wounds?

I found it all pathetic and sad, but apparently many of my fellow veterans were more than happy to accept these accolades, however belated and cynical.

For while this transformation of the veteran from unwitting perpetrator to American hero was taking place, U.S. policymakers were slowly but surely reasserting U.S. military intervention as a legitimate and necessary instrument of foreign policy. Reagan's intervention in Lebanon ended in disaster when hundreds of American Marines died

What We Can and Can't Afford

in a suicide bombing, but Reagan was smart enough to cut his losses, and quickly displaced that setback with his successful invasion of the tiny Caribbean island of Grenada, claiming falsely that the Cubans were building an airfield for Russian bombers and that the lives of American medical school students were in jeopardy. This ridiculously lopsided affair was hailed in the halls of power and touted to the American people as a great victory, even though our "enemy" had a military force with the size and firepower of the Providence, Rhode Island, police department, and our military was so unprepared that soldiers had to use tourist maps of the island and call the Pentagon on a pay telephone to ask for naval support.

By the time George H.W. Bush invaded Panama in 1989, few Americans questioned what Bush and Washington had named "Operation Just Cause." And when Bush committed over 500,000 U.S. military personnel to put the Emir of Kuwait back on his gold-plated toilet, most Americans didn't bother to ask why the U.S. ambassador to Iraq had said to Saddam Hussein in August 1990 that the U.S. had "no opinion in your Arab-Arab disputes." Or if Saddam's claims were true that the Kuwaitis were slant drilling and stealing Iraqi oil. Or why the U.S. had supported and protected Saddam all through the 1980s if he was such a tyrant. Operation Desert Storm might more accurately be called Operation Desert Stomp, so lopsided was this brief little war, but it was celebrated with a massive victory parade in Washington, D.C., and demonstrated for all the world to see that U.S. military might was once again a force to be reckoned with. As Bush triumphantly declared, "By God, we've kicked the Vietnam syndrome once and for all." Sadly enough, as the 2nd Gulf War, our endless war in Afghanistan, and our interventions in Somalia, Libya, Yemen, Pakistan, and elsewhere make clear, Bush seems to have been right.

This rehabilitation of American military legitimacy was, as I said, dependent upon rehabilitating the image of military service and the American serviceman (and now woman, too). By the late 1960s and early 1970s, as detailed by Heinl and in such powerful documentaries as *Sir! No, Sir!*, the junior ranks of the U.S. military were in something close to full revolt against the Vietnam War and those who were ordering them to fight and die in a war that could no longer be explained as anything other than hopelessly wrongheaded and perhaps even criminally insane. What Americans saw on television in the late 1960s and early 1970s was not returning veterans being spat upon and denigrated, but thousands of veterans in the streets protesting the war they had

12. The American War in Vietnam

fought, challenging the falsehoods foisted upon them and the American people, even hurling their medals onto the steps of the U.S. Congress.

The draft, by this time, had been thoroughly discredited as grossly unfair, and within the military leadership itself, a large portion of the blame for the breakdown of the military was attributed to the draft and the number of young men who were in the military and sent to Vietnam against their will.

The solution to this problem—the lesson learned, if you will—by the military and the foreign policy establishment was to get rid of the draft and replace it with an all-volunteer army. It took a decade and a half to build a new, more loyal and unquestioning military, but in conjunction with other efforts such as the rehabilitation of the Vietnam veteran as noble hero and the recasting of the Vietnam War as noble cause, the effort succeeded. The U.S. now has a relatively small military made up of a high percentage of careerists whose loyalty is to their armed service, whose ethos is defined by their unit identity and sense of comradeship, and who have minimal contact with the civilian society on whose behalf they are supposedly serving. Moreover, a high percentage of these soldiers are drawn from the lower economic strata, those groups with the least voice and the least clout in the American political system.

I teach high school at an elite private boys school that costs $22,000 just for a year of kindergarten; by the time the boys get to high school, their parents are paying $35,000 a year—and this is for a day school and does not include the cost of school lunch. While some of our boys do receive scholarship aid, the majority of their families range from financially well off to fabulously wealthy, and even our scholarship kids, by virtue of graduating from my school, have gained a distinct advantage in life.

I teach the children of the powerful and the influential, people with clout: captains of industry, political leaders, prominent citizens. And in my fourteen years at this school, not one of my students—now numbering in the hundreds after so many years—has chosen to forego college and enlist in the U.S. military instead. Except for a very few who attend one of the service academies each year and will eventually serve as officers, not one student I have taught here will ever serve a day in uniform, let alone be required to serve against his will or because he has no better options available to him.

Why should the parents of the boys I teach care what the U.S. government is doing in the world in our names and with our tax dollars?

What We Can and Can't Afford

They and their children will never have to pay the blood price, which is now borne by less than one percent of the American people—mostly people the parents of my students will never meet or know or care about. Indeed, not a few of these parents and alumni benefit financially, directly or indirectly, from the system as it now operates. Where do you think their wealth comes from?

Toward the end of the American War in Vietnam, policymakers discovered that most Americans didn't really care about the death and destruction of others so long as it was not American kids who were doing the dying. The lesson was learned too late to apply it on a large scale in Vietnam, but the Reagan administration applied the principle to its wars in Central America, spending millions of dollars a day to crush popular revolutions in El Salvador and Nicaragua with only a tiny handful of American lives lost in the process.

And now we have the modern miracle of drone warfare and Hellfire missiles, enabling us to kill anywhere in the world without having to put U.S. soldiers' lives in jeopardy or do anything more than, quite literally, lift a finger. Thanks to the lessons of the Vietnam War, the U.S. government has learned how to wage war with minimal domestic political opposition. Is this what Obama meant when he boasted that "the true legacy of Vietnam" is that "we now use American power smarter"?

Obama also bragged that "we honor our military more and take care of our veterans better." What does this mean? Every NASCAR auto race begins with a color guard and military flyover. Every baseball game and basketball game and even high school lacrosse match begins with the Star-Spangled Banner. At every Philadelphia Flyers ice hockey game, a serviceman or woman is ceremoniously given a Flyers team jersey with his or her name on it, and everyone in the arena stands and applauds. What are soldiers and veterans supposed to do with a Flyers jersey or a military flyover? Eat it? Put it in the bank? Pay the mortgage with it? As the saying goes, "Talk's cheap."

I call those empty displays "crocodile patriotism," meaningless posturing designed to make us all feel good about ourselves, less guilty about letting others bear the entire blood price of our government's military adventurism. Meanwhile, our servicemen and women and our veterans are committing suicide at the rate of 22 per day, according to the Veterans Administration, which also admits to a current backlog of 161,000 unadjudicated claims along with an additional 287,000 claims being appealed by veterans who believe their cases were not fairly settled.

Moreover, private organizations such as the Wounded Warrior

12. The American War in Vietnam

Project and Vet2Vet routinely ask for donations from the American public in order to provide care and services to our veterans. If, as Obama claimed, "because of Vietnam and our [Vietnam] veterans ... we [now] 'take care of our veterans better,'" why do these private organizations need to exist? Isn't this what my tax dollars are supposed to be doing by way of the Veterans Administration? The U.S. government has enough money to own over 9,000 Abrams main battle tanks costing $4.3 million each. Enough money to own 10 aircraft carrier battle groups with a whole new and larger class of carriers costing three times as much now under construction, 79 submarines, 363 drone aircraft, but private organizations have to beg for money from the U.S. public because the government doesn't have enough money to adequately care for the veterans our president insists we honor and care for?

To my amazement and dismay, few of my fellow citizens seem to be asking themselves these questions. I think it is because they have been gulled into accepting and internalizing a version of history that is largely fiction. Indeed, if one goes to the Vietnam War Commemoration website itself, prepared and sponsored by the U.S. Department of Defense, one will find that the timeline for the Vietnam War begins only with Ho Chi Minh's declaration of Vietnamese independence on September 2, 1945. There is nothing about the 80 years of brutal and exploitative French colonial rule. Nothing about Ho's attempt to meet with Woodrow Wilson in 1919. Nothing about U.S. support of and collaboration with Ho during the latter stages of the Pacific War against Japan. Nor about Ho's letters to President Harry Truman in 1945 and 1946. Nor about the French naval bombardment of Hai Phong in November 1946.

A search of the Department of Defense website for references to Martin Luther King, Jr., and his landmark 1967 speech "Beyond Vietnam: A Time to Break Silence" turns up nothing. A search for Daniel Ellsberg and the *Pentagon Papers* turns up nothing. The most powerful antiwar movement in the history of our nation is all but invisible in the government's official commemoration of the Vietnam War, as if it had never even existed.

The entire website is riddled with such oversights as well as distortions, misrepresentations, and falsehoods. The mass murders at My Lai show up on the timeline, but it is not called a massacre; it also reports that only one man—Lt. William Calley—was convicted of murder, saying that he was sentenced to life in prison, but neglecting to add that he served just three years under house arrest before being pardoned by President Richard Nixon. Meanwhile, the timeline includes the name of

What We Can and Can't Afford

every American who received the Medal of Honor. Each Medal of Honor winner gets a multi-page entry describing in detail his heroism while the entry on My Lai receives three short sentences and Ho's declaration of independence is covered in two sentences.

The whole point, of course, is to whitewash what actually happened in Vietnam—what the U.S. did to the Vietnamese—and focus only on the nobility and heroism and sacrifice of America's Vietnam War veterans, who, as Obama says in his speech, "did your job. You served with honor. You made us proud." The official flag of the Commemoration says, "Service, Valor, Sacrifice," and "A Grateful Nation Thanks and Honors You."

During my thirteen months in Vietnam, I regularly witnessed and participated in the destruction of civilian homes, the most brutal interrogations of civilians, and the routine killing of men, women, and children along with their crops and livestock. The people we were supposedly defending in fact hated us because we destroyed their forests with chemical defoliants, burned their fields with napalm, flattened their villages with 500-pound bombs, and called them gooks, chinks, slopes, dinks, and zipperheads, turning their sons into shoeshine boys and their daughters into whores. Is this what the president meant when he said, "You made us proud"?

But the new version of the American War in Vietnam does not contain any of these facts. It contains very few facts at all. Consider again the Department of Defense's 50th Anniversary Commemoration. Fiftieth anniversary of what? Apparently, the official version of the war does not begin until 1965 when the Marines first landed at Danang. Not when French soldiers returned to Vietnam aboard U.S.-flagged ships in 1945. Not when the U.S. began to pay the cost of the French War in 1950. Not when the U.S. plucked Ngo Dinh Diem from a Maryknoll seminary in New Jersey and installed him as head of a "nation" the U.S. created, hailing him as "the Winston Churchill of Asia." Not when John Kennedy sent "advisors" and air squadrons to Vietnam. Not when the U.S. backed a coup against Diem, nor when the U.S. Congress passed the Gulf of Tonkin Resolution after being deliberately lied to about what had happened in the Gulf of Tonkin and why.

But this is very much in keeping with Obama's insistence that "history will honor [Vietnam veterans'] service, and your names will join a story of service that stretches back two centuries." For the story Obama refers to is mythology, not actual history. It does not include 283 years of almost continuous warfare against the native peoples who were

12. The American War in Vietnam

living in North America when Europeans first arrived and who needed to be removed and ultimately exterminated in order to make room for John Winthrop's City Upon a Hill and the Manifest Destiny of white Anglo-Americans. It does not mention that those gallant Texans at the Alamo were fighting for the freedom to keep their Black slaves. It does not mention that President James Polk deliberately provoked a war with Mexico in order to steal half of Mexico's land. It does not mention that wealthy American sugar planter Sanford Dole used the U.S. Marines to depose Queen Liliuokalani and steal Hawaii from the Hawaiians. It does not mention that Theodore Roosevelt and his powerful friends provoked a war with Spain in order to embark on the creation of an American overseas empire, then betrayed both the Cubans and the Filipinos. It does not mention that for much of the 20th century, the U.S. government used the Marines in Central America and the Caribbean to create a favorable business climate and collect debts for Big Business, Wall Street, and American bankers. The words of Marine Major General Smedley Butler, two-time Medal of Honor winner, are worth repeating here:

> I spent 33 years and 4 months in the Marine Corps. And during that period I spent most of my time being a high-class muscle man for Big Business, for Wall Street and for the bankers. In short, I was a racketeer for capitalism. Thus I helped make Mexico and especially Tampico safe for American oil interests in 1914. I helped make Haiti and Cuba a decent place for the National City Bank boys to collect revenues in. I helped in the raping of half a dozen Central American republics for the benefit of Wall Street. The record of racketeering is long. I helped purify Nicaragua for the international banking house of Brown Brothers 1909–12. I brought light to the Dominican Republic for American sugar interests in 1916. I helped make Honduras "right" for American fruit companies in 1903. In China in 1927 I helped see to it that Standard Oil went its way unmolested.

You won't find any mention of Butler in most US high school history textbooks. Nor that US financiers stood to lose vast fortunes if Germany had won the First World War. Nor that the Pacific War in World War Two was mostly a matter of multiple empires competing for the same geographical territory. Nor that by the mid–1950s the US had the Soviet Union ringed with nuclear missiles, all of them pointed at Moscow.

There is a great deal that seldom gets mentioned about American history. My students are continually amazed by what they have never heard before in their lives. Most Americans have never heard the

What We Can and Can't Afford

history of their country, a history that includes much to be proud of, but equally as much to be ashamed of. The great American poet Walt Whitman once said, "The real war will never get in the books." He was referring to the American Civil War, but it pertains equally to just about any and every American war. And as James Loewen makes clear in his book *Lies My Teacher Told Me*, real American history will never get in the books, either. At least not in the books that most Americans read and accept as fact.

Thus, most Americans, if they think about the Vietnam War at all these many years later, are content to accept the fallacy that it was a noble cause fought by valorous young men who sacrificed for the greater cause of freedom against an evil communist enemy hellbent on conquest, and who were unfairly abused and unappreciated by unpatriotic cowards when they returned home. Meanwhile, the wrong people learned that by removing most Americans from any responsibility for or consequences of U.S. foreign policy, by placing the entire blood burden of U.S. foreign policy on the shoulders of a small segment of the American population—and that segment with the least voice in public affairs—the American military industrial complex that President Dwight Eisenhower warned against, but did nothing to stop or change, can do whatever it wants to do in the world without fear of domestic political consequences.

Meanwhile, the one lesson that no one in power in Washington seems to have learned is that no amount of military might can achieve goals that are unrealistic and incompatible with the beliefs, desires, and cultures of those at the other end of the rifle barrels and Hellfire missiles, and thus unachievable. If the Vietnam War did not drive home that lesson, certainly subsequent U.S. forays into Iraq, Somalia, Afghanistan, Libya, and now Syria should have made that lesson clear. But there really is such a phenomenon as "the arrogance of power," and we are watching it in action on a daily basis.

13

When the Chickens Came Home to Roost
The Vietnam War and the 60s Generation

(*LA Progressive*, April 16, 2016)

In early 1970, Vice President Spiro Agnew had this to say about the so-called Sixties Generation:

> As for these deserters, malcontents, radicals, incendiaries, the civil and the uncivil disobedients among our youth, SDS, PLP, Weathermen I and Weathermen II, the revolutionary action movement, the Black United Front, Yippies, Hippies, Yahoos, Black Panthers, Lions and Tigers alike—I would swap the whole damn zoo for a single platoon of the kind of young Americans I saw in Vietnam.

This is a fascinating statement for multiple reasons and on multiple levels. To begin with, a single platoon of the kind of young Americans he saw in Vietnam went into a village we remember as My Lai and murdered 504 unarmed men, women and children. On the same day, in the nearby village of My Khe, another unit of the same division murdered an estimated 155 additional Vietnamese civilians.* While I personally did not participate in or witness killing on that scale, I and my fellow Marines routinely killed, maimed, and abused Vietnamese on a near-daily basis, destroying homes, fields, crops, and livestock with every weapon available to us from rifles and grenades to heavy artillery to napalm. We thought it was funny to run Vietnamese off the

---

* According to John Marciano, in an e-mail to me dated 4/17/16, the figures are 407 and 97 respectively. In my opinion, and in his, this in no way lessens the atrocity.

What We Can and Can't Afford

roads with our vehicles and throw cans of C-rations at children as if we were hurling baseballs for strikeouts. We called the Vietnamese slopes, dinks, slants, zipperheads, and gooks.

It is no wonder, it turns out, that Agnew should be so fond of the kind of young Americans he saw in Vietnam, since he himself turned out to be a criminal who was forced to resign his office in public disgrace.

Meanwhile, a great many of the kind of young Americans he saw in Vietnam became the deserters he excoriates (it is a fact that most military desertions occurred after service in Vietnam, not before). Many other soldiers and former soldiers—motivated by feelings of shame, anger, betrayal, conscience, patriotism, decency, honesty, and every conceivable combination thereof—joined the malcontents, radicals, incendiaries, civil and uncivil disobedients, becoming heavily involved in the anti–Vietnam War movement through organizations like Vietnam Veterans Against the War, the Concerned Officers Movement, and the American Servicemen's Union.

As for the Black United Front, the Black Panthers, and other discontented minorities, one wonders if Spiro T. ever wondered why no one was prosecuted for the 1963 bombing of the 16th Street Baptist Church, though the FBI knew who had done it by 1965,* ever pondered the impact on Black Americans of the murder of Martin Luther King, Jr., ever noticed that in 1970 the infant mortality rate among white Americans was 13.8 while for black Americans it was 22.8.

Yippies, Hippies and Yahoos sounds colorful—like nattering nabobs of negativism—though it would have been even more alliterative if he'd said Hippies, Yippies and Yahoos, a distinction only a poet might notice, and Agnew was certainly no poet. And I suppose it's just coincidence that the National Football League Lions and Major League Baseball Tigers are both Detroit athletic teams, the city where major riots occurred in 1967 after the cops raided a party celebrating the safe return home of two Black Vietnam War veterans.

But how did such a large portion of my generation become deserters, malcontents, radicals, incendiaries, civil and uncivil disobedients, Yippies, Hippies, Yahoos, and Black Panthers? How did Nat King Cole and the Lettermen morph into Janis Joplin and Jefferson Starship? How did Students for a Democratic Society become the Weather

---

* One man was finally charged in 1977, and two others in 2001 and 2002 respectively; a fourth died without ever being charged.

13. When the Chickens Came Home to Roost

Underground? How did "My country 'tis of thee" turn into "We gotta get out of this place"?

We were, after all, raised by The Greatest Generation, weren't we? They'd survived the Great Depression and defeated the Nazis and Imperial Japan. They'd given us Levittowns and McDonald's and drive-in movies and fluoride and "one nation under God."* We'd grown up watching wholesome American families on shows like *Father Knows Best* and *Ozzie and Harriet,* learned about good and evil from shows like *Gunsmoke* and *Bonanza,* and came to understand the insidious ever-present threat of communism through shows like *I Led Three Lives.*

In my hometown of Perkasie, Pennsylvania, as far back as I can remember, we had a parade every Memorial Day that included the Pennridge high school and junior high school marching bands, complete with majorettes and color guards, uniformed members of the American Legion and Veterans of Foreign Wars marching in formation, the trucks of Perkasie Volunteer Fire Company No.1, Boy Scouts, Girl Scouts, Cub Scouts, Brownie Scouts, and assorted kids on bicycles decorated with red, white & blue crepe paper. Every school day started with a reading from the Bible (at least until 1963, when a suspiciously liberal Supreme Court ruled the practice an unconstitutional mixing of church and state) followed by the Pledge of Allegiance (under God). I Liked Ike, and when John Kennedy said, "Ask not what your country can do for you; ask what you can do for your country," I was old enough to be inspired, and inspired enough to enlist in the Marines only a few years later.

College could wait. I had watched with growing alarm as Communism spread its tentacles over the face of the globe: the violent repression of the Hungarian Revolution, the Berlin Wall, the Cuban Missile Crisis, communist insurgency in Laos (China had already been lost before I was old enough to remember), Khrushchev shouting, "We will bury you!" Kennedy dead, killed by a traitorous defector who had lived in the Soviet Union before returning with a Russian wife to murder the hero who had created the Peace Corps. And now his successor was saying that if we did not fight the communists in Vietnam, we would one day have to fight them on the sands of Waikiki.

I wasn't naïve, or perhaps more accurately, I didn't think I was naive. I knew the United States of America wasn't perfect. By the early 1960s, I could see on television young Black Americans being beaten

---

* "Under God" was not added to the Pledge of Allegiance until 1954.

What We Can and Can't Afford

in bus stations for trying to ride a bus, having ketchup and mustard poured over their heads while sitting at segregated lunch counters, being attacked with fire hoses and vicious dogs while singing the same hymns I sang in St. Stephen's United Church of Christ. George Wallace might declare, "Segregation now, segregation tomorrow, segregation forever," but that was the South, the Old Confederacy, the sore losers. And the American government and the American people were doing something about it. It was a wrong that would be righted, was even now in the process of being righted before our very eyes.

But as the decade of the sixties moved forward, the luster began to fade. The progression, or perhaps I should say decline, was gradual, slower for some than for others, but it was steady. As the televised images of white violence against peaceful blacks asking only for the right to vote and the decency to be treated as human beings went on and on, year after year, with the gains incremental and often hard to see, and with racial tensions erupting not just in the Old Confederacy, but in Philadelphia, Los Angeles, and New York City, the liberty and justice for all proclaimed in the Pledge of Allegiance seemed increasingly like empty words.

Meanwhile, my generation's shining knight having been struck down in his prime and just as we were truly expecting a golden age of Camelot (clichéd, I know, but nevertheless how could one *not* believe a new beginning was in the offing with so handsome and vigorous and young a president and his beautiful, glamorous wife), his replacement, an aging Texan with big ears and a ponderous drawl, kept insisting the U.S. wanted only peace and not a wider war while he took the U.S. deeper and deeper into a nightmare where Buddhist monks burned themselves to death in public, supersonic jets dropped jellied gasoline on fields plowed by water buffalo, and American boys came home in body bags in ever-increasing numbers with nothing at all to show for it but the hot air that rose from politicians' and generals' mouths.

Perhaps most frustrating of all, it did not seem as if either our government or our elders cared in the least what we thought or felt. Twenty-five hundred antiwar demonstrators became 25,000 antiwar demonstrators became 250,000 antiwar demonstrators, but it did not matter. One president was driven from office and another who promised to end the war was elected, but the war simply went on and on and on. Meanwhile, programs designed to help the poor and advance civil rights were crippled by a lack of commitment and gutted by the need to fund the war in Southeast Asia.

13. When the Chickens Came Home to Roost

That Black efforts to achieve equal rights became more militant and strident and angry as the decade progressed, that the antiwar movement transformed from peaceful marchers wearing jackets, ties, skirts and blouses into chanting protestors wearing tie-dyed t-shirts and love beads are to me measures of the increasingly frantic efforts of my generation to get our parents' generation to stop behaving as if they were out of their minds.

I know I am generalizing broadly here, but I think I do represent a broad swath of my generation. And I was raised to believe absolutely that the United States of America was the pinnacle of civilization, the epitome of freedom, the finest nation that had ever existed. We were truly the land of the free and the home of the brave, a nation of the people by the people and for the people, the country that most stood for equal opportunity, goodness and decency, the hope of oppressed peoples everywhere.

I wanted my country to be what I had believed all my life that it was. When I went off to Vietnam, I honestly believed that John Kennedy and Abraham Lincoln were smiling down at me from on high, that I was going to save the Vietnamese from the scourge of communism, that my country needed me to preserve all those freedoms we hold so dear. What evidence I already had that what I believed might not be entirely accurate, I was able to hold at bay because it takes a lot of force to dislodge a lifetime of conditioning. A week traveling through the Deep South when I was 16, an English teacher who tried to show me a wider world, a Quaker friend who told me just before I left for Vietnam, "Please try not to kill anyone," could hardly begin to make a dent in the certitude I had been conditioned to think was truth.

And then I ran headlong into reality in the rice fields and villages of Vietnam. It was a bewildering and horrifying and shattering awakening. Profoundly disturbing. Life-altering. I cannot begin to detail here all that happened over the course of my thirteen months in Vietnam or the path those experiences set me on, but suffice it to say that I finally had to confront the reality that what my parents' generation had taught me about who and what my country was—was bullshit. It was lies, delusions, hypocrisy, fiction. And when I finally began to understand that, it made me angry.

Other members of my generation have different stories to tell, different paths they followed, different experiences that shaped them. But I think most of us ended up at the same conclusion: that America, our United States of America, was not what we had been taught to believe

What We Can and Can't Afford

it was. That our parents' generation, the Greatest Generation, wasn't so great after all. The Generation Gap didn't just invent itself or develop out of thin air. We didn't start saying—and believing—that you couldn't trust anyone over 30 just because it sounded good. Our elders might blame our behavior and dress and beliefs on Dr. Spock and too little application of the belt, but Dr. Spock didn't raise us; their generation did. The generation that criticized us for enjoying the materialism they had created for us. The generation that was now sending so many of us off to die on the other side of the world. The generation that had lived their entire lives complacently ignoring the plight of Black Americans south and north. The generation that mocked us as "Yippies, Hippies, and Yahoos."

Long before the '60s painfully rolled over into the '70s, bringing us the invasion of Cambodia, the murders at Kent and Jackson States, the Pentagon Papers, and the invasion of Laos, if long hair and colorful clothes and marijuana pissed off the older generation, hurray for that. If amped-up drums and screeching guitars and politically charged lyrics upset our elders, we figured we must be doing something right. If women and gays and Latinos and Native Americans were demanding equality, it was about goddamned time.

There was, of course, no shortage of people in my generation that aren't covered by my sweeping generalizations. There were members of my generation who hated people like Bayard Rustin and Tom Hayden and Dick Gregory and Abbie Hoffman and Phil Ochs. Dick "Dick" Cheney and John Negroponte, Rush Limbaugh and Bill O'Reilly, John Boehner and Robert Zoellick are all more or less my contemporaries. And as the late Paul Lyons amply demonstrated in his book *Class of '66: Living in Suburban Middle America*, a large portion of the Sixties Generation neither fought in Vietnam nor protested the war, but merely sidestepped it and went on with their lives. That's why they had no problem with draft-dodging Dan Quayle as vice president and draft-dodging George W. Bush as president; in these men, who avoided risking their lives in Vietnam without personal or political consequence, much of my generation saw themselves and their own choices during the Sixties.

But a lot of us did find unavoidable the contradictions between what we'd been taught and what we could see, and chose not to ignore what we were seeing. We wanted America to be what we had been taught to believe that it was. For a while, many of us believed we could make it so.

13. When the Chickens Came Home to Roost

And for all my discouragement about the reactionary backlash that has consumed the United States since the rise of Ronald Reagan, a backlash that has seen huge numbers of Americans voting against their own self-interests election after election, the removal of the consequences of American foreign policy from domestic politics, the terrifying rise of the national security state, and the most obscene maldistribution of wealth this country has seen since the Gilded Age, the Sixties Generation—our generation—has had a lasting impact.

Who would ever have thought we'd live to see a Black president? (Even if he isn't really African American with the full heritage of slavery, poverty, and systematic de-humanization imbedded in his ancestry and his DNA, but is quite literally half–African and half–American, and even if he's disappointed many of us who had actually believed "Yes He Could," the mere fact of his election was something I never thought I'd live to see.) Who would have thought the Supreme Court of the United States—this Supreme Court in particular—would ever rule that banning gay marriage is unconstitutional? Who would have imagined Muhammad Ali lighting the torch at a U.S.-hosted Olympic Games, or a Gold Medal Olympic decathlete publicly going transgender? Or the legalization or decriminalization of marijuana in 26 states and counting? Or a woman as a viable candidate for president? Or a Socialist making a serious bid for the White House?

Okay, I'm well aware that these developments don't challenge the fundamental tenets of the military-industrial-security state. But tell the gay couple who are finally being treated with equality under the law that the Supreme Court's decision is of no real importance. Tell the thousands and thousands of transgender Americans that cultural acceptance of Caitlin Jenner isn't significant. Tell Black Americans that electing a Black president isn't progress. Tell people receiving chemotherapy that being able to smoke marijuana to relieve their nausea makes no difference. Tell American girls it doesn't matter that a woman might finally become president (even if, alas, this one happens to be a warmongering Wall Street toady, the very fact of her gender would have been unthinkable to previous generations).

One only needs to look at how the Democratic party and the mainstream media stacked the deck against Bernie Sanders to realize that the system is still so deeply entrenched as to seem invulnerable, unassailable, impervious to change or improvement, let alone to being dismantled. But what do you do with that conclusion? Jump off a bridge? Move to Tahiti? Drink yourself under the table? I prefer to take satisfaction in the things progressives have accomplished since I was a young man, to live my life as if real change is still possible.

Not long ago in my fair city, as the Democratic National Convention was anointing the Wicked Witch of the West as their candidate for president and Feeling-the-Bernie was breaking the hearts of progressives by proving himself to be, in the end, just another politician, I took to the streets with some thousands of other people whose heads are not up their backsides.

The official theme of the march was "Clean Energy," but I marched with members of Philadelphia Chapter 31 of Veterans for Peace, and all sorts of other causes and issues were represented from Black Lives Matter to Code Pink to the Granny Peace Brigade. Moreover, it wasn't just us old aging hippies and peaceniks. A huge number of the march's participants were a younger generation, men and women in their 30s and 20s. One of them was my 29-year-old daughter, who is the one who induced me to take to the streets again, something I hadn't done in years.

And in the midst of that raucous, high-spirited, good-natured crowd of people who refuse to accept The Way Things Are, I found myself thinking that maybe, just maybe, the sixties aren't over yet. Poor old Spiro T. must be turning in his grave. I certainly hope so.

14

Samuel Johnson Was Right[*]

(*New Hampshire Gazette*, November 10, 2017)

While I haven't yet chosen to kneel during the playing of our national anthem, I don't take off my hat and place my hand over my heart either. I don't even wear a hat to events where the anthem might be played, at least in part so I don't have to take it off. And rather than putting my hand over my heart, I only stand with my hands at my side.

I joined the U.S. Marines when I was 17 years old and voluntarily fought in Vietnam, where I was wounded in combat, and eventually promoted to sergeant and awarded an honorable discharge.

By no stretch of the imagination can any knowledgeable person construe what I did in Vietnam as having anything at all to do with your right to go to the church of your choice or marry the person you love or choose the brand of shampoo you want. I did serve proud and arrogant men who, however well-meaning they may (or may not) have been, were utterly ignorant of what was happening in Vietnam and why, but I most assuredly did nothing to protect my country, let alone serve my country or the best interests of humanity. That anyone would respect me or want to thank me for my "service" always leaves me wondering.

And I wonder how many of today's American servicemen and women are actually engaged in protecting our country. Do we really need to deploy U.S. military forces to at least 150 other countries around the world? Do we really need twelve aircraft carrier battle groups to protect our country when the next largest carrier fleet consists of one used ship the Chinese bought from Ukraine? Is deploying NATO troops to former East Bloc countries and placing missile defense systems in

---

[*] Back in 1775, according to James Boswell, his biographer, Johnson famously said, "Patriotism is the last refuge of a scoundrel."

What We Can and Can't Afford

Romania any less aggressive or provocative than Russia annexing Crimea?

We could debate these points, perhaps, but here are some other points to think about:

According to the World Health Organization, the United States ranks 37th in healthcare (quality, accessibility, and cost) behind such nations as Portugal, Colombia, and Morocco. Our infant mortality rate is the highest in the developed world, surpassing such nations as Slovakia, Belarus, and Cuba.

Depending on which barometer one uses, U.S. secondary education ranks as low as 29th (behind Slovenia, Latvia, and Vietnam) or as high as 14th (behind Russia and Poland). No survey in recent decades has placed the U.S. in the top ten.

The U.S. puts more of its citizens behind bars than any other nation on earth: 724 out of every 100,000. Our closest competitor is Russia at 581 per 100,000.

African Americans comprise 13.2 percent of our population, but since 1976 have made up 34.6 percent of those we put to death by state-sanctioned execution.

If the number of Americans living in poverty were organized as a sovereign state, those 45 million Americans would be a nation larger than 165 of the 195 countries in the world today. Meanwhile, the top 1 percent of our population possesses 40 percent of our national wealth while the bottom 80 percent possesses only 7 percent of our national wealth.

For the most recent figures I could fine (2013), 11,208 Americans were murdered by other Americans using firearms. Between 2005 and 2015, 71 Americans died by acts of terrorism in the U.S. while 301,797 died by gun violence.

Annual U.S. military spending is greater than the next 17 countries combined. We spend six times as much on defense as China does, and 11 times more than Russia. At the same time, we provide 50 percent of all arms sales to the rest of the world. Russia, our closest competitor, provides less than a third of that amount.

And we haven't even gotten to the problems Colin Kaepernick was trying to bring to public discussion when he chose to kneel last year during the playing of the anthem: police brutality and minority oppression. In 2015, for instance, 102 unarmed Black Americans were killed by police; only ten officers were charged with a crime, and only two were convicted. While unarmed whites are also killed by police, Blacks make

14. Samuel Johnson Was Right

up 37 percent of the total although they are only 13 percent of the population, figures which uncannily reflect our legal execution rates as well.

While one might quibble with the exact statistics in any given example above (as Mark Twain famously said, "There are lies, damned lies, and statistics"), the substance of each of these statements is true.

So, when we play the national anthem before sporting events as a sign of "respect," I wonder just exactly what it is that I'm being asked to respect. It seems to me that I'm being asked to forget, ignore, overlook, or condone a whole lot of stuff we all ought to be ashamed of and trying to do something about.

When I hear people accusing these NFL players of disrespecting our country, or our servicemen and women, or our flag, I find myself wondering what any of them have been doing besides feeding at the trough. Consider, for instance, our current commander-in-chief's military service record. Oh, wait! He doesn't have one. It's easy to stick an American flag pin in your lapel and get all teary-eyed when "The Star-Spangled Banner" gets played. But Carl Schurz* didn't say, "My country right or wrong." What he said was, "My country right or wrong; if right, to be kept right; if wrong, to be set right." What have those who've been dumping on Colin Kaepernick and his fellow kneelers done to set our country right?

And if Kaepernick or anyone else wants to sit through the national anthem, or kneel, or stand on their heads and blow bubbles, that's their right. Not their privilege. Not an act of treason or a lack of patriotism. It is their right as Americans.

When the symbols of freedom replace the substance of freedom, we're all in a whole lot of trouble.

---

* Civil War general, U.S. senator and Interior Secretary.

15

Remarks at the Horsham Air Guard Station

Drone Facility
October 28, 2017

What prompts Luke Skywalker to join the Resistance? Death from the sky perpetrated by a powerful Empire.

George W. Bush ordered 57 drone strikes during his presidency. Obama authorized 542 strikes in 8 years (1 every 5+ days). Trump ordered 75 in his first 74 days (1+ per day). But you know the substance of all this, if not the exact statistics.

I am sure the men and women operating this facility think that what they are doing is justified and necessary. Given that I joined the Marines when I was 17 and eagerly volunteered to fight in Vietnam, fully believing that I was doing good and fighting evil, I'm not inclined to pass judgment on the young men and women who believe what they are told by people they trust.

It is the people they trust who are the criminals.

But so what? Who's going to arrest them? You? Me? What are we doing here today, anyway? Who are we kidding? You think anybody's listening? For all the difference we're making, we might as well be home picking lint out of our navels.

Except that I have to live with myself. And I suppose you're all in the same bind. I know that nothing I do will make a damn bit of difference, but I also know that if I do nothing, I'm as guilty as the folks who are doing things I believe are not only wrong in a moral or humanitarian sense, but counterproductive and guaranteed to produce more recruits for "the Resistance."

Now I do have to admit that I don't usually participate in these kinds of vigils. They make me feel too conspicuous and even a little silly.

15. *Remarks at the Horsham Air Guard Station*

I mean seriously, I can't imagine that the folks inside here are doing anything other than laughing at us. I wouldn't even be here today except that the Brandywine Peace Community's Bob Smith asked me to come, and I always have a hard time saying no to Bob. So here I am.

But my usual form of protest is writing. Writing I can do in the privacy of my own home. No one's laughing at me. I don't run the risk of being arrested. Or beaten up by folks like those "good people" Trump said were demonstrating in Charlottesville a month or so ago. And then I publish my poems, and some people read them and get all inspired, and *they* go out and look silly or get arrested or beaten up, or sometimes all three.

But today, as long as I'm already here, I'll just share a few of my poems with you. Indeed, this first one I'll read is at the request of Bob Smith himself:

For Mrs. Na
Cu Chi District
December 1985

> I always told myself,
> if I ever got the chance to go back,
> I'd never say "I'm sorry"
> to anyone. Christ,

> those guys I saw on television once:
> sitting in Hanoi, the cameras rolling,
> crying, blubbering
> all over the place. Sure,

> I'm sorry. I never meant
> to do the things I did.
> But that was nearly twenty years ago:
> enough's enough.

> If I ever go back,
> I always told myself,
> I'll hold my head steady
> and look them in the eye.

> But here I am at last—
> and here you are.
> And you lost five sons in the war.
> And you haven't any left.

> And I'm staring at my hands
> and eating tears,
> trying to think of something else to say
> besides "I'm sorry."

What We Can and Can't Afford

Manning the Walls

The day the towers came down, goggle-eyed
we stared in disbelief at death for once
so close to home we couldn't hide
our terror in the rubble of Manhattan:
complacency turned upside down and strewn
across a Pennsylvania field in burning pieces,
even Mars, our God of War, in flames.
Who'd have thought it possible? What next?

Overnight the world had changed forever,
all bets off, all the rules suspended
in the urgency to save our way of life
from lethal challenges so sinister
we need the Stars-n-Stripes in every classroom
and the FBI needs secret access
to the records of the books we're reading:
Dostoyevsky, Danielle Steele—you never
know what might be useful to a terrorist.

Well okay, I was as scared as anyone
that day, and I won't deny the world
we live in is a dangerous place.

But I remember gazing at the tiny
dot of Sputnik in the darkness
over Perkasie when I was only nine,
my country at the mercy of the Reds,
the world changed forever overnight.

I learned to Duck-n-Cover at my desk
in Mrs. Vera's room at Third Street School.
I learned to recognize the yellow signs
on public buildings reassuring us
of shelter from the Russians' atom bombs.
I learned we had a missile gap, a fail-
safe point, a hotline to the Kremlin.

That's how I grew up: Nikita Khrushchev,
Ich bin ein Berliner, Armageddon
always just a missile strike away.

One hell of a lot of good the basement
of the Bucks County Bank & Trust would do
against a thermonuclear warhead,
but anyone who tried to point this out
was either nuts, naive, or communist.

15. Remarks at the Horsham Air Guard Station

Most of us got lucky in the Cold War—
provided we ignore Korea,
Vietnam, the brushfire wars our proxies
fought around the globe for forty years,
the millions dead and maimed and dispossessed.
At least we never dropped the Big One, and
the good old USA came out on top.

No wonder our surprise on 9–11
to discover Huns outside the gates again.
Cry havoc, sound alarums, man the walls!

But any history buff can trace the rise
and fall of empires: Pax Romana,
Rule Britannia, Persia, Babylon,
Ottomans and Incas by the sword
made arrogant, and by the sword brought down.
Catastrophe is history's middle name,
and taking off our shoes in airports,
locking up librarians, inventing
threats that don't exist, I pledge allegiance
to the flag, one nation under God or not,
isn't going to save us from the Visigoths,
the Mongol hordes, Bin Laden, or ourselves.

Barbarism, communism, terrorism,
name your ism, something's always out there
in the darkness wanting in. You'd think
by now—we're talking generations here,
millenia, the whole of human time—
we'd figure out we're all in this together
and it's time to learn to share. Ask the Greeks.
Ask the Hittites. Ask the dinosaurs.

16

In Memory of Horace Coleman

(*VVAW Veteran*, Fall 2017)

I am deeply saddened by the news that Horace Coleman has died, though it doesn't come as a surprise. I had known he was in poor health for some time. I only ever met Horace twice: a long time ago when a group of us veteran-poets read in New York City—I think it was at the Public Theatre in the early 1980s—and again at the VVAW 40th Anniversary in Chicago, but I've known of him and been in touch with him

Horace Coleman at VVAW's 40th Anniversary in Chicago, 2007 (photo courtesy of Brooke Anderson and Vietnam Veterans Against the War).

16. In Memory of Horace Coleman

since 1975 when Jan Barry and I were compiling *Demilitarized Zones: Veterans After Vietnam*. We used several of Horace's poems in that book. He subsequently published several collections of his own, including *Between a Rock & a Hard Place* and *In the Grass*, and when I was putting together *Carrying the Darkness: The Poetry of the Vietnam War* in 1985, *and Unaccustomed Mercy: Soldier-Poets of the Vietnam War* in 1988, Horace ended up with multiple poems in both books. I am sorry Horace is gone, but I am glad that his voice will continue to be heard through his poetry.

17

A True Spat-Upon Soldier Story

(*New Hampshire Gazette*, September 29, 2017; *LA Progressive*, October 7, 2017; *Monthly Review*, October 15, 2017)

One of the most widely promulgated and enduring myths of the American War in Vietnam is the belief—indeed the conviction among countless Americans young and old—that soldiers returning from Vietnam were accosted by antiwar demonstrators, spit on, called baby killers, verbally and even physically assaulted and abused.

That does not accord with my own experiences. I returned to the U.S. from Asia twice in full military uniform, March 1968 and June 1969, both times passing through San Francisco airport—the heart of hippiedom—on my way home to Philadelphia. No one ever accosted me.

In May 1970, after the killings at Kent State, I joined the antiwar movement, but I did not spit on myself or call myself "baby killer." Moreover, I never saw anyone else around me abusing soldiers or veterans.

Vietnam War veteran Jerry Lembcke reinforces my anecdotal evidence in his book *The Spitting Image: Myth, Memory, and the Legacy of Vietnam* (NYU Press, 2000), which thoroughly investigates and debunks these stories of abuse.

I, however, do have a true "spat-upon veteran story." It goes like this:

The day after I came home from Vietnam in early March 1968, I took the money I'd saved in those 13 months and went to West German Motors in Ft. Washington, PA, and bought a brand-new Volkswagen. VW Beetle. Red with black interior.

Only I didn't buy it. I had to give the money to my father, and he bought it because I was not legally old enough to buy a car. The owner's card remained in my father's name for the next year and a half until I turned 21, which was the age of majority then in Pennsylvania.

The day after that, I went to McKeever Insurance, in my hometown

17. A True Spat-Upon Soldier Story

of Perkasie, PA, to get insurance for my car. But Mrs. McKeever told me I couldn't get a policy in my name. I would have to be carried on my parents' policy as a dependent child.

Understand what I'm saying here: I had just spent 13 months fighting in Vietnam. I was a combat-wounded Marine Corps sergeant, but the state of Pennsylvania recognized me only as a child dependent on my parents.

Let me say that again: I had just spent 13 months fighting in Vietnam. I was a combat-wounded Marine Corps sergeant, but the state of Pennsylvania recognized me only as a dependent child.

Indeed, I could not even legally buy a beer in my own hometown.

And when I began college in the fall of 1969, unlike the World War II and Korean War veterans who received full college tuition plus monthly living expenses in recognition of their service, I got $135 a month for every month I spent in the Marines, which was hardly enough to buy my books and cover the cost of my dorm room; it didn't begin to cover my tuition.

You want to talk about abuse and disrespect? I was indeed abused and disrespected when I came home from the Vietnam War, but it wasn't the antiwar people who were abusing and disrespecting me.

And in perpetuating the myth that I was abused by the very antiwar movement I joined, rather than by the government that sent me to Vietnam in the first place, my fellow citizens are distorting history, placing blame where it does not belong, and allowing the real abusers to avoid responsibility for the terrible damage they caused.

18

God, Jesus, and the Vietnam War

(*New York Times*, November 10, 2017)

I arrived in Vietnam in early February 1967, and was assigned to 1st Battalion, 1st Marines. After falling away from the Church in my mid-teens, I'd had a religious re-awakening at Parris Island, where I found myself much in need of God's mercy because we got none from our drill instructors. I took my renewed religious fervor to Vietnam with me, and soon got to know our battalion chaplain, a Jesuit priest, pretty well.

Many months later, in November, the battalion was on an operation near the DMZ. Night was approaching, and I was digging in when Father Lyons came by. The conversation, which I still remember vividly, went something like this:

"Hello, Corporal Ehrhart. How's it going?"

"Not bad, Father." I said. "Can't complain."

"You know, Corporal, I don't mean to put you on the spot, but I do miss the talks we used to have when you first got here. You were more faithful than my Catholic boys," he laughed.

"Things change, Father."

"What happened, Corporal Ehrhart? What's wrong?"

"What's wrong, Father? Take a look around. And you're asking me what's wrong? Look, I'm sorry, sir; I'd rather not get into it."

"You can talk to me, son; that's what I'm here for."

"Man to man?"

"Of course. Making me an officer wasn't my idea."

"Father, when I enlisted, I thought I was doing the right thing. I thought I was doing right by my country—gonna help the Vietnamese, and all like that. I really believed it. I guess that sounds pretty corny, doesn't it?"

18. God, Jesus, and the Vietnam War

"Not at all, son. We all want to believe we're doing the right thing."

"Well, I don't believe it anymore. I don't know what I believe, but I sure don't believe that. We're not doing anybody any good around here, and any fool can see that. Well, anyway, the thing is, there I'd be, going to chapel every week and praying to God to forgive what I'm doing, knowing all the time I was just gonna go out and do more of the same thing the next day. Father, any God worth His salt isn't gonna buy that for a minute. It got to where I could almost hear Him up there while I was praying: 'Don't hand me this crap again, Ehrhart. Just don't bother me unless you're serious.' After awhile, every time I'd try to pray, there'd be that Voice."

Cpl. Ehrhart with Vietnamese detainees rounded up for questioning, Operation Pike, August 1967 (author's photo).

What We Can and Can't Afford

"God's always ready to listen, son. He's always been ready to comfort people like us, and He still is. I really don't mean to preach a sermon at you, but you mustn't let your own fear keep you from Him."

"Father, that's not right. You can't just say you're sorry, and then go out and deliberately keep doing the same stuff over and over again. You got no business telling guys like me it's okay to deal like that."

"I'm not saying it's okay, Corporal Ehrhart, and I never have. I can't presume to judge men. But you boys are as much a part of Jesus' flock as anybody else; maybe you're the part He cares about most. Jesus broke bread with publicans and sinners, didn't He? Can I do any less, and still be a priest?"

"Well, if you're just here to look after us sheep, how come you got that?" I pointed to the M-16 Father Lyons held.

He looked down at the weapon and shook his head slowly. "I'd be happy not to have to carry one of these, and I hope I never have to use it," he said, "but I'm afraid the VC don't make exceptions for Catholic priests."

"I understand that, sir, but that's the point. You've got an excuse. Colonel Gravel's got an excuse. General Westmoreland's got an excuse. President Johnson's got an excuse. I'm up to my earlobes in everybody's excuses. Either you're a Christian, or you're not a Christian. There's nothing ambiguous about 'Thou shalt not kill.'"

"You're right, of course," said Father Lyons. "But it's just not that simple. Nobody's perfect, son. We're all human beings. God made us in His image, and He knows we're going to fail. That's what Jesus Christ is all about."

"That just don't get it, Father. These guys believe in you. They trust you. You tell 'em they're gonna be forgiven, and they just keep praying and shooting and praying and shooting, and thinking they're gonna go to heaven. You think God gives a big rat's ass about communism and democracy and domino theories? I just hope to high heaven there ain't any God, because we're all in a whole lot of trouble if there is."

"Corporal Ehrhart, have you ever thought about applying for a discharge as a conscientious objector?"

"Oh, no; no way. End up in Portsmouth Naval Prison for twenty years? I've got enough trouble as it is. I've got four more months to go in this cesspool, and then I'm outta here."

"But if you're really this troubled, maybe I can help you. I can talk to Colonel Gravel."

"Listen, Father, you said I could talk straight with you, so I am. But

18. God, Jesus, and the Vietnam War

this is just between you and me, and I'm trusting you to keep it to yourself. I've got a good record, and I want to keep it that way. It's gonna be hard enough to live with myself for the rest of my life. And then get drummed out of the service on top of that? I'm not gonna hang that albatross around my neck. No, sir."

Father Lyons sighed deeply. "Well, that's your decision," he said. "If you change your mind, let me know. But think about this, will you? Don't let what men do in God's name turn you away from God's love. Just because we fail to live up to what God asks of us doesn't mean He won't forgive us. It's God's world, after all; He knows what we're up against."

"Well, that's a heck of a way to send somebody to sea, isn't it, sir? Knock a hole in the bottom of the lifeboat, and then tell 'em, 'Do the best you can, folks; good luck.'"

"I'm afraid I just can't seem to find the right things to say to you, can I?"

"I guess not, sir. I'm sorry. Really; it's nothing personal. You're a nice man, Father."

"I'm sorry, too, son," said Father Lyons, his voice sounding very tired and lonely. "I just don't have all the answers. God works in mysterious ways sometimes, I suppose. Let me know if you change your mind."

But I did not change my mind. At that stage of my life, CO didn't mean "conscientious objector." It was only the first two letters of "coward."

Later on that same operation, I lost my dog tags. When we got back to battalion, I had the company clerk make me a new set. On the line for religion, which originally read "UCC" for United Church of Christ, I had him put "None."

I still have those dog tags. But I've spent fifty years wondering if and how my life would be different if I had had the courage to take Father Lyons up on his offer.

19

The Tail Wagging the Dog

(*LA Progressive*, March 10, 2018; *New Hampshire Gazette*, March 30, 2018; *Peace in Our Time*, Spring 2018)

I was dismayed to hear that Florida's Republican governor had signed a bill raising the age of gun purchase from 18 to 21, extending a three-day waiting period, and banning "bump stocks" while at the same time authorizing teachers to carry firearms, a bill that manages to be at once both cowardly and insane.

Cowardly in that the "gun control" provisions are all-but-meaningless: raising the age of purchase has no practical impact because a shooter can get something with which to shoot easily enough; consider that the 20-year-old shooter in Sandy Hook used an assault rifle his mother had purchased legally. And one can easily fire a semi-automatic weapon 60 to 100 times a minute simply by pulling the trigger for each shot. Pulling a trigger doesn't take very long.

Meanwhile, arming teachers as a solution to school shootings would seem utterly unbelievable if it were not actually happening. Witness this new Florida law.

As a Marine veteran of combat in Vietnam, I have an understanding of what happens when people start shooting. Even with the vaunted training I received in the Corps, I can tell you that it takes tremendous willpower and self-control to remain functional when someone is shooting at you.

Now picture a school cafeteria where someone is blasting away with an AR-15 and several 30-round magazines. Children are dead. Children are wounded. Blood is everywhere. People are screaming and crying and running helter-skelter. Pandemonium such as you cannot imagine unless you have ever been under fire.

And you think some high school biology teacher is going to step into this situation, calmly pull out his or her 9-millimeter pistol, take

19. The Tail Wagging the Dog

careful aim, and deftly kill the child who is blazing away? Cool thinking, expert marksmanship, steady nerves. Problem solved. Right? In your dreams.

Yet 18 states allow K-12 teachers to carry firearms on the job. Or does Florida make it 19?

But here's the best part. The day after the Florida bill was signed, I woke up to discover that the National Rifle Association has filed a federal lawsuit blocking this new law because, says the NRA, it violates the 2nd Amendment by punishing law-abiding citizens for the actions of a few deranged whackos.

Yet I am a law-abiding citizen, and I am being punished every day, having to live in fear of being gunned down in the school where I teach, or at the mall, or at a Flyers hockey game, or a rock concert, or anywhere else in these United States of America because of the deranged whackos of the NRA who think the 2nd Amendment gives them the right to make millions of law-abiding citizens live in terror on a daily basis.

Indeed, the NRA is the most insidious and lethal terrorist organization on earth, and it is perfectly legal, operates in the open, spends millions of dollars buying spineless politicians, and blames gun violence on everyone and everything under the sun except the guns.

Look, you want to have bolt-action hunting rifles? Okay. Shotguns? Okay. Handguns, even though most firearms deaths are caused by handguns? Okay, I can even live with those. But AR-15s, AK-47s, and their ilk? They're not called "hunting rifles." Or "self-defense rifles." They're called "assault rifles." They are designed to do one thing: kill as many people as possible in the shortest time possible. The Marine Corps didn't give me a deer rifle in Vietnam, or a shotgun, or even a pistol. I was given an M-16 assault rifle. My job was to kill people with it.

The 2nd Amendment gives the people the right to keep and bear arms, but it qualifies that right by placing it within the context of a well-regulated militia. Neither Devin Kelley nor Adam Lanza nor Stephen Paddock nor any other of these mass killers belonged to a well-regulated militia.

And the amendment doesn't say that Tom, Dick and Harry have the right to own 20 or 30 or 50 high-powered assault rifles. Or even one high-powered assault rifle. It doesn't give people the right to own bazookas or M-60 machineguns or 81-millimeter mortars. Why should any civilian be allowed to own a weapon that is designed to do the same thing as bazookas, machineguns, and mortars?

When will law-abiding, responsible, patriotic Americans finally

What We Can and Can't Afford

decide to put a stop to the NRA tail wagging the American dog? When will we throw out of office the craven politicians who kowtow to an organization that terrorizes the rest of us daily?

And as for arming teachers: when I joined the Marines, I expected to be given a weapon and trained how to use it. When I became a teacher, I did not expect to be expected to kill my students. If you expect me to do that, you are stark-raving mad.

20

America's Modern Military
Who Serves and Who Doesn't

[Originally delivered as a talk for the Temple University Dissent in America Teach-In Series on February 16, 2018.]

(*LA Progressive*, June 20, 2018; *VVAW Veteran*, Fall 2018)

> "A standing army, however necessary it may be at times, is always dangerous to the Liberties of the People. Soldiers are apt to consider themselves as a Body distinct from the rest of the Citizens."—Samuel Adams, 1776

For most of the first 165 years of American history, the United States maintained only a minimal standing army when not engaged in a war. The figures—before, during, and after each of our significant wars through the end of World War II—look like this:

1812:	6,700	1815:	38,200	1816:	10,000	1821:	6,000
1845:	8,500	1847:	44,700	1849:	10,000		
1860:	16,000	1865:	1,000,700	1866:	57,000	1877:	24,000
1897:	27,800	1898:	210,000	1905:	67,000		
1914:	98,000	1918:	2,400,000	1920:	204,000	1925:	137,000
1939:	190,000	1945:	8,300,000	1948:	554,000		

Since 1948, however, our standing army has been considerably larger than previous peacetime periods, varying from half a million to a million and a half. When we include the navy, air force, and Marine Corps, our standing military has added up to between one and a half million and three million at any given time.

During the Revolutionary War, various states attempted to institute military drafts, but efforts were not very successful; there were

What We Can and Can't Afford

many loopholes, and even flagrant refusal. The burden, not surprisingly, fell disproportionately on the poor.

There was no federal national draft until 1863, but again this was only partially successful; exemptions were available by purchase or by hiring a substitute. Again, the burden fell disproportionately on the poor, and in any case this draft was disbanded at the end of the war.

The federal government did not attempt a national draft again until 1917 and U.S. entry into the Great War (only later called World War I). It was somewhat more equitable than the Civil War draft, but farmers, the poor, and people of color were still more likely to be drafted. Like the Civil War draft, when the Great War ended, so did this draft.

The first peacetime draft in U.S. history did not occur until 1940; it was put in place in anticipation of U.S. entry into World War II, and it remained in place through 1946.

As the Cold War heated up, however, the federal government instituted a second peacetime draft in 1948. This draft remained in place continuously until 1973 through both the Korean and Vietnam Wars as well as periods of peace in between.

Finally, in 1974, the government ended the draft entirely, and went to the so-called All Volunteer Force (AVF) that we still have today.

Why was there a peacetime draft at all? Was the threat from the Soviet Union so dire? Or did it have more to do with the post–World War II transformation of the United States from a world industrial power to *the* global giant: economically, politically, militarily? Did it have to do with maintaining what had become, after 1945, an American Empire? And why disband the draft in 1973? If the reason for a peacetime draft was fear of the USSR, why end the draft while the USSR was at the height of its power?

Perhaps it had more to do with reducing—indeed, eliminating—domestic opposition to U.S. foreign policy and the use of the American military to enforce American will on the unwilling.

Certainly, it is well known and well documented that by the later stages of the American War in Vietnam, opposition to the draft as inherently unfair to the poor and minorities led first to a switch from the old deferment system to a somewhat more equitable lottery system, and then to an end of the draft altogether.

At the same time, by the early 1970s opposition to the Vietnam War had reached critical proportions even within the military itself. Reference, for instance, Colonel Robert D. Heinl, Jr.s', "The Collapse of the Armed Forces," *Armed Forces Journal*, June 1971. Resistance to the

20. America's Modern Military

American war in Vietnam was widespread by then, and the breakdown within the military was catastrophic.

The U.S. military and the U.S. government both wanted (and needed) docile and obedient soldiers who would not question their role in whatever circumstances in which they might find themselves along with an American public who would not question whatever wars and adventures the government wished to undertake.

In this regard, the attacks on 9/11 were a boon to the creation of a pliant citizenry that would not question the exercise of U.S. military might, but the process of creating a pliant citizenry and an unquestioning soldiery began in the 1970s.

Currently, the U.S. military maintains 800 bases in 70 countries worldwide with U.S. forces stationed in another 60 countries. What are we doing in all these places? Most Americans do not know, and do not care.

Instead, we "honor our military" by having 16 Medal-of-Honor winners participate in the ceremonial coin toss at Super Bowl LII, by giving a service person his or her very own Flyers jersey at every home hockey game, by staging military flyovers at the start of NASCAR races, and all sorts of other public displays that in fact do nothing to benefit active-duty military personnel or veterans.

What am I supposed to do with Delaware's Vietnam Veterans Memorial Highway? I still have to pay the same $4.00 toll everyone else pays when I use the Delaware Turnpike.

We have been at war continuously since October 2001, yet who among us has sacrificed anything? For most of us, life goes on day after day without the least awareness that a very small number of our fellow citizens are at war: as of May 2016, 5500 in Iraq; 9800 in Afghanistan; we are not told how many in Syria, and who knows where else? Not long ago, several U.S. soldiers were ambushed and killed while on a military operation in Nigeria. Nigeria?! But who cares?

Americans are further isolated from the military by two additional and newer developments. One is the use of mercenaries in place of American soldiers: as of May 2016, there were 7,770 hired contractors in Iraq, and 28,600 in Afghanistan (more than three times the number of our uniformed service personnel). And make no mistake, these "contractors" are mercenary soldiers, hired guns.

The second development is drone technology, which allows us to kill at will with no risk to the killers, no U.S. casualties, no fuss, no muss, no bother. During Barack Obama's presidency, the U.S. launched

What We Can and Can't Afford

drone missiles nearly once a week, week in and week out for eight years. God only knows what's happening during the Donald Trump presidency, but who cares?

So, who serves in the U.S. military today? Who enlists? Let me tell you about my students at the Haverford School in suburban Philadelphia. I have taught there for 17 years. In that time, approximately 1600 young men have graduated from the Haverford School. Not one single young man has gone directly from high school graduation into the U.S. military as an enlisted soldier, sailor, airmen, or Marine. Not one.

This year, it will cost a family about $37,000 to enroll their son in my school for a single year of high school. And if he wants to eat lunch, that costs extra. Our clientele are generally well-heeled, educated, and focused on their own success and the success of their children.

We do offer scholarships, and nearly 40 percent of our boys are receiving some amount of scholarship aid, some of them up to 100 percent. But even the scholarship kids, once armed with a diploma from my school, have options that are often not available to many young people in the U.S. Every one of our boys gets into college somewhere. They don't all go to Harvard or Stanford, but they all go somewhere.

A few of them go to one of the service academies every year, where they will get a free education and a guaranteed job as an officer, not as an enlisted private starting at the bottom of the ladder. A few have opted for ROTC and eventually have been commissioned as officers. But the overwhelming number of the boys I've taught will never serve a day in uniform in any capacity, let alone risk their lives for "freedom" or the Koch brothers, because they have other options.

So why should they or their parents care what the U.S. government is doing out there in the world in their names and with their tax dollars? It isn't their children on the pointy end of the stick and isn't ever going to be. Today's U.S. military is largely inhabited by people who have far fewer options than my students have, who need money for college and can get it only by enlisting first, who have few prospects for any decent job that pays a living wage; a few are that much smaller number of young people who are looking for adventure and excitement ("Be All You Can Be," "An Army of One," "A Force for Good," etc.), and who have had drummed into them the ethos of the "warrior," the Band of Brothers mythology foisted on the world by England's King Henry V via William Shakespeare.

The wrong people learned the wrong lessons from the American war in Vietnam, and learned those lessons very well. Today, the

20. America's Modern Military

consequences of U.S. foreign policy have been completely removed from domestic politics. And those who do the bidding of our policymakers and their masters come by and large from those strata of American life with the least political clout, the least voice in American affairs, the least influence on how and why they are being asked to risk their lives, or to what end.

It is a sorry situation, and with the fox in charge of the henhouse, it isn't likely to change.

21

From Pennridge to Vietnam
What I Knew and Didn't Know

A presentation to the students of Pennridge Senior High School Perkasie, PA, May 31, 2018 (VVAW *Veteran*, Spring 2020)

Let me start by telling you that I am a 1966 graduate of Pennridge High School. I am also a veteran of the American War in Vietnam. I was not drafted. I volunteered for the U.S. Marine Corps when I was 17 years old, went to Vietnam when I was 18 years old, and earned the rank of sergeant by the time I was 19 & ½ years old. I was wounded in combat, and eventually received the Good Conduct Medal and an Honorable Discharge.

My first memories of television were of Soviet tanks crushing the Hungarian Revolution in 1956. I'd seen and heard Nikita Khrushchev pounding his shoe on the podium at the UN while shouting, "We will bury you." I'd awakened one morning to the Berlin Wall, and I'd lived through the Cuban Missile Crisis. When Lyndon Johnson said that if we didn't fight the Reds in Vietnam, we'd be fighting them on Waikiki Beach, it sounded very much as if my country needed me.

I didn't know that Franklin Roosevelt had all-but-handed Eastern Europe over to the Soviets at Yalta in 1945. Or that the Soviet Union had lost as many people in World War II as all other nations combined, and was not about to see this slaughter repeated in another war with the West. Or that the Soviet Union was, by 1962, completely encircled by U.S. nuclear ballistic missiles. Most of all, I did not know that what was happening in Vietnam had nothing to do with whatever worldwide struggle between communism and capitalism was actually taking place. I did not know that Ho Chi Minh had spent a lifetime trying

21. From Pennridge to Vietnam

to free his country from foreign domination. That the Americans had simply replaced colonial France in that struggle. That in fact Ho Chi Minh was deftly playing Russians and Chinese off against each other in order to navigate between them and pursue his own agenda, which remained what it had always been: independence for his country. I did not know that the nation I thought I was defending from the scourge of communism—the Saigon-based Republic of Vietnam—never really existed. I did not know that Vietnam posed no danger to my country, nor that I was in danger only because I'd gone halfway around the world to make trouble for the Vietnamese. Interestingly enough, as soon as I went home, the Vietnamese communists stopped trying to kill me. But I digress.

Because of what I did not know when I got to Vietnam, imagine my confusion when I discovered that the people I was sent to help didn't welcome me with open arms, didn't seem to like me, didn't seem to want me there or appreciate my help. But as my thirteen months in Vietnam slowly ground forward, I regularly witnessed and participated in the destruction of civilian homes, the most brutal interrogations of civilians, and the routine killing of men, women, and children along with their crops and livestock. And I began to realize that the Vietnamese people hated us because we destroyed their forests with chemical defoliants, burned their fields with napalm, flattened their villages with 500-pound bombs, and called them gooks, chinks, slopes, dinks, and zipperheads while turning their sons into shoeshine boys and their daughters into

Ehrhart as high school senior, Pennridge High, 1966 (author's photo).

What We Can and Can't Afford

Ehrhart in Vietnam, 1967 (author's photo).

whores. No wonder my so-called allies and brothers-in-arms, the South Vietnamese army, seemed to be indifferent cowards with no will to fight while my enemies, the Viet Cong, seemed willing to fight to the bitter end, though they possessed only the most rudimentary of resources.

I once, for instance, killed a man in an ambush who was dressed in thin cotton shirt and pants with sandals made from discarded tires (we called them Ho Chi Minh sandals). He had in one pocket a few balls of rice wrapped in a banana leaf. His weapon was a 1936 French bolt action MAS-36 with a bent hide-away bayonet, a stock held together with wire, and a bamboo strip to replace the leather sling that had rotted away a decade or more earlier. He had five bullets, and the barrel of his rifle was so pitted that I dared not fire it for fear it would explode in my face. And that is how that man had gone out to do battle with the most powerful army on earth. You can kill people like that, but you cannot defeat them.

One has to wonder why one side that seems to have everything going for it won't fight while the other side that has nothing going for it won't surrender, and I sure as heck did wonder. But I had no way to find

21. From Pennridge to Vietnam

my way through the myriad welter of information and experience that was pouring in on me as my time in Vietnam unfolded. It simply did not make sense. Nothing made sense. It was all just crazy. Or seemed so.

I returned to the United States from Vietnam in March 1968. I spent the next two years and two months trying to convince myself that it didn't matter to me what was happening in Vietnam anymore because I was out of it, and I still had all ten fingers and all ten toes; it was no longer my problem.

Then in early May 1970, soldiers of the Ohio National Guard opened fire on students protesting the war at Kent State University, murdering four of them and leaving another permanently paralyzed. The news stunned me. It wasn't enough to send us halfway around the world to die, I thought; now our own government was killing us in the streets of our own country.

That was the day I joined the antiwar movement. It was also the day I set out to discover what was happening in Vietnam and why. What I discovered was even more shocking than what had happened at Kent State.

I learned that Ho Chi Minh and his Viet Minh army had been allies of the U.S. in fighting Japan during the Second World War, that American OSS officers had worked with Ho, training and equipping his men. I learned that State Department diplomat Abbott Moffat had spent time with Ho, and had determined that Ho was first and foremost a nationalist, and urged the U.S. to support Ho's bid for independence from French colonial rule. I learned that instead, the U.S. had supported France's war to retake its colony, paying 80 per cent of the cost of the French War, and when France finally threw in the towel, I learned, the U.S. had plucked an obscure Vietnamese Catholic mandarin from a Maryknoll seminary in New Jersey and set him up to be the leader of South Vietnam, a nation invented by none other than the United States.

I learned that the regime this man, Ngo Dinh Diem, created was no more democratic than Ho chi Minh's regime in North Vietnam, nor— when Diem failed and was overthrown by a U.S.-backed *coup d'état*— were his successor military governments any more concerned with democracy. I learned that the attack on the USS *Maddox* in the Gulf of Tonkin in early August 1964 was *not* unprovoked, the *Maddox* was *not* operating in international waters but within the territorial waters of North Vietnam in support of combat operations against North Vietnam, and the Johnson Administration knew it at the time. The second attack a few days later never actually happened, and the Johnson

What We Can and Can't Afford

Administration knew it at the time. The Johnson Administration knowingly and flagrantly lied to the American people and the Congress of the United States. This is not speculation. This is fact, provable by examining the documents compiled at the order of Robert McNamara himself and commonly known as the *Pentagon Papers*.

I learned a whole lot more than these few facts, but time does not permit me to give you a complete history lesson. If you're interested, you might read Marilyn Young's *The Vietnam Wars: 1945–1990*, which is by far the best single-volume history of the war.

But perhaps the most important thing I learned about is the long history of China and Vietnam. From the second-century BCE to the tenth-century AD, China occupied and ruled Vietnam. Maps of China all through this long millennium show what was then Vietnam, extending down as far as Hue, as a province of China. The Vietnamese saw things differently, however. All through this period, there was rebellion after rebellion after rebellion—the Trung Sisters, Li Bi, Ly Tu Tien & Dinh Tien, Mai Thuc Loan, Phung Hung, Duong Thanh, or Hwang Chao—all led rebellions, and all were crushed, until finally in 938 the Vietnamese rebelled yet another time, and this time succeeded in defeating their Chinese occupiers and throwing them out. Three successive Chinese invasions, along with two Mongol invasions and a Siamese invasion, were all defeated over the next nine centuries before the arrival of the French on Vietnamese shores. A thousand years of resistance to Chinese occupation, nine hundred years of successfully defending Vietnamese independence, and—what I have not yet mentioned but will now—immediate and unceasing resistance to French colonization even before French rule had been fully consolidated.

The U.S. began to intervene in Vietnam in 1945, first by proxy via the French, then from 1954 to 1965 through increasing levels of direct support to a succession of dictatorships in South Vietnam, and finally by direct insertion of U.S. combat troops on a massive scale. Within three years of the arrival of the first Marines in 1965, the American people were growing skeptical of the war. Within five years, huge numbers of Americans wanted the war to end. Within seven years, most Americans no longer cared what happened in and to Vietnam so long as young Americans stopped dying there.

The Vietnamese resisted Chinese domination for a millennium. For one thousand years. Americans were tired of it within a decade. When you understand that the Vietnamese were prepared to fight us for as long as it took: 10 years, 50 years, 500 years; when you understand that there

21. From Pennridge to Vietnam

never would come a time when the Vietnamese would lay down their arms, accept foreign domination, register Republican, and go shopping at the mall, the idea that Americans could ever have won the Vietnam War becomes, quite frankly, chimerical, absurd, even ridiculous.

Let me tell you about an interesting evening I spent in post-war Hanoi in 1985. I was having dinner with two old North Vietnamese generals who between them had six stars and 85 years of experience with war and fighting. When I learned that one of them had commanded a unit fighting against the Marines at an outpost where I'd been stationed called Con Thien, I asked him what he thought of the Marines.

"You were—brave," he'd replied, a twinkle in his voice.

"You are too diplomatic," I'd said. "Seriously, what did you think of us?"

"Your fixed positions were useless," the general replied. "And you were too dependent on your helicopters and air support. You did not know how to become one with the land, and so you sacrificed true mobility for a false sense of security."

"Would it have mattered if we had done things differently?" I had asked.

"No," he'd replied after a pause. "Probably not. History was not on your side. We were fighting for our homeland. What were you fighting for?"

After an even longer pause, the only honest answer I could give him was, "Nothing that mattered." And indeed, though the communists won and the U.S. was sent ignominiously packing, the world did not come to an end, the universe did not implode, all of you are still able to worship in the church of your choice and marry whomever you like and think whatever you want to think.

Not only that, but the U.S. and Vietnam are now great friends. The Vietnamese government and military receive financial and technical aid from the U.S. The U.S. and Vietnam regularly hold joint naval exercises. Just recently, the aircraft carrier *USS Carl Vinson* paid a port call to Da Nang, the first place in Vietnam where U.S. Marine combat forces had come ashore in March 1965.

Why are the U.S. and Vietnam so chummy these days? Because the U.S. needs all the help it can get to counter the rising influence of China in Southeast Asia. But the question should not be "why are we so chummy these days," but rather why didn't U.S. policymakers know enough in the 1940s and 1950s and 1960s to realize that we could have made Vietnam an ally over 70 years ago, saving millions of Vietnamese,

What We Can and Can't Afford

Laotians, Cambodians, and Americans a whole lot of blood and grief and treasure.

And it makes me wonder what obvious realities and truths are U.S. policymakers missing in the world today as we wage war in Iraq, Afghanistan, Syria, Yemen, and elsewhere in the Muslim and Arab worlds. What preconceived notions and arrogant assumptions are U.S. policymakers making today that will appear, in the cold light of history, to be sheer folly and head-shaking stupidity.

But that's another topic. Let me close by giving you a sampling of what I did in the service of my country:

"Just for Laughs"
"Souvenirs"
"Hunting"
"The Next Step"
"Guerrilla War"
"Time on Target"
"Making the Children Behave"
"Beautiful Wreckage"

You might want to ponder all that a while before you thank me for my service.

[All of these poems can be found in *Thank You for Your Service: Collected Poems* published by McFarland & Company. If you don't yet own a copy, you should correct that deficiency immediately.]

22

"A Band of Brothers"
Senior Dinner Remarks

The Haverford School for Boys
June 7, 2018

As nearly as I can count, I've sat through and listened to at least two dozen commencement speeches: my own, of course, from high school back in 1966, and again from college in 1973; at least one of my older brothers' that I can recall; my daughter's high school and college graduations; and sixteen Haverford School commencements. I can't honestly remember a word of any of them. They all say the same thing, pretty much: you're about to set sail on the rest of your life, you're embarking on a new adventure, the world stands before you like an open door, you'll do great things, you can make a difference, it's your turn now, yak, yak, blah, blah, blah, & et cetera. I did not even bother to show up for the graduation exercises when I earned my master's degree or doctorate. I'm only coming tomorrow because I have to. Oh, and for the faculty gauntlet at the end of the ceremony; that's always pretty cool.

I have no idea who tomorrow's commencement speaker is. I haven't asked. I love surprises, and I assure you that I'm looking forward to it with the same eager anticipation I feel when I'm on my way to the dentist to have another root canal.

Not that commencement isn't a big deal, especially and in particular high school commencement. It *is* a big deal. You've all looked forward to this for as long as you can remember. You should relish the moment, revel in it, bask in its glory and yours. But it seems to me that the real beauty and power and significance of tomorrow is the fact, the realization, the sadness, and the joy of you young men being together for one last time on this journey you've all shared—some of you for three or four years, some of you for over a decade, but all of you together.

What We Can and Can't Afford

You are brothers in no figurative sense of that word. You have shared the same classrooms and halls, the same athletic teams and venues, the same stages and studios, the same teachers and coaches and mentors. You will remember the Haverford School and these years and these experiences for as long as you live. The good times and the bad. The tough times and the easy times. The sad times and the happy times. And you will remember each other. Take a look to your left and right. To no small degree, the guys on either side of you have helped to make you who you are and who you will be for the rest of your lives. You owe each other more than any of you will ever begin to realize for years to come.

That is what makes tonight significant. That is what will make tomorrow significant. You are together—all of you as a class—for the last time. I look forward to seeing you all up there on stage together, each of you happy and sad and proud all in the same breath, a band of brothers not in that hackneyed way that Shakespeare turned into a cliché in *Henry V*, but in the day-to-day comings and goings, the mundane trials and tribulations, the confusion and pain and joyfulness of transforming from boys into men.

Who needs old fogeys like me giving you sage advice at a joyful time like this? But surprise, surprise—I told you I like surprises—I'm going to give you some advice anyway. It applies especially to the next few days when you're all celebrating graduation, and to your arrival on your various college campuses, but—well—pretty much for the rest of your lives:

- Don't drink and drive.
- Don't smoke that funny stuff and try to operate heavy equipment (and remember: a car is "heavy equipment").
- Put away your cellphones, especially when you're driving.
- Treat women with respect. Your mother and your sister are women. How do you want men to treat them? Treat other women, every woman, the way you want your mother and your sister to be treated.
- Remember that every day is Game Day. Every spring for 17 years I have watched a depressing number of VI Formers think they no longer have to give me and their other teachers their best effort. It happened again this spring. It is more disappointing than I can express, and as fondly as I will remember all of you, I will also remember who quit before the race was over. Try not to make a habit of that in the years ahead.

22. "A Band of Brothers"

- Read poetry. If you don't like poetry, you're reading the wrong poems.
- Make it your goal in life to leave a better world behind you than it was when you got here.

Okay, that's enough. I will close by saying that I have seldom been accorded so wonderful and affirming an honor as this year's *Haligoluk* Appreciation, and I am doubly honored that you have asked me to speak to you tonight. Thank you. Really. Thank you. I love you all very much. I will miss you all. Now get out there into the world and do something worthwhile with yourselves.

23

A Foolproof Solution to Gun Violence in the U.S.

(*LA Progressive*, August 4, 2018;
New Hampshire Gazette, August 16, 2018)

Most people who pay attention to the issue of gun violence know the grim statistics. According to the BBC, 21,386 Americans committed suicide in 2014 using a firearm, while 11,008 Americans were murdered with firearms. In addition to deaths, firearms cause nearly three times as many nonfatal injuries, upwards of 75,000 annually. Figures vary from year to year, but the trend is upward. Americans are in possession of 270,000,000 firearms, roughly nine firearms for every ten Americans. This is nearly twice as many as the next most heavily armed nation—Yemen, which is in the midst of an ongoing civil war—and almost three times as many as third-place Switzerland, where universal military service is mandatory and citizen-soldiers keep their weapons at home.

My gun-toting acquaintances argue that without their guns, they and their loved ones are at the mercy of the criminals; that any gun controls at all are the slippery slope toward banning firearms entirely; and that the 2nd Amendment to the Constitution is sacred and inviolable.

But while there are all sorts of anecdotes bandied about, demonstrating how "a good guy with a gun" is the antidote to "a bad guy with a gun," the overwhelming evidence makes it clear that being in possession of a legal firearm actually increases the risk of injury or death rather than reducing it.

And as for the arguments involving the Constitution, unlike the late Antonin Scalia and others who claim to be "strict constructionists" following the "original intent" of our Founding Fathers, I am a *true* strict constructionist. I believe the 2nd Amendment should be strictly interpreted as the Founding Fathers originally intended.

23. A Foolproof Solution to Gun Violence in the U.S.

And I cannot believe, even for a nanosecond, that when those men wrote the 2nd Amendment, they could possibly have envisioned high-powered military assault rifles with 30-round magazines or pocket-sized .45-caliber handguns or shotguns capable of firing ten rounds in succession before reloading.

What did those Founding Fathers intend? A typical weapon of the day was the "Brown Bess" muzzle-loading flintlock smooth-bore musket, nearly five feet long, over ten pounds in weight, and capable of firing no more than three rounds a minute, even in expert hands.

Like our Founding Fathers, I believe absolutely that every American citizen has the fundamental, constitutional right to keep and bear one of these weapons. I'd like to see somebody rob a bank with a Brown Bess. Or shoot up a nightclub. Or commit suicide.

But what about all those Americans who love to hunt? Easy. State-run and regulated armories where hunters—once they've fulfilled certification requirements (much like drivers have to do)—can rent out a rifle or shotgun, and purchase ammunition. When their hunting adventure is over, they turn in their weapons along with the spent cartridges and unused ammo. Weapons not turned in or ammo not accounted for, you're under arrest.

As for the argument that when guns are outlawed, only outlaws will have guns: that one's easy, too, if we're really serious about ending gun violence in the U.S. Any person caught in illegal possession of a firearm goes to prison for life, period. Any person committing a crime while in possession of a firearm: automatic death penalty, no appeals, no fifteen years on Death Row. Either criminals will stop carrying guns or all the criminals will eventually be disposed of. Either way, no more criminals with guns.

Cruel and unusual punishment? I'll tell you what's cruel and unusual punishment: that I and my family have to live every day of our lives wondering when some whacko with a gun is going to shoot up the movie theater we're in or the store where we shop, or the classroom where I teach, even though we've done nothing wrong or illegal.

I am as law-abiding as all those law-abiding gun owners who argue that law-abiding gun owners are not the problem. Yet because those law-abiding gun owners demand the right to have unlimited access to all the guns and ammunition they can cram into their houses and garages and cars, I have to live 24/7 in the slaughterhouse that has become ordinary life in America, where 96 people are killed with guns every single day, where 50 women are shot to death each month by

What We Can and Can't Afford

Walk-out in honor of the students and faculty killed at Marjorie Stoneman Douglas High School by students and faculty at the Haverford School for Boys (author's photo).

intimate partners, where 4.6 per cent of the world's population accounts for 82 percent of gun deaths worldwide.

You think my solution is too draconian? If you've got a better solution, I'd like to hear it. Or maybe it's best just to keep doing what we've been doing for the past 50 years as Congress and state legislatures have knuckled under to the National Rifle Association and the gun manufacturers. That would be nothing. We can continue to do nothing. How effective has that approach been so far?

24

Earth Songs II
A Review

(*VVAW Veteran*, Spring 2019; *VFP Newsletter*, Fall 2019)
Earth Songs II: Poems of Love, Loss and Life,
Jan Barry, 2018, *www.janbarry.net*

If Veterans for Peace were reconstituted as Veteran Poets for Peace, Jan Barry would be its hereditary king, prime minister by acclamation, and president for life. Just consider the titles of the anthologies he has edited or co-edited: *Winning Hearts and Minds, Demilitarized Zones, Peace Is Our Profession*, and most recently *Sound Off*. His own collections include *War Baby, Veterans Day, Earth Songs*, and *Life After War & Other Poems*. And now comes *Earth Songs II*, a compilation of new work written in the past fifteen years.

I readily admit that I am not exactly an impartial critic. I've known Barry for forty-seven years, and he has been one of the major influences in my life. We first met when he

Jan Barry (photo by Paula Rogovin).

What We Can and Can't Afford

was editing *Winning Hearts and Minds* with Larry Rottmann and Basil Paquet back in 1972. I was trying, without much success, to cope with the flood of emotions coursing through me in the wake of my encounter with the American War in Vietnam. A few years later, he and I co-edited *Demilitarized Zones* together, and it was during those years—1975 and 1976—that Barry showed me how to direct my rage and confusion into constructive channels through poetry and literature.

He believed then in the power of the word, and all these years later he still does. His refusal to give in to despair, his fundamental belief in the goodness of humanity, and his willingness to keep moving forward in spite of the obstacles life throws in his path are nothing short of astounding. And he has once again demonstrated all these qualities in the 105 poems collected in this new volume.

The poems themselves range widely, touching on issues of war and peace, the debilitating impact of combat on the human spirit, aging parents, the devastating loss of his wife of decades, trying to date again, his own advancing age, and the rejuvenating power of nature.

Think about this description of our current hyper-militarized culture the next time you're watching an NFL game and they cover the whole field with an American flag while the 82nd Airborne Division chorus sings the national anthem:

> Our flag flapping, sword saluting
> Sworn to secrecy
> Stiff upper lip, suck it up
> He-man, iron man military mindset
> ("Singing Out")

Or these last few stanzas from "Dummies Guide to Chemical Warfare":

> Spewing arsenals of chemical weapons—
> Chlorine, mustard gas, phosgene, sarin,
> A-bombs, H-bombs, depleted uranium
>
> 'Til we run out of cutesy mots
> And slam into S for suicide—
> And that's all she wrote.

Some of the most heartbreaking poems deal with the loss of his wife Paula. Just when you think he's going to be okay, the poem "Bad Day Blues" ending:

> Having a bad day—
> Then a cat meows,

24. Earth Songs II

> Wanting a companion—
> Ah, come here

The very next poem, "Death Is Never Done" concludes:

> The cat disappeared
> One night—
> Like your embrace,
> Your face, your light.

Still, that refusal to give in or give up is captured in "Alone":

> Learning to be alone,
> Sleep alone, eat alone,
> Dream alone.
> On my own.
>
> You're surely gone,
> Can't help me carry on.
> Have to find
> Some other sign.

Some of the most poignant poems are about his parents, who lived long lives, were married seventy years, and died within a year of each other. Other poems explore an uncle killed in a dive bomber in the World War II Pacific ("the tail gunner jumping / from the rear seat engulfed in fire"), the encroachment of "civilization" on the natural world ("the silence / Of this forty mile lake is shattered / By shore to shore boats, / Door to door cottages, / Year round houses"), and the refusal of nature to give in to that encroachment:

> **Summer Wildflowers**
>
> Flaming fields of purple loose strife
> Flicker along country highways
> Beside gleaming epaulets of golden rod
> Twirling in stride with fluttering
> Scarfs of Queen Anne's lace
> And shimmering sky blue
> Clusters of chicory.

Few poets have so consistently insisted that peace is possible and poetry matters. In "Gold Star Grandson," Barry sums up his life's work in a single stanza:

> So I went off to war
> And when I came home
> Transformed silences
> That replaced the missing

What We Can and Can't Afford

> Into poetry
> And sought to tell
> Stories of fallen sons
> Whose voices were stilled.

The quiet strength of Barry's voice and the simple decency of his vision are blessings to anyone who cares about the world we live in and the future we will leave to coming generations. Here is "Memorial Highways" in its entirety:

> There's a memorial highway
> For veterans of every major war—
> Can you imagine
> A memorial highway
> For peace treaties—
> Peace served
> And died, too.

25

Chiseled in Stone by God's Hand?

(*LA Progressive*, August 5, 2019;
New Hampshire Gazette, August 17, 2019)

On Saturday afternoon, August 3, I turned on my computer, and what is the first headline I see? "**Mass Shooting in El Paso, Texas.**" Again? Yes, again. According to CBS News, as of July 31, there have now been 248 mass shootings in the United States of America in 2019 resulting in 246 dead and 979 wounded. So far.

And these figures don't include the incident on August 2 in Promfret, Maryland, that killed three and injured one. Nor do these figures include the incident in El Paso, Texas, that killed 20 and wounded 26.

But it gets better ... or rather, worse. Less than 24 hours after the Texas shootings, another mass shooting occurred in Dayton, Ohio, this time with nine more dead and 27 wounded.

I really thought—or at least hoped—that the slaughter of six teachers along with *twenty* 6- and 7-year-olds in Newtown, Connecticut, would finally have left most Americans horrified, disgusted, and sickened enough to force their cowardly state and federal elected representatives to put a stop to this slaughter.

Fat chance, it turns out. Since then, we've had hundreds of additional mass shootings resulting in over 2,000 dead and almost 10,000 wounded, including 50 dead at a nightclub in Orlando, Florida, 59 dead at a music festival in Las Vegas, Nevada, and 17 dead at a high school in Parkland, Florida.

Here is the kind of weapon the men who wrote the 2nd Amendment to the Constitution in 1787 had in mind:

Land Pattern Musket (aka "Brown Bess")
Length: 4 feet, 8 inches

What We Can and Can't Afford

Weight: 10 & ½ pounds
Action: muzzle-loaded flintlock
Rate of fire: 3 rounds per minute in very skilled hands
Muzzle velocity: 785 feet per second
Effective range: 50 yards.

Here is a typical weapon available 232 years later:

AR-15 (dubbed "America's Rifle" by the NRA)
Length: 3 feet, 3 inches
Weight: 7 & ½ pounds
Action: semi-automatic with 10, 20, or 30-round magazine
Rate of fire: 60 rounds a minute (in the hands of a rank amateur)
120 rounds a minute (in the hands of an adrenalin-charged killer)
Muzzle velocity: 3,300 feet per second
Effective range: 600 meters

There is absolutely no way on God's Green Earth that James Madison, George Washington, John Adams, John Jay, John Dickinson, Roger Sherman, Alexander Hamilton, or *any* of the other men who created our present Constitution would have said it is okay for any Tom, Dick or Harry to "keep and bear arms" like what are available today.

People who claim to be "strict constructionists" on the Constitution, arguing that the document should be interpreted exactly as the framers originally intended, don't seem to grasp that AR-15s, AK-47s, and 40-round magazines were not what the original framers had in mind. The original intent of the 2nd Amendment did not include mass murder on a mass scale on an almost daily basis.

Indeed, the men who wrote the Constitution recognized that situations and circumstances change, and that is why they provided a mechanism to amend the Constitution when deemed necessary, which has happened 27 times so far. The Constitution was not chiseled in stone by the hand of God.

And that includes the 2nd Amendment, which is no more sacrosanct than any other part of the Constitution. It is only the National Rifle Association and its supporters and minions who would have us believe that the 2nd Amendment alone is immutable, unchangeable, and eternal. Yet our elected officials at both the state and federal levels dance like marionettes to the strings pulled by millions and tens of millions of NRA dollars in the form of direct contributions to candidates at both state and federal levels, lobbying at both state and federal levels, public relations campaigns, and financial support for gun advocacy groups.

25. Chiseled in Stone by God's Hand?

I don't know about you, but I'm tired of living in a shooting gallery. Indeed, the American tolerance of guns and gun violence has become the laughingstock of the world (and this even before #45 took office and gave the world even more cause for laughter).

The National Rifle Association is right about one thing: I do indeed wish to take their guns away. Repeal the 2nd Amendment.

Well, no, that's not exactly accurate. To be more specific, I believe every American citizen should have the right to keep and bear a flintlock muzzle-loading smoothbore musket. That's what our Founding Fathers intended, and I believe intently in the original intent of the men who wrote our Constitution.

I'd like to see how many people would have died if Stephen Paddock, Omar Mateen, Adam Lanza, or Nikolas Cruz had been armed with a Brown Bess musket. Come on, folks, put some heat on your elected representatives.

26

Veterans Day vs. Armistice Day

(*BigCityLit*, Fall 2019/Winter 2020)

I've never paid much attention to Veterans' Day. None at all, really. The day I've always noted, at least in passing, is November 10, which is the birthday of the U.S. Marine Corps. I have a very curious relationship with the Corps, which is not worth trying to explain here; suffice it to say that, for better or worse, the three years I spent in the Marines were instrumental in shaping who I am today.

But being a veteran means nothing to me. I certainly didn't serve my country, let alone the greater good for humanity. Quite the contrary. When people say to me, "Thank you for your service," it is all I can do to reply politely. I long ago lost patience with such empty and empty-headed vacuity. Nothing I did while in uniform deserves either honor or commemoration.

Armistice Day, on the other hand, was something very different. That people should honor and reverence the end of the greatest carnage powerful elites had ever visited upon ordinary human beings—at least up until that time—was a great idea. It still is. I would very much like to see Armistice Day restored to its original meaning and intent: a celebration of peace.

Even in a world where war seems to be the perpetual state of affairs, a day to remember and celebrate peace seems to me both worthwhile and instructive. I really don't need a free dinner at Appleby's or NFL coaches wearing military-style camouflaged jackets or the false thanks of posturing politicians.

But a little peace? That would be nice.

27

Bernie Sanders
Extreme Radical Socialist

(*LA Progressive*, March 20, 2020;
New Hampshire Gazette, March 27, 2020)

I have long since grown weary of hearing Bernie Sanders characterized as "extreme," a "radical," and "socialist." No one will ever accuse The Donald of being a socialist. But telling over 16,000 lies in his first three years in office seems pretty extreme to me. And if denying the undeniable scientific evidence of human-induced climate change and dismantling the entire regulatory system put in place over the 20th century to protect American citizens from rapacious industrialists and financiers isn't radical, I need a new dictionary.

Meanwhile, President "I-knew-it-was-a-pandemic-all-along" did away with the National Security Council's pandemic unit in 2018, and now our private for-profit healthcare system is being overwhelmed by the coronavirus pandemic, unable to provide sufficient hospital capacity or healthcare workers, and our capitalist economy cannot produce enough test kits, face masks, hand sanitizer, or even toilet paper to meet demand.

What's so extreme about providing adequate medical care for everyone? I've heard we can't afford it. But we can afford to pour $2,000,000,000,000 (count all those zeroes, folks: that's two trillion dollars) into the black hole of Afghanistan? We can afford ten new aircraft carriers at a cost of $13,000,000,000 each (still a lot of zeroes: that's thirteen billion bucks per ship) even though our current carrier fleet is at least five times larger than the next largest carrier fleet in the world? We can afford 500 F-35 fighter planes at between $79,000,000 and $109,000,000 (depending on the model: A, B, or C) for each airplane?

What We Can and Can't Afford

But the richest nation in human history can't afford decent healthcare for its citizens?

Elsewhere in the world, French president Emmanuel Macron, not exactly a flaming Lefty, has suspended rent payments, utility bills, and taxes during the COVID-19 pandemic while the Spanish government has nationalized all private hospitals. Germany is providing direct payments to millions of self-employed workers and microbusinesses. Radical? More like taking action for the common good. And these are countries that already have broad social safety nets the envy of anything provided in the United States of America.

As for the accusation that Sanders is a socialist, how do folks think their roads get paved, their sewage gets treated, they get drinkable water when they turn on their taps? Collecting money from the body politic and using that money for the common good: that's socialism. Indeed, one of the largest socialist undertakings in the entire world is the U.S. military, those uniformed heroes we ostentatiously honor at every sporting event and public gathering in America. Our service members and their families are provided with government housing, government healthcare, government education, and in most cases food, clothing, and entertainment. All of this, good people, is socialism at work.

Indeed, I submit to you that Jesus of Nazareth was himself a socialist. He threw the moneychangers—the capitalists—out of the temple. He told the 1 percent they were going to have a hard time getting into heaven. Something about the eye of a needle. He provided healthcare to the poor, and never asked for a shekel in return. He hung around with prostitutes and sinners. His disciples were ordinary working men. He fed the hungry multitude fish and bread at no cost to those he fed.

And you're telling me that I shouldn't support Bernie Sanders because he's a radical? An extremist? *A socialist*? Maybe if we had a little more socialism in this country, our neighborhood electrical systems wouldn't short-circuit every time there's a storm. Maybe if we had a little more socialism, we wouldn't have 47,000 structurally deficient highway bridges in danger of collapse. Maybe if we had a little more socialism, the richest 10 percent of our population would not own 77 percent of the wealth (including 38 percent held by the top 1 percent) while the bottom 40 percent of our population would own a bit more than nothing at all, which is the total amount of wealth owned by 120,000,000 Americans.

We can argue about specific figures and actual numbers, and what constitutes "no wealth," but anybody more observant than a blue

27. Bernie Sanders

point oyster can see that something is seriously amiss when Michael Bloomberg can shell out $500,000,000 (all those zeroes again) on a vanity run for president while major corporations like Walmart and McDonald's are paying fulltime employees poverty-level wages.

Meanwhile, the Democratic Party is about to give us Joe Biden, who has little to offer us beyond the fact that he's not Donald Trump. He is part and parcel of the same Democratic Party that turned its back on the majority of Democratic voters during the Clinton years, and did nothing to reverse the creation of Republican Lite during the Obama years, thus paving the way for Number 45 and the disaster that has befallen us all.

The Democratic powerful want to get rid of Donald Trump and get back to the system they were happy with. Bernie Sanders wants to get rid of that system. No wonder the *New York Times*, the *Washington Post*, MSNBC, and CNN are all screaming at the top of their lungs: Radical! Extremist! Socialist! No wonder Cory Booker, Kamala Harris, Diane Feinstein, John Kerry, and an avalanche of other party stalwarts have endorsed Biden. They've all been working the system all their lives, and it's paid big dividends for them.

Looking at all of this in the cold light of reality, I don't imagine Bernie Sanders has a snowball's chance in Hell of getting the Democratic nomination. The system really is rigged, as we learned in 2016 when the party stalwarts denied him the nomination the first time around. But I voted for Bernie in the Pennsylvania primary four years ago, and if the coronavirus doesn't get me first, he'll get my vote in my state primary again this April.

28

Captain Crozier Deserves a Medal

(*LA Progressive*, April 5, 2020;
New Hampshire Gazette, April 10, 2020)

Let me get this straight: Captain Brett Crozier, commanding officer of the USS *Theodore Roosevelt* has been relieved of his command for "poor judgment," "unprofessional conduct," and damage to his "national security mission" because he wrote a letter asking the U.S. Navy for resources to help his crew of nearly 5,000 sailors deal with a coronavirus outbreak on his ship.

Meanwhile, his—and our—Commander-in-Chief got elected at least in part through the help and intervention of Russian President Vladimir Putin, a man for whom our president often expresses affection and admiration. Our Commander-in-Chief has gone through Secretaries of Defense and National Security Advisors as if they were itinerant peddlers, at least one of whom is now a convicted felon. He has handed over one of the most sensitive areas of diplomacy, the Middle East, to a 30-something relative with absolutely no diplomatic experience. He has murdered in cold blood the second most powerful man in the Iranian government.

Our Commander-in-Chief believes that a few years at a military school is pretty much the same thing as being in the armed forces. He has expressed the thought that he ought to award himself a Purple Heart Medal (perhaps for bone spurs miraculously discovered by podiatrist Larry Braunstein, who rented an office in a building owned by the father of our Commander-in-Chief). He ridiculed former prisoner of war John McCain, saying, "I like people who weren't captured."

Our Commander-in-Chief has alternately threatened and cuddled up to that pudgy pompadoured man in North Korea. He threatened to

28. Captain Crozier Deserves a Medal

withhold vital military aid to an ally at war with Russia unless the president of Ukraine took action to enhance the domestic political career of our Commander-in-Chief. He continues without skipping a beat his support for the Saudi ruler responsible for the murder of a U.S. resident whose children are American citizens. He has alienated our NATO allies repeatedly, those countries that most support and reflect our most admirable American aspirations of freedom, tolerance, and democracy.

Our Commander-in-Chief has made a mockery of American diplomatic integrity, withdrawing from, pulling out of, or outright abrogating the Intermediate-Range Nuclear Forces Treaty, the Paris Agreement on Global Warming, the Transpacific Partnership, and the Iran Nuclear Arms Pact. What sovereign nation will ever again in our lifetimes trust the signatures of U.S. leaders on any diplomatic document or treaty?

Indeed, our Commander-in-Chief utterly dismisses global warming as "fake news," ignoring the overwhelming scientific evidence to the contrary, and even dismissing his own military leadership's concerns about the national security implications of global warming. He has placed in charge of the Environmental Protection Agency a succession of advocates for the fossil fuel industries, and repeatedly rescinded federal restrictions on the exploitation of our environment.

Our Commander-in-Chief dispensed with the National Security Council's pandemic unit several years ago, and when the coronavirus outbreak began, he insisted first that it wasn't a threat, then that it was no worse than the common flu, then that he knew it was a pandemic all along, then that we should stop social isolating and all go back to work to save the economy, meanwhile offering federal assistance only to those states whose governors, in his words, "Treat me well." At the same time, he now considers himself a "wartime president," and insists on calling coronavirus "China virus" (perhaps because it's less exciting to be at war with a corona—whatever that is—than to be at war with the Chinese).

Our Commander-in-Chief has left dozens of countries without a U.S. ambassador, and even embassies with ambassadors are frequently badly understaffed. There has been a massive exodus of career civil servants from the State Department since January 2017. He has publicly and repeatedly undermined and questioned the integrity of both the Federal Bureau of Investigation and the Central Intelligence Agency.

I won't even go near the Commander-in-Chief's taunting of the physically disabled, his flagrant disparagement of women, his serial lying, his grotesque boasting about how intelligent he is and how

What We Can and Can't Afford

extensive his vocabulary is and how successful he is in business since these things may not bear directly on issues of national security (though even these things certainly fall under the categories of poor judgment and unprofessional conduct).

And certainly just about everything else I've discussed here very much touches on the security of the United States of America in addition to issues of judgment and conduct. Yet Captain Brett Crozier has been relieved of his command for acting in the best interests of the men and women for whom he is responsible.

Would that our Commander-in-Chief would show such concern for the men and women to whom he is responsible. He could start by awarding Capt. Crozier the Navy & Marine Corps Medal, the highest decoration available for heroism *not* involving armed combat.

29

Tom McGrath
*A Political Poet**

(*In These Times* 1978)

"Little as it is, what have we, comrades, but love and the class struggle?" asks Thomas McGrath in is 214-page long poem, *Letter to an Imaginary Friend* (Swallow Press, 1970). "Love and hunger!—That is my whole story."

But it is *our* story as well. And McGrath tells it better than any other poet writing in America today. His great achievement, as Fred Stern says in his forthcoming book, *Where the West Begins*, is the ability "to integrate personal experience, the events and feelings befalling his 'persona,' with his vision of class struggle and struggle for a socialist society."

At 61, McGrath, almost alone among his contemporaries, is a true "political poet," holding the reins of that volatile team with just the right tension so that neither horse runs away with the wagon. His shorter poems, most of which have been collected in *The Movie at the End of the World* (Swallow, 1973), are often brilliant. His long poem is an American masterpiece which may well find a place beside Whitman's *Song of Myself*, Williams' *Paterson*, and Pound's *Cantos*.

Though he says *Letter to an Imaginary Friend* is only "pseudo-autobiographical," the poem revolves around major benchmarks in McGrath's own life: his childhood on a North Dakota farm, his wartime service in the arctic boredom of the Aleutians, his involvement in the radical labor movement, his refusal to cooperate with the House Un-American Activities Committee, and his two marriages.

---

* I don't know why I didn't include this essay in my first essay collection, *In the Shadow of Vietnam*, published by McFarland back in 1991. But McGrath deserves to be recognized and appreciated, so I am including it here.

What We Can and Can't Afford

But one need not know the details of McGrath's life to understand and appreciate the poem, for McGrath weaves these into a broader, more generalized social—and socialist—awareness. the details he chooses are those which intersect with "something bigger"—the common experiences of all underdogs seeking the Fifth World, the Saquasohuh of Hopi prophesy.

The people we meet are at once themselves and symbols of "something bigger": Cal, "one of the bundle teamsters ... read *The Industrial Worker* ... last of the real Wobs"; Jenny, "the female kachina ... filling the field with light"; Cassidy, "simple as a knife, with no more pretension than bread"; "Showboat" Quinn of the National Maritime Union ("What part in the fuckin' pageant of history did *you* play?"); Bill Dee of "the bronc-stompers from the gone days of Montana mustangs"; Genya, "innocence/beauty/valor ... miner's-light ... girl with a handful of debts."

All of them move in the great circle of the Round Dance, the cycle of struggle, joy, despair and struggle, shifting stars "in the permanent sky." We move with them because they are people we have known and loved; they are us. What they seek, we seek also: "the commune of pure potential.... Communitas / Circle of warmth and work."

McGrath's juxtaposition of joy and despair propels us incessantly forward. Yes, we live in "a criminal nation / Of the rich and mighty ... a compromised country / Half dead at the bottom and rotten ripe on top." Nevertheless, *"that's* not the point and never was the point." What matters, McGrath insists, is "the generosity, expectant hope, / The open and true desire to create the good.... The beginning is right here / ON THIS PAGE. / Outside the window are all the materials."

To that end, says McGrath, "I offer as guide this total myth. / The legend of my life and time.... It is only required to open your eyes—/ Come: / We'll walk up out of the night together."

Letter to an Imaginary Friend is a tale of personal courage and collective energy, a monument in words to all those who have brought us that much closer to the world we want for our grandchildren, and in inspiration to those of us who must carry on.

No other contemporary American poet has offered us so much. Yet McGrath and his work command a depressingly small audience. Even well-read lovers of poetry often return blank stares at the mention of McGrath, and he is still published almost exclusively in the "little magazines."

Undoubtedly, his politics ("unaffiliated far left," he says these days)

29. Tom McGrath

are the major cause of McGrath's relative obscurity. Mainstream America, or rather mainstream poetical America—for mainstream America doesn't pay any attention to anybody's poetry—isn't comfortable with a poet who writes passionately about *real* change in the language of Marxism and the radical left, about commitment to revolution and the uprooting of existing political and social structures.

Yet it is just those politics, and McGrath's ability to turn his political ideals into good poetry, which makes McGrath so appealing. Too many poets never force their poetry beyond the narrow confines of their own private lives. Others who do, like Robert Bly, Muriel Rukeyser, Adrienne Rich, or Galway Kinnell, seldom offer more than criticism of what is.

Thomas McGrath offers a true vision of how to change what is, and what to change it into. His tenacity in maintaining that singular vision through forty years of writing on the margins of the world is awesome: "…my purpose," he says, again in *Letter to an Imaginary Friend*, "is nothing less / Than the interpositioning of a fence of ghosts (living and dead) / Between the atomic sewing machines of bourgeois ideology / (Net where we strangle) and the Naked Man of the Round Dance…. In other words to change the world/—Nothing less."

Author's note: I wrote this essay review in 1978 when I was not yet 30 years old, and my own writing career was barely underway. A great deal has happened between the time it was published and my rediscovery of it on a rainy afternoon in the midst of the coronavirus pandemic of 2020—to me, to my country, to the world. McGrath himself died in 1990, largely unknown and unheralded to the end, and now almost entirely forgotten.

But I still think he deserves better, and who knows what history will finally decide. I am pretty sure McGrath would be appalled by the ignorant, grasping grifter who has finally laid bare the magnitude of the criminality this nation is capable of. I imagine he would have been pleased that a Socialist has actually been a serious candidate for the presidency, and disappointed that Bernie Sanders did not get beyond the politics of a party to which he never really has belonged. And I remain convinced that *Letter to an Imaginary Friend* is the greatest poem of the 20th century.

30

A Letter to My Daughter
Election 2020

(*LA Progressive*, May 11, 2020; *New Hampshire Gazette*, May 22, 2020)

Dear Leela,

Whatever you think of my wish that the Green Party not complicate this particular presidential election—and I know you and many other Millennials don't agree with me, fed up as you justifiably are with both major political parties—please understand that I do care about your future and the lives of the rest of your generation and the generations to follow. And that includes the daughters.

I do not for a moment wish to underrate or dismiss or minimize the hurt and damage and pain and disrespect the sexual abuse of women engenders. My mother was a woman. My wife is a woman. You are a woman. It pains me deeply to think that you have been subjected to this kind of abuse. Last year I broke off a friendship of over thirty years in large measure because I could no longer bear the man's disrespect for women, his serial philandering, and his disparagement of the Me Too Movement.

But to equate the lifetime history of abuse of women by Donald Trump with something Joe Biden may have done over thirty years ago—when weighed against the damage Donald Trump has already caused this nation and the world, and will continue to cause if he is reelected—seems to me out of proportion.

I don't really much care what happens with the rest of my own life. I have been able to brush off this cancer I've been battling, for instance, because I'm not really all that eager to go on living anyway. Most of what I have hoped for and worked for over the course of my life has come to

30. A Letter to My Daughter

nothing. The world and my country are worse off now than they were when I was your age. It certainly isn't my future I give a rat's ass about because there isn't much left of it.

It is your future that really does concern me. If you think the two parties are tweedle dee and tweedle dum, consider who the Democrats have appointed to the Supreme Court during your lifetime:

Ruth Bader Ginsburg
Stephen Breyer
Sonia Sotomayor
Elena Kagan

And the Republicans?

Clarence Thomas
John Roberts
Samuel Alito
Neil Gorsuch
Brett Kavanaugh

Ginsburg is going to be very lucky to survive as long as January 2021. She has no chance of surviving another four years of a Republican administration. And if Trump gets the next appointment, that will make the court an insurmountable 6–3. You can kiss *Roe v. Wade* goodbye, along with a lot of other fundamental freedoms and liberties.

Moreover, Trump and his minions in the Senate have been appointing scores and scores of equally odious judges to lifetime appointments at the district and appellate levels, packing the entire federal judiciary with rightwing ideologues who are even now in the process of reversing every progressive gain made since the Warren Court when I was a youngster.

Under Donald Trump, the deterioration of the very fabric of our nation is occurring at hyper-speed. Trump has dismantled and eviscerated the Environmental Protection Agency, the Food and Drug Administration, the Securities and Exchange Commission, the Federal Election Commission, the National Institutes of Health, the Department of Education, the Justice Department, and the Department of State. And that's not the half of it. He has repeatedly thumbed his nose at the Constitution, and repeatedly gotten away with it. The so-called USA PATRIOT Act was bad enough, but Trump has reversed, nullified, or thrown out literally all of the civil and legal protections provided for ordinary citizens so painstakingly won over the past ninety years.

Moreover, he genuinely seems to think that global warming is fake

What We Can and Can't Afford

news, and is not only doing nothing to slow it down, but actively supporting and activating policies that are only increasing the impossibility of ever reversing the situation. You think I'm not thinking about your future? I'm not going to be around when this particular hammer comes down. It isn't my future I'm worried about.

I am not a Joe Biden fan. I supported Bernie Sanders with my writing and my money right up until he withdrew from the race. I am underwhelmed that Joe Biden is who I'm going to have to vote for. But Trump is in a league of his own. Like no other president in my lifetime, he has actively promoted the services of, and openly encouraged the support of, misogynists, racists, and bigots. Over the past three and a half years, I have come to believe that another four years of Donald Trump will render your future something very close to untenable, and perhaps even uninhabitable. I am not convinced that the damage he has already done can be reversed. I am certain another four years of this disaster will be fatal to just about everything you and I care about.

Vote your conscience. I would and will never tell you not to. But I won't apologize for writing to the Green Party and asking them to step aside this time around. I am not trying to silence them or dismiss their concerns. But I am terrified that Donald Trump will be reelected. I believe this election really is, for the first time in my life, well and truly *not* a time for a protest vote. I am seeing profoundly disturbing changes in this country unlike anything in all my 71 years. And I will say this one more time: it's not my future I'm terrified for. My future is already history. You are who matters.

I love you,

Dad

31

Racism

As American as Apple Pie

(*LA Progressive*, June 7, 2020;
New Hampshire Gazette, July 3, 2020)

For much of my adult life, I have taught high school English and history, most recently including eighteen years at the Haverford School for Boys in suburban Philadelphia, retiring in June 2019 at the age of 70. In my U.S. History course, I always teach a unit I call "Race in America," which begins with the first shipload of Africans arriving in Jamestown, Virginia, in 1619, and goes right up to Rosa Parks and the modern Civil Rights Movement.

I sugarcoat nothing. We cover slave life on the plantation with its whippings and brandings and castrations and amputations, the almost infinitely repeated rape of female slaves by their masters (how else can one account for the range of skin tones we call "black"), the separation of families. We look at the failure of Reconstruction and more importantly *why* it failed (the refusal of the federal government to enforce the 14th and 15th Amendments, the disinterest and racism of northern whites, and the reclaiming of political power by the same southern white racists who had fought to destroy the Union). We study not only "legal" disenfranchisement through poll taxes, literacy tests, and grandfather clauses, but also Ku Klux Klan violence, lynching, and the imposition of penal servitude, "slavery by another name," that existed extensively from the 1880s into the 1940s.

We look at photographs of thousands of hooded Klansmen and Klanswomen marching down Pennsylvania Avenue carrying American flags with the capitol dome behind them. And photographs of lynchings with the white lynchers proudly facing the camera and smiling happily.

What We Can and Can't Afford

And videos of enraged whites pouring mustard over the heads of black Americans sitting passively at Woolworth lunch counters.

I think it is fundamentally necessary for young Americans to understand that slavery and racism are not a sidebar to American history, but central to that history. We look at the progression represented by 1857's *Scott v. Sandford* to 1898's *Plessy v. Ferguson* to 1954's *Brown v. Board of Education of Topeka*. We study the hard fought, sometimes murderous, but finally successful Montgomery Bus Boycott, the lunch counter sit-ins, and Freedom Summer.

I want to believe, and I want my students to believe, that as Dr. Martin Luther King, Jr., said, "The arc of the moral universe is long, but it bends toward justice."

My white students often wonder why I keep harping about racism. Once, when I was teaching the poetry of Langston Hughes and Claude McKay in an English class, one boy blurted out, "I never owned any slaves. Why are you trying to make me feel guilty?" My reply was, "I'm not asking you to feel guilty about what your ancestors did. I'm asking you to live your lives in such a way so that your descendants won't have to feel ashamed of you." Six months later, at the end of the school year, Ian gave me a ceramic bowl that he'd made. Painted around the rim of that bowl were those words.

So, pat myself on the back and think, "Oh, what a good boy am I." But I need to remember that this isn't about me.

Nor is it about my white students, who can walk in my suburban neighborhood without others eyeing them suspiciously, who can shop at the drugstore or the hardware store without being followed by an employee, who will never have to explain how they came to be driving a BMW or Mercedes. What do I say to my African American students in the face of Eric Garner, Freddie Gray, Tamir Rice, Philando Castile, Breonna Taylor, George Floyd, and 1,252 others killed by police just since January 1, 2015?

One of my former students, a young man named Dan, posted this message on social media:

> More than ever, I'm overwhelmed and confused. I'm overwhelmed when I hear on the news another black man or woman's life was cut short due to senseless violence and racism. Overwhelmed to see my community continue to hurt while our voices continue to be suppressed and our feelings minimized. Overwhelmed when we say "Black Lives Matter" and the response is "All Lives Matter," but the actions don't match the words. I'm confused as to how cops can act off of impulse with lethal weapons, but

31. Racism

black civilians must remain cool with guns drawn to their faces and hands behind their backs in cuffs. Confused as to how when we kneel or we protest, we need to find a different way. Confused as to how one can 'see both sides' in such calamity. It's disheartening to see that we as a country need to take into consideration any racist's feelings because our protest may hurt their ego. Meanwhile, lives continue to be lost and families and communities continue to mourn. Where is the solace for the black community?

It's easy to post and spread awareness on social media, and it is appreciated, but let's take the next steps: signing petitions, making calls demanding justice, and continuing to educate ourselves; most importantly, have the uncomfortable conversations at home, where it all begins.

Don't think because it doesn't pertain to you that it doesn't pertain to you.

Those are not the words of an incendiary black man full of rage and ready to lash out at whatever and whoever gets close. They are the words of a thoughtful 20-year-old full of pain and hurt, trying to come to terms with the situation in which he finds himself, his community, and his country floundering.

I don't know what to say to him. This is not the United States of America I want to be living in. This is not the country I want to bequeath to him. I owe him something better than this. Every caring American—black, white, yellow, red, pink, and blue—owes him and his generation something *much* better than the racism that has plagued this nation since before it was a nation, that plagues the nation to this day, that makes it difficult to be an African American in America, and downright dangerous to be a young African American male in America.

Dan offers some very constructive actions that each and every one of us can take to try to help change the current sorry state of affairs in this country, to which I would add: get out and vote for candidates who promote inclusion rather than division, get out on the streets and exercise your 1st Amendment right to peaceably assemble and petition the government for redress of grievances, write to your elected officials at every level from your local municipality to those who represent you at the national level (and then write again, and again; most of them can be reached easily by e-mail).

Our national anthem claims that this is the land of the free and the home of the brave. How brave are *we* willing to be in order to ensure that *all* of us are free? As my young friend so wisely observes, "Don't think because it doesn't pertain to you that it doesn't pertain to you." This pertains to all of us. We really are all in this together.

32

Trump and the Military
Is Anyone Really Surprised?

(*LA Progressive*, September 9, 2020; *Intelligencer*
and *Bucks County Courier Times*, October 1, 2020;
New Hampshire Gazette, October 9, 2020.)

A recent article in September's *The Atlantic* titled "Trump: Americans Who Died in War Are 'Losers' and 'Suckers'" details our current commander-in-chief's flagrant disrespect for the men and women in our armed forces together with the generations of American service personnel who went before them. I need not repeat the insults and ignominies he heaps upon those who have served their country. You can readily find the article online and read it for yourself, if you haven't already done so.

What amazes me is not what the article says, but the fact that so many people are only now expressing their outrage over Trump's disrespect for the military of which he is constitutionally commander-in-chief. The storm of shock and anger at Trump's aspersions leaves me scratching my head.

Who did we think this guy was before that article appeared?

This is the man who believes he "served in the military" because he attended a military academy for high school.

This is the man who was deferred from the draft during the Vietnam War because he was diagnosed with bone spurs by a doctor who rented office space in a building owned by Donald Trump's father.

This is the man who claims he knows "more about ISIS than the generals do."

This is the man who called Navy torpedo bomber pilot George H.W. Bush a loser for being shot down by the Japanese during World War II.

This is the man who says of former prisoner of war John McCain, "I like people who weren't captured."

32. Trump and the Military

This is the man who proclaims, "I always wanted to get the Purple Heart."

This is the man who belittled Khizr and Ghazala Khan, Gold Star parents whose U.S. Army captain son was killed in combat in Iraq.

This is the man who told the widow of another U.S. soldier killed in an ambush in Niger that he "knew what he signed up for."

This is the man who accused Lieutenant Colonel Alexander Vindman of his own National Security Council staff of being "very insubordinate" because Vindman testified honestly to the U.S. Congress about Trump's dealings with Ukraine.

This is the man who declared his own Secretary of Defense, General James Mattis, a 44-year veteran of multiple wars, "the most overrated general in the world."

This is the man who said his own chief of staff, John Kelly, who served as an enlisted Marine and rose to the rank of sergeant before becoming a commissioned officer and rising to the rank of general, "couldn't handle the pressure of the job."

And now, all of a sudden, we're surprised to discover that Donald Trump has no respect for the military of which he is commander-in-chief, who believes the members of our military are "suckers" and "losers," who looks at the graves in Arlington and wonders aloud what was in it for them?

What upsets me is not so much what's in that article, which is really nothing we didn't already know or at least could have inferred, but rather the moral cowardice of the anonymous sources the writer based his article on. Their refusal to identify themselves, whatever excuses and rationales they may be telling themselves to justify their anonymity, only allows Trump and his Trumpsters to claim the whole story is completely fabricated. Never mind that Trump's entire life bespeaks the truth of that article. Without attribution, he and his minions can claim that it's all just idle rumors, malicious speculation, Fake News.

Indeed, one wonders if those anonymous sources are actually working for the Trump campaign. They have certainly played right into Trump's hands. Unless those anonymous sources step forward, identify themselves, and explain how they know what they purport to know, the article merely seems to confirm, just as Trump claims, that the lying liberal media are simply out to get him.

33

Why I'm Not Voting for Donald Trump

(*LA Progressive*, October 12, 2020;
New Hampshire Gazette, October 23, 2020)

Just a few days ago, an e-mail acquaintance of mine sent me this:

Gotta admit I'm voting for Trump because I fear what happens if he loses. Who is Trump running against? I don't think that Joe's cognitive skills are up to the task. I think almost everything he says has been scripted for him.

Harris? I'm not even sure Joe picked her. Look at the horrible claims she made against him while she was still campaigning—and now they're buds? I have to believe that powers behind the scenes have designs on how they'll direct Joe on what his policies will be. If, for some reason, he's unable to complete four years and Harris takes over, she'll have to go along with the plans made for Joe. If she didn't agree to those terms, she wouldn't have been picked for the VP slot. If the democrats take the white house, I'm afraid we're in for an extreme radical-leftist shift. Maybe some folks think that's what we should have.

Here is my reply:

I have to admit that I was taken very much by surprise when I read your e-mail yesterday. I spent a good deal of last night awake, thinking about all of this. This morning I went back and re-read our entire exchange of e-mails and letters going back to June 9th, 2019. And I see a very distinct, clear pattern.

In your very first letter, you write, "I highly value your opinions. My question is about the aftermath of Tet. If the Americans would have/could have followed it up with smashing great force against the Viet Cong and NVA, would the war's end have been different? It seems that Tet was a military disaster for the communists. The American media did everything it could to portray the United States as the Tet Offensive's loser." And you go on to repeat multiple popular myths about the war that have no basis in fact.

In response to your first letter, I sent you a long and detailed e-mail

33. Why I'm Not Voting for Donald Trump

explaining the reality of what was happening in Vietnam, citing for you a number of factual historical sources and references. Over the next weeks and months, you returned with a number of questions, each of which was based—forgive me, please—on a serious lack of factual knowledge. (One I particularly remember was your staggering misbelief that "the Chinese effectively still are in charge" of Vietnam when in fact the two peoples are mortal enemies.)

I had hoped that by my taking the time to respond to so many of your questions in such detail, you would begin to realize that what you believe and how you see the world are based on a serious lack of knowledge. You subscribe to a view of the world that is without foundation or support in historical reality.

If I managed to teach you anything at all about history, none of that translated into an understanding of the political situation we are facing in this country today. You believe that if Biden wins, the country will become "extreme radical-leftist."

Joe Biden is about as vanilla mainstream as a politician can get. There is absolutely nothing "extreme radical leftist" about him. His record over the years is almost painfully moderate, middle-of-the-road. (Indeed, a big reason I am not hugely enthusiastic about him is because he is *not* progressive enough.)

And as for Kamala Harris, she was a prosecutor and state attorney general. This is not exactly "extreme radical-leftist," even in California.

And who are these ominous "powers behind the scenes" who are directing Biden, and will direct Harris if she takes over? The evil Deep State that is out to hand the USA over to China or Antifa or the Mexicans? The secret supporters of Bernie Sanders, who have somehow infiltrated and taken over the Democratic party even though they couldn't manage to finagle Bernie's nomination? Are you a follower of QAnon? Where do you get these ideas? What knowledge are your beliefs based on?

I happen to know Joe Biden as it turns out. His nephew went to the school where I taught, and I coached him for four years, advised him for three years, and taught him for two years. I got to know the boy and his parents very well, and through them met Joe Biden on a number of occasions. He is not a doddering old senile septuagenarian. He is sharp as a tack and in far, far better physical health than our current president. Moreover, Joe Biden is a decent man.

Meanwhile, our current president is a bullying, blustering, narcissistic, racist, sexist, lying, cheating, selfish, truly ignorant grifter who has spent four years thumbing his nose at the Constitution, dismantling the institutions created by that document, and riding roughshod over the separation of powers. He has seriously damaged American democracy, courted dictators, insulted allies, and encouraged rightwing violence. And he has done this with the support of Republicans like Mitch McConnell and Lindsey Graham. He has made our nation the laughingstock of the world—I have

What We Can and Can't Afford

contacts in Britain, Germany, France, Spain, Italy, Austria, India, Japan, Thailand, and Vietnam, and I can tell you that people in those countries are scratching their heads and wondering if Americans have lost their minds.

I will also say this: I am far less afraid of a disorganized mob in the streets throwing bricks through store windows than I am of organized militias dressed in full body armor and carrying AK-47s and AR-15s. If you could listen to Donald Trump tell the Proud Boys to "stand back and stand by," and not feel the shivers running up and down your spine, then you and I really do have nothing in common.

I sincerely hope that is not the case. In the first letter you ever wrote me, as I said, you wrote, "I highly value your opinions." I hope that is true. And I hope that you will reconsider your beliefs about the possible consequences of this election. Historical analogies are never completely accurate because every situation is different. But it is worth remembering that Joseph Stalin, Benito Mussolini, and Adolph Hitler all came to power legally, as did Vladimir Putin. I fully believe that if Donald Trump remains in office—by hook or by crook—another four years, you can kiss American democracy goodbye.

If you truly value my opinions, you will think long and hard about what I've said in this e-mail.

34

The Democratic Party Has One Last Chance

(*LA Progressive* and *New Hampshire Gazette*, November 20, 2020)

I have been feeling increasingly bleak and anxious ever since last March. And these past couple of weeks, as the presidential election has loomed larger and larger, have left me almost dysfunctional. The thought of another four years of this Monster in the White House left me wallowing in the depths of despair because suicide is not a viable option, and I'm too old and not rich enough to emigrate to any country I'd be willing to spend my last years in, but I have felt that I could not endure another four years of this Monster. Some of the fantasies I've been having lately have been so vivid that they have frightened me.

And then Friday morning, November 6, my cat caught me in an unguarded moment, and I realized that she had no idea what is going on, and moreover could care less. She is happy with food, warmth, and attention. And it made me think hard about the frame of mind I'd worked myself into lately. I ended up writing this poem:

Beanie the Cat
November 6th, 2020

Anne and I have been holding our breath
for three days, trying not to think,
or feel, or contemplate the implications
of another four years of madness
if our current president should win,
astounded it should be so close
we still don't know who won.

What We Can and Can't Afford

What kind of country could this be
to have so many voters ready
to return to office such a man?
Dishonest, criminal, amoral,
pathologically narcissistic,
ignorant, uncaring, vile. A grifter.
One struggles to avoid despair.

But then there's Beanie, curled up
beside my wife, sound asleep. She's
had her breakfast, asked and gotten
some attention, belly scratched, ears
massaged, green eyes almost iridescent,
happy, I suppose, at least content
if purring signifies contentment.
What goes on behind those glowing eyes
we'll never know, but she's not worried
in the least about elections, this
or any other. She's got us. Moreover,
we've got her. Reason enough, perhaps,
to face whatever's coming next.

Only 24 hours later, Biden finally collected Pennsylvania's Electoral College votes, giving him 273 and the election, and the circumstances that gave rise to my poem disappeared. The magnitude of my relief has so far been beyond expression.

Of course, we still have the problem of some 70,000,000 fellow citizens who—is there a polite way to say this—have their heads so far up their backsides that they can see daylight. Already I am trying *not* to think about 2024, knowing that Trump may be vanquished, but the Trumpsters and Trumperdom are here to stay. Since most of them are aging white men, however, I hope we can outlast them. Well, not me, actually—I'm as aged as they are—but my daughter and the generations who still have a future ahead of them. They may live long enough to see the demographics of this country change enough to leave aggrieved white men and their benighted partners politically irrelevant.

But this is no time to sit back and gloat, or even bask in the relief so many of us are feeling, as if we are finally out of the woods. Our task now is to put pressure on a Biden Administration to keep its promises and act on progressive issues like climate change, health care, racial justice, and income inequality.

My own daughter voted for Biden only with extreme reluctance,

34. The Democratic Party Has One Last Chance

believing—rightly so, in my opinion—that Biden represents the kind of politics-as-usual that led to the election of Donald Trump in the first place. The Democratic Party has this one last chance to make itself worthy of my daughter's vote.

As fervently as I wished for the defeat of Donald Trump, I hope Joe Biden and his party understand this and act accordingly.

35

Insurrection

Are We Really Surprised?

(*LA Progressive*, January 11, 2021;
New Hampshire Gazette, January 15, 2021)

Let's review the facts.

Our 45th president openly bragged about grabbing women by their genitals, and declared that he could murder someone in broad daylight in Manhattan without consequences. He has paid hush money to prostitutes he was "screwing" (please substitute the F-bomb) even as his third wife was nursing their newborn child.

Our 45th president has declared that he and North Korean dictator Kim Jong Un "fell in love," and that Russian dictator Vladimir Putin "is really very much of a leader," while calling German chancellor Angela Merkel "stupid," French president Emmanuel Macron "nasty," and Canadian prime minister Justin Trudeau "two-faced."

Our 45th president has gone through secretaries of defense, secretaries of state, and national security advisors like he's trying on new shoes, Imelda Marcos–style, looking for a pair that might fit. He has had a 91 percent turnover rate among senior-level advisors since he took office.

Our 45th president has, from even before he took the oath of office, declared that any news he doesn't like is "fake news," while he himself has subscribed to what his own press secretary called "alternative facts." Speaking of lies, our Liar-in-Chief has so far told over 20,000 of them, averaging 50 per day every single day of his presidency.

Our 45th president has openly mocked the disabled, urged police "not to be gentle" with Black Lives Matter protestors, incited his supporters to punch out his critics, praised "body-slammers," called the leadership of the National Rifle Association "great American patriots,"

35. Insurrection

repeatedly demanded that former Secretary of State Hillary Clinton be thrown into prison, and described his own former secretary of defense and ex-Marine James Mattis as "the world's most overrated general."

Our 45th president has failed at just about everything he has put his hand to. Trump Taj Mahal, Trump's Castle, Trump Plaza Casinos, Trump Plaza Hotel, Trump Hotels and Casinos Resorts, and Trump Entertainment Resorts have all gone bankrupt. Trump Steaks, GoTrump, Trump Airlines, Trump Vodka, Trump Mortgage, Trump: The Game, Trump Magazine, Trump University, Trump Ice, The New Jersey Generals, Tour de Trump, and Trump Network have all gone belly up.

Our 45th president promised to build a wall to keep Mexican immigrants out and insisted that the Mexicans themselves would pay for it. He promised to "drain the swamp," but instead placed family members and close friends into key positions of power within his administration, earned millions of dollars by violating the Emoluments Clause of the U.S. Constitution, directing U.S. taxpayers' dollars to Mar-a-Lago, Trump Turnberry Golf Resort in Scotland, and various Trump hotels, and arranged for his daughter Ivanka to receive fast-tracking approval for seventeen different trademarks from the Chinese government in return for lifting trade sanctions.

Our 45th president has pardoned liars, perjurers, corrupt politicians, war criminals, and murderers. He has been exposed for defrauding the U.S. government and the state of New York of millions and millions of dollars in taxes, and cheated his own niece and nephew out of their fair share of their grandfather's inheritance.

Our 45th president has called the white supremacist KKKers in Charlottesville, Virginia, "good people." He has claimed that removing statues of men who waged war on our nation—that's called treason, by the way—in an effort to keep millions of Americans enslaved is "an attempt to wipe out our history." He has directed rightwing armed militia groups to "stand by."

Our 45th president began laying the groundwork for his claim that his electoral defeat would be fraudulent many months before the election ever took place. He continued to claim the election had been stolen from the moment Pennsylvania's electoral votes were declared for Joe Biden a few days after the election, and he has continuously claimed a "stolen election" ever since.

We have been watching this dangerous buffoon for the past forty years. He has been performing his disgraceful carnival act on the world

What We Can and Can't Afford

stage for the past four years. He has been regularly and consistently demeaning the dignity of the presidency, to the detriment of the nation, while enablers from Ted Cruz, Mitch McConnell, and Josh Hawley to Sean Hannity, Tucker Carlson, and Laura Ingraham have encouraged and egged him on.

And now we are shocked that Trump-inspired insurrectionists finally stormed the capitol building in the capital city of the United States of America, smashing, looting, vandalizing, and desecrating the very heart of American government?

Now Education Secretary Betsy DeVos, Transportation Secretary Elaine Chao, Special Envoy Mick Mulvaney, Deputy National Security Advisor Matthew Pottinger, Deputy Assistant Secretary of Commerce John Costello, Acting Chairman of the White House Council of Economic Advisors Tyler Goodspeed, and Melania Trump Chief of Staff Stephanie Grisham have all resigned, claiming in various ways to have "reached a breaking point"? After one thousand, four hundred, and forty-seven days of this crap? Only now have they're reached a breaking point? How courageous.

Now Lindsey Graham says, "Enough's enough. Count me out"? Now Mitch McConnell says he never wants to speak to our 45th president again? Now Ted Cruz calls what happened Wednesday a "despicable terrorist attack," but denies any responsibility for what happened on January 6?

Oh, *please*! I mean, just, for cryin' in a bucket: PULEEZE!!!

How could what happened on Wednesday surprise *anyone*?! You'd have to be deaf, dumb, blind, and living under a rock in Outer Mongolia *not* to have seen this coming for days, weeks, months, and years.

But what do we do now? What do we do with the 74,000,000 of our fellow citizens who voted for this madman even after the past four years of lunacy and chaos? I know what I'd like to do, but it would be neither ethical nor practical nor legal. So, we simply have to live with them and hope that somehow there are still enough sane Americans to neutralize the damage these damaged people can do.

I may be pipe dreaming, but I find myself thinking back to when I was 16 years old and watching the Alabama police attacking peaceful civil rights marchers in Selma with vicious dogs, billy clubs, and high-powered fire hoses. A lot of Americans watched that unfolding, and had to ask themselves, "How could this happen in the United States of America?" Nothing changed overnight, but the weight of public

35. Insurrection

opinion and political will did in fact begin to shift in favor of putting an end to the segregated South and Jim Crow America.

What happened last Wednesday in Washington was certainly a very different situation. Indeed, the perpetrators at the capitol, in another time and place, would have been the ones using vicious dogs and billy clubs. But I can only hope that enough Americans watched what happened on January 6, and have and will continue to ask themselves, "How could this happen in the United States of America?"

And then I hope they will make up their minds to be and act and do whatever they can to see that such a disgraceful scene is never enacted again. Nor such a disgraceful human being ever again elected to the presidency.

36

Is This Who We Are?

(VVAW Commentaries, January 15, 2021)

"The only thing necessary for the triumph of evil is for good men [and women] to do nothing." —Edmund Burke

In the wake of the insurrectionary and seditious attempted *coup d'état* on January 6, 2021, I've repeatedly heard many people argue that "THIS is *not* who we are." Just the other night, President-elect Joe Biden said the exact same thing: "This is not who we are."

But even a cursory review of American history reveals that this is indeed who many of us are. Bigotry and hatred and intolerance are, I'm sorry to say, as American as apple pie. Consider, for instance, the Pequot Massacre of 1637, during which a bunch of white Christians burned a Native village (the wrong tribe at that) and shot, stabbed, and bludgeoned to death some 500 men, women, and children who tried to escape the flames.

Then there were Pennsylvania's "Paxton Boys" of 1763 who, in two separate attacks, exterminated the last of the peaceful, unarmed, and Christianized Conestoga Indians, taking their scalps for good measure.

Or we might take the time to reflect on the Cherokee Trail of Tears when thousands of Native Americans were forced to march from Georgia to Oklahoma in the dead of winter, four thousand of them dying along the way, even though the U.S. Supreme Court had ruled that the U.S. government had no right to force them to move ... to which President Andrew Jackson replied, "Mr. Marshall has made his decision. Now let him enforce it." (As we try to deny who and what we are as a people and a nation, we might do well to remember that #45 is not the first U.S. president to give the middle finger to our Constitution.)

How about the American Civil War, in which over one-quarter of a million Americans died trying to keep enslaved almost four million of

36. Is This Who We Are?

their fellow citizens, whom they did not consider even as human beings, let alone citizens?

In the wake of the Civil War, we had a hundred years of Jim Crow segregation, accompanied week after week and year after year by lynchings, beatings, and constant intimidation. And when the lynchers were not off lynching somebody, they would get dressed up in their white sheets and pointy-headed hats (oh, the irony), and hold parades. (Check out the photos of the Ku Klux Klan marching down Pennsylvania Avenue in Washington, D.C., on August 9, 1925, for instance.)

Even *before* World War II, some of our fellow citizens were treated to huge signs saying things like: "Japs Keep Moving. This is a White Man's Neighborhood," and "No Japs Wanted Here." And all through the 19th and 20th centuries, others of our fellow citizens were greeted at the doors of stores and restaurants with signs reading: "We don't serve Spanish or Mexicans" and "No Dogs, Negroes, or Mexicans."

And when I was a teenager in the 1960s, I regularly watched on television as snarling police dogs and snarling police repeatedly attacked peaceful civil rights marchers singing the same hymns I sang in my own church on Sunday mornings.

So don't try to tell me the January 6 insurrectionists with their Confederate flags and Viking horned helmets and bear spray and hockey sticks wielded as weapons and noose to hang Vice President Pence with are *not* who we are. For a great many of my fellow citizens, this is *exactly* who we are. This is not "fake news." The facts of history speak for themselves. As one of my heroes, Megan Rapinoe, recently said: "This *is* America."

The only question that really matters is: What are you and I going to do about it?

37

Will You Settle for Returning to Politics as Usual?

(LA Progressive, March 23, 2021;
New Hampshire Gazette, March 26, 2021)

It took Joseph Robinette Biden, Jr., Commander-in-Chief #46, only about five weeks to start dropping bombs on other countries. And he's decided that he's not going to penalize Saudi Arabian Crown Prince Mohammed bin Salman for ordering the brutal murder and dismembering of *Washington Post* columnist Jamal Khashoggi. And so I was very quickly reminded of the only reason why I voted for Uncle Joe: he's not Cadet Bone Spur.

It isn't all bad, of course. Biden's cabinet appointments have been nothing short of historic: a gay secretary of transportation, a Native American secretary of the interior, a Black secretary of defense, a secretary of education who's actually an educator, an attorney general who Moscow Mitch and Graham Cracker wouldn't even let the senate vote on for a Supreme Court appointment.

And a whole raft of executive orders reversing—for now at least—some of the damage done by C-in-C #45 to environmental protection, immigration, voting rights, transgender military service, collective bargaining for federal workers. Biden has rejoined the World Health Organization and the Paris Climate Accord, and canceled the Keystone XL pipeline.

But dropping bombs on Shiite militias in Syria to "send a signal" to Iran is simply a return to pre–Trumpian politics as usual. Refusing to treat the ruler of a medieval country run by Sharia law like the murdering tyrant he is because he and his country are useful to Biden in dealing with another medieval country run by Sharia law is pre–Trumpian diplomacy as usual.

37. Will You Settle for Returning to Politics as Usual?

The simple fact is that Joe Biden, though infinitely preferable to his predecessor, is part and parcel of the same stale, unresponsive, we-respond-to-the-folks-with-the-money, dysfunctional political system that led to the election of a congenital liar and criminal grifter in the first place. Between 1976 and 2016, millions of Americans came to believe—with very good reasons—that neither major political party cared about them or was looking out for their interests.

By the third year of Bill Clinton's presidency, the Democratic Party had made itself over as Republican Lite, and Joe Biden was a part of that transformation. When Barack Obama became president, he appointed to key positions many of the same Wall Street playmakers who had helped to bring on the Crash of 2008. His secretary of state was Hillary Clinton, who subsequently gave highly paid speeches to Wall Street firms in which she tacitly approved of cuts to Social Security and praised unfettered international trade. Need I remind you who was Obama's vice president?

And then there is the infamous photo of former vice president Biden giving the Liberty Medal to former president George W. Bush. This just boggles the mind. The medal Biden is putting around Bush's neck is not just for "work with veterans" as the original caption said, but for work with disabled veterans in particular, veterans disabled in the wars of aggression waged by the Bush administration under false pretenses and outright lies. Does Biden not understand the irony here? Surely he could have gracefully declined to participate in this charade, which is about as hollow as giving Donald Trump a Purple Heart for his bone spurs.

And speaking of gracefully declining, does Biden really have to end every public speech with: "May God bless our troops"? For what? Waging forever war in Iraq and Afghanistan? Dropping drone missiles on wedding parties and school buses? I assume Biden is referring to the Old Testament God who killed off the entire human race aside from Noah and his family. The God of Joshua who flattened the city of Jericho. The God of Lot who obliterated Sodom and Gomorrah.

Surely Biden can't mean the Father of Jesus of Nazareth, the Lamb of God, the Prince of Peace, the man who healed the sick and broke bread with sinners, the guy who said turn the other cheek and love thy neighbor. Any God who would bless me for what I did as a U.S. Marine in Vietnam ought to go talk to a priest.

So where does all this leave us? Soon after last November's election, I wrote in an essay titled "The Democratic Party Has One Last Chance":

What We Can and Can't Afford

This is no time to sit back and gloat, or even bask in the relief so many of us are feeling, as if we are finally out of the woods. Our task now is to put pressure on a Biden Administration to keep its promises and act on progressive issues like climate change, health care, racial justice, and income inequality.

My own daughter voted for Biden only with extreme reluctance, believing—rightly so, in my opinion—that Biden represents the kind of politics-as-usual that led to the election of Donald Trump in the first place. The Democratic Party has this one last chance to make itself worthy of my daughter's vote.

As fervently as I wished for the defeat of Donald Trump, I hope Joe Biden and his party understand this and act accordingly.

Now it's Showtime, and while we are seeing some improvements over the previous four years, so far we haven't seen much to suggest that "politics as usual" are no longer acceptable. It is time to start delivering on changes that will benefit ordinary Americans and restore faith in the Democratic Party as the party of working people: affordable healthcare; increases in living wages and the standard of living for the 99 percent; fair and equitable taxation; decent housing; withdrawal of American military forces from many—perhaps most—of the one hundred and fifty countries where they are now stationed; reduced spending on a grotesquely outlandish "defense" budget and corresponding increases in spending for education, mass transit, highway and electrical infrastructure; consumer protection and regulation of financial marketers and investment firms.

Think this is too much to ask, let alone expect? I'm no clairvoyant, but I'm willing to bet that if a Biden/Harris administration doesn't start delivering on a significant portion of such an agenda, the Retrumplican Party will be back in the saddle by 2024.

So, what can you yourself do about any of this? When is the last time you wrote to your U.S. senator, your U.S. representative, your state senator, or your state representative? If you already have, write to them again. And again. And again. How about your county commissioner? Your town councilperson? All politics, after all, really is local. And get involved with at least one public action group:

Veterans for Peace (*https://www.veteransforpeace.org/*),
Ready for 100 (*https://www.sierraclub.org/ready-for-1000*),
Everytown for Gun Safety (*https://everytown.org/about-everytown/*),
Black Lives Matter (*https://blacklivesmatter.com/*).

37. Will You Settle for Returning to Politics as Usual?

There are dozens, perhaps hundreds, of ways you can become engaged locally, regionally, and nationally. The last four years have been a nightmare, but the next four years are likely to determine the future of this country for all time to come. President Biden and his party need to be pushed, poked, prodded, and pestered into recognizing that politics as usual is no longer acceptable, affordable, or allowable.

38

Welcome to the Shooting Gallery

(*LA Progressive*, April 2, 2021;
New Hampshire Gazette, April 9, 2021)

Welcome to the Shooting Gallery, folks, at the Great American Firearms Bazaar! Step right up and win your sweetheart a Kewpie doll! No background check required! No waiting period! Just plunk down your $$$$$, pick up a gun, and start blasting away! It's easy! It's fun! Guaranteed to win a prize every time!

Just when we thought things were looking up—coronavirus vaccinations increasing by the week, Cadet Bone Spur relegated to Maybe-Lar-Gesse and facing dozens of lawsuits and maybe some criminal prosecutions too, a real president in the White House, and the crocuses and daffodils beginning to bloom—we get forcefully and depressingly reminded that this country we live in is still the most insane gun culture on Planet Earth.

In the space of two weeks in late March, twenty-one more unarmed innocent Americans and the police officer who tried to protect some of them were murdered by men who had legally acquired the firearms they then used to kill people who had never done them any harm: eight shot dead in Atlanta, Georgia, March 16; ten shot dead in Boulder, Colorado, March 22; four shot dead in Orange County, California, March 31. And as I type this, I wonder how many more murders will happen before this essay is published.

Meanwhile, once again, out come the handwringing calls for background checks, waiting periods, banning of assault rifles, limiting magazine capacities. Once again, the National Rifle Association declares that guns don't kill people. Once again, the dust will settle, and the 24-hour news cycle will go on to the latest shenanigans of the British

38. Welcome to the Shooting Gallery

royal family and the NCAA men's basketball tournament and President Biden's proposed two trillion dollar 21st century New Deal.

And nothing will change. It's like that movie *Groundhog Day*. Only it's not a movie, and it's not entertaining. It's just real people dead. Different ones each time. Young, old, male, female, white, Black, Asian. Sooner or later your friends and family, my friends and family. Maybe you and me.

And you know what? Even if Congress mandated national background checks and waiting periods, and outlawed assault rifles and large capacity magazines, the slaughter would continue. None of those changes to our current gun laws would mean a tinker's damn in Hell.

If I choose to, I can pass a background check, wait two days, walk out of a gun store with a .45 caliber pistol that holds eight bullets, and kill eight people in eight to ten seconds. I can replace that magazine in three to four seconds, and kill another eight people. Sixteen people dead in less than thirty seconds. Who needs assault rifles and high-capacity magazines?

There is a reason why the men who wrote our Constitution made provisions for amending that Constitution: they knew that situations and circumstances change, and they understood that our Constitution would need to be able to change, too.

Consider some of the changes we've made to that document over the past two and a half centuries: slavery has been abolished; Black Americans, Native Americans, and American women can now vote; senators are elected by the people instead of by state legislatures, presidents are limited to two terms. I was not eligible to vote until long after I returned home from Vietnam as a combat-wounded Marine, but the voting age is now 18, not 21.

It isn't easy to amend the Constitution, but the very fact that the men who wrote that document included the mechanism for changing it puts the lie to those who insist on knowing and acting on "the original intent" of the Founding Fathers. That the Constitution provides for amendment makes it perfectly clear that those wise men realized the world they lived in would not remain unchanged for all eternity.

So how in the world did the 2nd Amendment become the one tiny piece of the Constitution that is handed down directly from God and James Madison, unchangeable, immutable, sacrosanct for all time now and forever *ad infinitum*?

Back in 1787, a lot of Americans put food on their tables by hunting. Some of them lived in circumstances where self-defense was sometimes necessary. And the weapon they had was a muzzle-loading, smoothbore, flintlock musket that could maybe crank off three shots a minute if you were really good with it.

Seriously, I ask you: what do you think George Washington or Benjamin Franklin, or James Madison would have thought about fellow citizens who own three or eight or twenty-seven high-powered assault rifles and automatic pistols and pump shotguns? About gun stores on every other street corner that any Tom, Dick, or Harry can just walk into and buy an arsenal? About state legislatures who refuse to limit gun purchases to just one-per-month? (At that rate of purchase, at my current age I could now be the proud owner of 648 firearms, but the Pennsylvania state legislature says that such a law would limit my right to keep and bear arms.)

I must admit that the NRA has me pegged: I really don't want to regulate guns; I want to take them away entirely. I see no reason why any private citizen needs to own a gun. Most countries do not allow their citizens to own firearms. Those that do carefully regulate those guns. In this country, it is easier to buy a gun than to get a driver's license or apply for a passport or even adopt a pet from the SPCA.

But how would we ever retrieve all those guns that are already in the hands of Cliven Bundy and Lauren Boebert and Wayne LaPierre and hundreds of thousands of other Americans who think that God gave them their guns?

Back in 2018, I wrote an essay called "A Foolproof Solution to Gun Violence in the US" (*The New Hampshire Gazette*, v.CCLXIII, #24, 8/16/2018) in which I proposed a way to do that. I even took into account, and provided for, those who want to go out and shoot deer and pheasant instead of their neighbors and co-workers.

Many people thought my proposal was more than draconian, but the problem we face is itself draconian (that is, harsh and severe). Until we get guns out of the hands of people who neither need them nor have any legitimate use for them, the slaughter we live with on a yearly, monthly, weekly, and even daily basis will continue unabated.

39

"We Forced Them to Be Brutal to Us"

(*New Hampshire Gazette*, June 4, 2021;
VFP Newsletter, Summer 2021)

Does anyone ever notice those ubiquitous black-and-white POW/MIA flags anymore? You see them everywhere: post offices; federal, state, and municipal buildings; many banks and other privately owned properties; even at all the rest stops on the New Jersey Turnpike.

I'd be willing to bet that almost no one under the age of 40 has any idea what those flags are supposed to represent, or how and why they got where they are. Indeed, even most people over 40 probably don't know or have long since ceased to think about it.

But for over a quarter of a century, the issue of American prisoners of war and missing in action in Vietnam (POW/MIA) was seldom far from the headlines. It became the *raison d'etre* for Richard Nixon's continuation of the war, and the argument for refusing to grant diplomatic recognition to Vietnam for another two decades.

H. Bruce Franklin's *MIA, or Mythmaking in America* convincingly detailed how the myth of the POW/MIA became mythology. And Elliot Gruner's *Prisoners of Culture* explained how the POWs were transformed from survivors into heroes. Both books were published in 1993, and neither was a bestseller, but soon after they were published, the Clinton administration extended diplomatic recognition to Vietnam, and the POW/MIA issue faded into obscurity.

But now comes a new book that illuminates a side of the POW story that has been largely neglected: the story of POWs who willingly and voluntarily opposed and spoke out against the war while they were still in captivity: *Dissenting POWs: From Vietnam's Hoa Lo Prison to America Today* by Tom Wilber and Jerry Lembcke (Monthly Review Press, 2021).

What We Can and Can't Afford

The accepted understanding of those "dissenting POWs" is that they were cowards, traitors, weak, brainwashed, or seeking to curry favor with their captors. The authors argue otherwise.

Tom Wilber is the son of one of these "dissenting POWs," Commander Gene Wilber. Jerry Lembcke is the author of the myth-busting book *The Spitting Image* (1998). They have produced an important book that challenges the argument that dissenting POWs were somehow psychologically damaged, weak, or otherwise compromised, but were instead motivated by conscience, morality, and logic.

Wilber and Lembcke explain how senior ranking officers (SROs), all of them career military men, took control of their subordinates in the camps, and demanded adherence to what these men saw as their "duty" to sacrifice and suffer for the United States of America. As navy commander and future U.S. senator Jeremiah Denton admitted years later, "We forced them to be brutal to us."

In the wake of the apparent weakness of American POWs during the Korean War—largely mythology itself—for senior career military men like Denton, James Stockdale, and Robinson Risner "torture became a way to confirm their worth as American warriors.... When the torture they wanted from the Vietnamese wasn't forthcoming, they provoked it. When that didn't work, they inflicted their own damage." As Stockdale later wrote, he wanted his wife and his sons to be "proud" of him.

When a few SROs opted out of that masochistic approach, these men ostracized them and threatened them with court-martial in post-captivity, a threat that Stockdale and others tried unsuccessfully to carry out. They did, however, win the cultural war to portray the Vietnamese as sadistic, inhuman monsters who routinely and with relish resorted to torture, and few former POWs dared to challenge their version of captivity.

The public perception of that experience was powerfully fostered by the National League of Families of American Prisoners in Southeast Asia, the ubiquitous metal bracelets sold by the Victory in Vietnam Association (later renamed Voices in Vital America), and the Hollywood film industry through dozens of movies starring the likes of Sylvester Stallone, Chuck Norris, and Gene Hackman, not to mention the incredibly successful campaign to create and display the POW/MIA flag.

Like Franklin's and Gruner's books, *Dissenting POWs* is not going to make the *New York Times* Bestseller List, nor will it alter most

39. "We Forced Them to Be Brutal to Us"

people's perceptions of the American POW experience during the Vietnam War. But at least, for the sake of posterity and accurate history, the book exists for those who care to know. It illuminates an entirely neglected aspect of that sorry episode in American history that the Vietnamese call the American War.

40

It's Time to Dump the Filibuster

(*LA Progressive*, June 9, 2021;
New Hampshire Gazette, June 18, 2021)

Let's take a look at the Republican Party this spring of 2021.

We have Senator Josh Hawley of Missouri, who pumps a raised fist on January 6 in support of the MAGA insurrectionists.

We have Representative Andrew Clyde of Georgia, who likens smashing windows and beating police with American flags and hockey sticks to a "normal tourist visit," and insists that the supporters of former President Donald Trump who stormed the Capitol behaved "in an orderly fashion."

We have Representative Paul Gosar of Arizona, who says the Justice Department is "harassing peaceful patriots" who came to DC on January 6 to exercise their 1st Amendment rights.

We have Senator Lindsey Graham of South Carolina, who says of Trump, "Enough's enough," then travels to Mar-a-Lago to kiss Trump's ass.

We have House Minority Leader Kevin McCarthy of California, who says Trump "bears responsibility" for the violent insurrection by a mob of MAGA supporters, then flies to Mar-A-Lago to apologize to Trump.

We have Senator Roy Blunt, also of Missouri, who believes it's "too early" to create a commission, while Senate Minority Whip John Thune of South Dakota is worried about the commission "dragging on indefinitely."

We have Senate Minority Leader Mitch McConnell of Kentucky, who says there is already "no shortage of robust investigations" into January 6.

40. It's Time to Dump the Filibuster

We have Senator Tommy Tuberville of Alabama who is opposed to an investigation into January 6 "until they make it bipartisan," though the panel would consist of an equal number of Democratic and Republican appointees.

And as long as I'm mentioning notable Republicans, I just can't overlook Representative Marjorie Taylor Greene of Georgia, who equates proof of vaccination to gain access to the floor of the House with the Yellow Stars German Jews had to wear in Nazi Germany, and Representative Lauren Boebert of Colorado, who demands the right to carry her Glock automatic pistol onto the floor of the House.

Speaking of Republicans, the Republican-controlled Arizona Senate has hired Cyber Ninjas, a company that has never audited any previous election, and whose founder and CEO, Doug Logan, is a committed supporter of Trump, to audit the 2020 presidential election results in that state.

At the same time, 361 voter suppression bills have been introduced in 47 states, almost exclusively by Republicans. Georgia, Iowa, Utah and Arkansas have already passed such bills with Florida and Texas in hot pursuit. All of this to make our elections "fair and honest" in spite of the fact that voter fraud in U.S. elections at every level is statistically negligible, and every election official across the country insists that this 2020 election was the fairest in U.S. history.

Meanwhile, President Biden's sweeping recovery bills, announced with such fanfare and to overwhelming public support months ago, are still stalled in the Senate. His Infrastructure Jobs Plan, which would rebuild roads and bridges, boost broadband access, and make other improvements; and his Families Plan, which would expand preschool and college opportunities, create a national family and medical leave program, distribute child care subsidies, and make other similar investments, are both awaiting just ten Republican votes in the Senate to get beyond the filibuster threshold of 60 votes, as is the George Floyd Justice in Policing Act.

I fear Uncle Joe and his Democratic colleagues are going to be waiting until Hell freezes over—a terrible cliché, but sadly true—for those needed Republican votes. Already the Republicans have responded with badly watered-down counterproposals to the Jobs and Families Plans. As if they're actually willing to sign off on anything even resembling what's required. As if Moscow Mitch and his cronies have *any* intention of agreeing to bipartisan *anything.*

Meanwhile, support for Biden's proposals will end up dying quietly

What We Can and Can't Afford

of inertia as the Democrats fritter away their election goodwill and once again turn their backs on working Americans while ordinary people return in disgusted resignation to a sorry acceptance of the way things are and have been since at least the early Clinton years.

After the experience of the past 25 years—since at least that vile "Contract with America" Newt Gingrich foisted on the nation—how any Democrat with a functioning memory can imagine bipartisan government is utterly beyond me. (Joe Manchin, are you really this stupid or do you just like to be the center of attention?)

Yes, we run the risk of the Republicans steamrolling their own agenda through the legislature in the future if we get rid of the filibuster, but that's a risk we ought to be willing to take, considering that the Republicans have misused that same filibuster to stymie virtually every aspect of the Democratic agenda since the beginning of the Obama administration.

And if the present Democratic White House and Democratic Congress don't make significant progress in alleviating the distress of ordinary working Americans, visibly and soon, they may *never* get another chance to get *anything* done.

Don't get me wrong. I have no particular fondness for the Democrats, who, at least since the Clinton years, have behaved like Republican Lite, and bear a great deal of responsibility for delivering the country into the hands of #45.

But if I've learned anything since November 2016, I've learned that while the Democratic Party is hardly worthy of champagne and tickertape parades, the Republican Party has simply ceased to bear even a passing resemblance to a collection of sane and decent human beings.

And as long as the filibuster remains, Democratic control of Congress and the White House are largely meaningless, nothing of significance will get accomplished in Washington, and by the next election cycle millions of Americans will once again be willing to listen to rogues, charlatans, fascists, and demagogues.

It's time to put an end to an undemocratic and anachronistic legislative ritual.

41

Afghanistan
The Graveyard of Empires

(*LA Progressive*, July 11, 2021;
New Hampshire Gazette, July 16, 2021)

I've never taken any pride in my service to my country in Vietnam back in the 1960s. When people thank me for my service, I think about what I did in Vietnam and want to tell them to go see a priest.

But I've always taken a perverse delight in having participated in this country's longest and stupidest war. Kind of like being a pre–2004 Boston Red Sox fan or a post–Jim Brown Cleveland Browns fan.

Sadly, even that small pleasure was taken from me when the U.S. war in Afghanistan finally eclipsed the longevity and stupidity of the American War in Vietnam a few years back.

The Vietnamese were tough as nails, and didn't like foreigners, having handed the Chinese and the Mongols their asses on multiple occasions, not to mention the Siamese, the French, and the Americans.

But Afghanistan isn't called "the Graveyard of Empires" for nothing. Ask those pesky Mongols. Or the British. Or the Russians. And now you can ask the Americans, too, because after twenty years we're finally throwing in the towel. Bailing out. Or coming to our senses.

Though of course with the usual diplomatic mumbo-jumbo: we're not quitting, we haven't lost, we'll still support the Afghan government. Reminds me of Otto in *A Fish Called Wanda*: "We did not lose Vietnam! It was a tie!"

So, what have we accomplished after two decades? According to the Associated Press and the Watson Institute for International & Public Affairs at Brown University, as of April 30, we've caused between 66,000 and 69,000 civilian deaths in Afghanistan along with 47,245

What We Can and Can't Afford

dead Afghani military personnel. American casualties have been 2,442 killed in action with 20,666 wounded in action.

Over 3,800 American "private security contractors" have also been killed, but quite frankly, I don't feel too badly about that lot, who are actually mercenaries trained with our tax dollars in the Green Berets, Navy SEALS, Delta Forces, and other elite branches before jumping ship for higher pay and fewer restrictions on the exercise of violence.

Meanwhile, the cost so far to us docile U.S. taxpayers totals $2,260,000,000,000.* This includes $815,700,000,000 for actual warfighting costs: bombs, bullets, MREs, and all that good stuff.

Another $88,000,000,000 to train the Afghan army and police (who are, even as I type this, throwing down their weapons and turning tail in the face of a Taliban offensive).

Another $36,000,000,000 for reconstruction, infrastructure, and education (though roads, bridges, dams, and canals remain in notorious disrepair while new hospitals and schools stand empty).

And another $9,000,000,000 for reduction of heroin production (though opium exports are at an all-time high while 47 percent of Afghanis live in poverty).

Meanwhile, we taxpayers have shelled out $530,000,000,000 in interest payments to service our war debt, while ongoing costs of caring for our war veterans has claimed another $296,000,000,000, and both of these costs won't be going away any time soon; they'll just keep growing.

All those zeroes could be replaced with the word "billion" (except for the first figure, which would be "2.26 trillion"), but I use the zeroes because it's worth seeing them. That's a lot of zeroes. Through two Republican administrations and now into the second Democratic administration (though in all fairness, Uncle Joe seems finally to realize what's been obvious almost from the start: Ain't nobody gonna whup Afghanistan into shape).

Afghanistan isn't even a country except in some cartographer's imagination. Just a collection of tribes and chieftains and warlords. On a good day, the president of Afghanistan has about as much power as the mayor of Kabul. I'll bet you can't even name the president of Afghanistan.

Doesn't matter anyway because he and all his pals are syphoning

---

* This in a country where Kevin McCarthy and Mitch McConnell say we can't afford to provide free childcare or college education or rural and inner-city internet.

41. Afghanistan: The Graveyard of Empires

off all that U.S. aid money and stuffing it into Swiss bank accounts, and there's nothing you or I can do about it. (How do you think Nguyen Van Thieu managed to buy a palatial estate in England after he beat it out of Saigon back in 1975 and lived out the rest of his life in elegant seclusion?)

I do feel sorry for all those Afghan women and girls who are going to go back to what one counterterrorism expert calls "the Middle Ages," but I wonder why he and all those other folks who are wringing their hands over the fate of Afghan women and girls have no problem with Saudi Arabia, which has never left the Middle Ages.

But I also feel sorry for all those American women and girls who are living in poverty in our own country; all those American women and girls who are once again, slowly but surely, losing the right to control their own bodies; all those American women and men who are steadily being stripped of their right to vote; all those American women and girls and men and boys who are being murdered day after day after day in a country that has more guns and gun violence I would wager to bet than even Afghanistan.

I'm glad the U.S. is finally withdrawing from the Graveyard of Empires, but I can't shake off the conviction that I myself am living in an Empire's Graveyard.

42

Afghanistan
Vietnam Redux

(*Vox Populi,* August 20, 2021; *LA Progressive,*
August 21, 2021; *Bucks County Courier Times* and *The Intelligencer,*
August 22, 2021; *New Hampshire Gazette,* August 27, 2021)

Way back in March and April of 1975, I watched with profound sadness but absolutely no surprise as the South Vietnamese army (ARVN)—with only a brief exception at a place called Xuan Loc—turned tail and retreated without a fight in the face of a North Vietnamese offensive, and the government the U.S. had installed, paid for, and supported for two decades collapsed like a house of cards.

Eight years earlier, I had gone to Vietnam as an 18-year-old Marine believing that I would be defending the freedom-loving people of South Vietnam from the communist aggressors invading their country. I encountered, over and over again, ARVN forces that would not fight, though they had been trained and equipped and supported by the U.S., and Viet Cong guerrillas who were untrained, unpaid, and ill-equipped, but would not stop fighting.

I didn't then know anything about the history of the country or the war I found myself in. But I could readily see that one side believed in what it was fighting for and the other side did not. And it was painfully easy to see which side was which. So that final rapid collapse years later came as no surprise at all, though it did come with the unavoidable truth that what I and my comrades had endured had all been for nothing.

But at least, I had thought, perhaps somebody down there in Washington, D.C., had learned something. Perhaps policymakers would avoid such folly, such willful blindness to reality, such hubris, such wishful thinking in the future.

42. Afghanistan: Vietnam Redux

Fat chance, as it turns out.

Only a few days ago, as the Taliban were storming into Kabul, the *Washington Post* had written: "It seems certain that in coming years the use of military force will be informed by this searing experience. US foreign policy will be guided by more modest ambitions, especially when weighing the use of military power."

Seriously? Did the journalist who wrote this manage to do it with a straight face? I suspect that the person who wrote it is too young to know anything about the American War in Vietnam. I hope so because I shudder to imagine a mind that could remember the collapse of South Vietnam and still think U.S. policymakers will actually learn something *this time*.

So, yet another house of cards collapses after two decades of U.S. blood and treasure poured into a government that had no more legitimacy in the eyes and hearts of most people in Afghanistan than the Saigon regime had among the people of Vietnam. At least Vietnam was and is a country. Afghanistan, a collection of tribal societies and ethnic warlords, exists only in a cartographer's fantasy.

I feel badly for those Afghans who risked their lives to help the U.S. as interpreters and in other capacities, and are now in danger of who knows what. And I do honestly feel sorry for the women and girls of Afghanistan who had escaped the clutches of the Taliban at least temporarily. But if they are in such jeopardy, I wonder why their fathers and husbands and brothers will not fight to defend them.

Think about that: why should Americans fight and die to defend the women and girls of Afghanistan when their own fathers and husbands and brothers will not? We American taxpayers have spent $88,000,000,000—that's 88 billion dollars—training the Afghan army and police, and it's painfully clear that we might as well have tossed that money into the ocean or burned it in my oven. (Or maybe spent it on health care, education, infrastructure, and other useful projects in our own country? Now there's an idea. But I digress.)

Indeed, it turns out that the Taliban are in possession of thousands of Humvees and MRAP vehicles, tens of thousands of M4 and M16 rifles, M2 .50 caliber machineguns, grenades, communications equipment, night vision goggles, even airplanes and drones, all abandoned by fleeing Afghan National Army soldiers or simply handed over outright. Your tax dollars at work.

What has befallen the people of Afghanistan may or may not be a tragedy—apparently some significant segment of Afghan society wants

What We Can and Can't Afford

the Taliban to succeed—but the chaotic images of terrified human beings cramming into the bellies of huge U.S. transport planes at Kabul airport are as heartrending as heartrending gets.

Still, the real tragedy in all this is that the United States of America invaded yet another foreign country, imagining that we could bend it to our will and create a "Mini-Me" version of ourselves, and then spent twenty years, trillions of dollars, and thousands of lives ignoring what was obvious from the very outset.

43

Afghanistan
Who's Responsible?

(*LA Progressive*, September 6, 2021; *New Hampshire Gazette*, September 11, 2021; subsequently picked up by and included in various newspapers owned by the Gannett Co., Inc., including *Chambersburg Public Opinion*, *Erie Times-News*, *Pocono Record*, *Somerset Daily American*, and *York Daily Record*)

Surprise, surprise! Fox News and the Republican Party are blaming President Joe Biden for the chaotic U.S. withdrawal from Afghanistan and the horrific scenes of terror and confusion at Kabul Airport in the final days. House Minority Leader Kevin McCarthy—born in 1965—calls the evacuation "the biggest US failure in my lifetime" (Saigon fell in 1975. Well, I'm just sayin'). Senators Josh Hawley and Marsha Blackburn are demanding that Uncle Joe resign. Endlessly mindlessly Talking Head Tucker Carlson called Biden "the supposed president of the United States."

Never mind that Donald Trump brokered a treaty with the Taliban promising the withdrawal of U.S. troops by last May. (Check out the great photo of Secretary of State Mike Pompeo meeting with Mullah Abdul Ghani Baradar, the Taliban's de facto political leader, in Doha, Qatar, in September 2020.)

Never mind that George W. Bush invaded Afghanistan in October 2001 to destroy al Qaeda, but decided to take out the Taliban government while he was at it and create a U.S.-inspired democracy. (I think that's called Mission Creep. Or perhaps Creepy Mission?)

Never mind that 18 months later, "W" and his pals Dick "Dick" Cheney and Donald Rumsfeld decided to invade Iraq, which had nothing whatever to do with the attacks on 9/11 (the attackers were 15 Saudis, an Egyptian, a Lebanese, and two men from the United Arab

What We Can and Can't Afford

Emirates), thus turning Afghanistan into a neglected sideshow. (But of course, Iraqis would benefit by ending up living in another U.S.-inspired democracy.)

Never mind that beginning way back in 1979, a succession of U.S. administrations, Democratic and Republican, actively supported, funded, and supplied fundamentalist Muslims—including Osama bin Laden, and many of those who became the Taliban—in their successful effort to overthrow a secular modernist Afghan government in a country where, by the late 1980s, 50 percent of university students, 40 percent of doctors, 70 percent of teachers, and 30 percent of civil servants were women. Read that again. *Women! In Afghanistan.* And the U.S. helped to overthrow that government.

Then consider that, according to former *Baltimore Sun* reporter Arnold Isaacs's calculations, U.S. direct aid to the Kabul government's security forces over the last 20 years comes to $270,000 for each and every one of the 307,000 Afghan defense and security personnel supposedly on duty as of January 2021 to defend the country against the Taliban in the wake of a U.S. withdrawal. That's over a quarter of a million bucks for every single soldier and policeman in Afghanistan. (We American taxpayers don't seem to have gotten much back on that investment.)

Isaacs further points out, based on figures provided by the Special Inspector General for Afghanistan Reconstruction, that the U.S.—and that means you and me as taxpayers (at least those of us who actually do pay taxes, no need to name names here)—has spent $20,925 on each and every man, woman, and child alive in Afghanistan today.

As Isaacs points out, "That's way more than the entire income of the vast majority of Afghans during that period, especially if you leave out those who got rich from corruptly siphoning a lot of that money into their own pockets. Hard not to think we could have achieved a better result by just folding up some of those dollars in envelopes and handing them out to the population, including those subject to recruitment by the Taliban, to bribe them onto our side. That strategy apparently worked quite well for the Taliban this year."

I'm not surprised that the shameless Republicans who twice refused to convict a lawless grifter of impeachable offenses, who have described the January 6 insurrectionists as "peaceful protesters," "normal tourists," and "true patriots," who have obstructed and stymied every attempt to investigate the instigator of that attack or the administration he headed, who have engineered the most right-wing Supreme

43. Afghanistan: Who's Responsible?

Court since Roger Taney ruled on *Dred Scott v. Sandford* in 1857, would blame President Biden for what has unfolded in Afghanistan in the past month.

But what about the responsibility of those who engineered the overthrow of Afghanistan's moderate secular government? What about the responsibility of those who armed and trained the fighters who would one day become al Qaeda and the Taliban? What about the responsibility of those who threw unimaginable amounts of money into a government they knew to be corrupt and ineffective? What about the responsibility of those who told the American people year after year that our efforts were making progress and bearing fruit?

I hate to get personal here, but does anybody with a functioning brain in his or her head really think this is all Uncle Joe's fault? I feel pretty confident in arguing that Biden's decision to withdraw from Afghanistan is the first smart decision this country has made about Afghanistan in the past forty-two years.

44

Sanitizing American History

(*New Hampshire Gazette*, September 24, 2021)

In September 1814, as Francis Scott Key stood on the deck of a British warship watching the bombardment of Fort McHenry, he was inspired to write a poem that eventually became the "Star-Spangled Banner." We hear that song a lot these days: at every football game from middle school to the NFL; at NASCAR races and hockey games and commencement ceremonies, and, well, at just about any public event that attracts more than three Americans.

I wonder how many of my fellow citizens know that Key's original poem contains not just the stanza we sing, but three additional stanzas, one of which goes like this:

> And where is that band who so vauntingly swore,
> That the havoc of war and the battle's confusion
> A home and a Country should leave us no more?
> Their blood has wash'd out their foul footstep's pollution.
> No refuge could save the hireling and slave
> From the terror of flight or the gloom of the grave,
> And the star-spangled banner in triumph doth wave
> O'er the land of the free and the home of the brave.

In case you're not quite up on U.S. history, that bit in there about nothing saving "the hireling and the slave" from "flight" and "the grave" is Key's way of rebuking the British for granting freedom to any enslaved African American who escaped to the British side. Like so many Americans before and since, Key was certain that "the land of the free" was and is only for white people.

Then there's our Statue of Liberty, that beacon of hope, that icon of freedom. What schoolchild doesn't learn Emma Lazarus's famous words:

> Give me your tired, your poor,
> Your huddled masses yearning to breathe free,

44. Sanitizing American History

> The wretched refuse of your teeming shore.
> Send these, the homeless, tempest-tossed to me[.]

It is the essence of who we are, the best of what we are.

But a contemporary of Lazarus, Thomas Bailey Aldrich, penned a poem called "Unguarded Gates" in which he described "Liberty" as a "white Goddess," and warned that the nation was being overrun by "a wild motley throng" bringing "unknown gods and rites," "strange tongues," "accents of menace," "come to waste the gift of freedom." The poem ran in an 1892 issue of *The Atlantic Monthly*, then one of the most popular and influential journals in the country.

Another one of my favorite examples of American Exceptional Myopia is Woody Guthrie's "This Land Is Your Land." We don't hear this one nearly as often as the "Star-Spangled Banner," but we always hear it at events that want to celebrate how wonderful all we Americans are and what a wonderful country we live in.

Except that when we sing that song, written in the midst of the Great Depression, there's always a few stanzas we never sing. Indeed, if you even want to find them, you have to Google "original lyrics"; otherwise you get the sanitized version that doesn't include these stanzas:

> As I went walking I saw a sign there,
> And on the sign it said "No Trespassing."
> But on the other side it didn't say nothing.
> That side was made for you and me.
>
> In the shadow of the steeple I saw my people,
> By the relief office I seen my people;
> As they stood there hungry, I stood there asking
> Is this land made for you and me?

Then there's the memorial we erected to honor Martin Luther King, Jr. It contains fourteen different inspirational quotes from his various speeches. It's even got one from February 1967 that says: "I oppose the war in Vietnam because I love America." But the designers didn't include this one from just a few months later: "[T]he greatest purveyor of violence in the world today: my own government."

Too little time has passed since 9/11 to see how more recent events are going to be sanitized for public consumption, though the continued almost uniformly accepted fiction that Americans died in Iraq and Afghanistan defending this nation and our freedoms does not bode well, nor does the number of so-called responsible voices in government

What We Can and Can't Afford

and media who describe the January 6 insurrectionists as "normal tourists," "peaceful protesters," and "true patriots."

Meanwhile, I'll leave you to ponder a few of our misquoted heroes like Patrick Henry, who famously said, "Give me liberty or give me death." Okay, it's not really a misquote, but no one ever seems to mention that when he said, "Give me liberty," he really meant: *me; Patrick Henry. Never mind my 67 slaves. No liberty for them. It's all about me.* (There's even a widely used high school U.S. history textbook titled *Give Me Liberty*.)

Here's a good one: Ken Burns and Lynn Novick begin their 18-hour documentary *The Vietnam War* by asserting that the war was "begun in good faith by decent people." Well, okay, Burns and Novick aren't really what most of us would call American heroes—yet—but "good faith" and "decent people" don't really apply to men who actively courted and supported Ho Chi Minh during World War II only to turn their backs on him when the war was over; men who refused to allow elections in 1956 because they knew Ho would win any free and fair election by a landslide; men who said Asian boys should fight Asian wars, and then sent 3,000,000 American boys to fight in Vietnam (58,000 of whom came home dead).

Then there's the frequently misquoted Union General and later U.S. Senator Carl Schurz—this is one of my favorites—who did not say, "My country, right or wrong." What he said was, *"My country, right or wrong; if right, to be kept right; and if wrong, to be set right."*

45

Re-thinking American History

(*New Hampshire Gazette*, October 8, 2021)

I have spent my entire life reading. As Emily Dickinson wrote, "There is no Frigate like a Book / To take us Lands away." Even in Vietnam, as an 18-year-old, I read whatever I could get my hands on from John Updike's *Rabbit, Run* to Voltaire's *Candide* to John Cleland's *Fanny Hill: Memoirs of a Woman of Pleasure*.

I don't read many books more than once because there are so many good books to read, but I've read multiple times David Howarth's *1066: The Year of the Conquest*, and Cecil Woodham-Smith's *The Reason Why: The Story of the Fatal Charge of the Light Brigade*. I re-read Herman Melville's *Moby-Dick* every five years or so because it is the greatest epic poem in the English language.

A few books have caused me or forced me to alter my thinking immediately and significantly, mostly notably Paul Fussell's *Wartime: Understanding and Behavior in the Second World War*, and Paul Lyons's *Class of '66: Living in Suburban Middle America*, which changed my perceptions of the World War II and Vietnam generations respectively.

But never has a book offered such startling new information that it has required me to revise and re-think my entire understanding of the whole of American history. Until now, that is. Having recently finished Andrew Levy's *The First Emancipator: Slavery, Religion, and the Quiet Revolution of Robert Carter*, that is exactly what I have had to do.

Who even ever heard of Robert Carter III? Not me, and I'm a pretty solid student of history, especially American history. Yet he was one of the very wealthiest planters in 18th century Virginia, a contemporary and friend of Thomas Jefferson, George Washington, and Patrick Henry, a supporter of the American Revolution.

What We Can and Can't Afford

But what should have made him unavoidably famous was that in 1791, he filed a Deed of Gift with Virginia's Westmoreland District Court providing for the emancipation of his nearly 500 slaves. Go back and read that sentence again. Yet I've never heard of him until a few weeks ago, nor have most of you who are reading this.

Moreover, this was not a precipitous and immediate emancipation, but rather a carefully thought-out and gradual freeing of his slaves over time with adequate provision for elderly and infirm slaves as well as for children.

Thus, while our larger-than-life heroic Founding Fathers were writing eloquently of liberty, freedom, and equality, privately and sometimes publicly deploring slavery, they nevertheless insisted that it was economically impossible to escape the tangled web of slavery, and culturally infeasible to free the slaves without also removing them from white society by sending them all west of the Mississippi or back to Africa.

No wonder no one has ever heard of Carter. His story was buried almost before he died in 1804 because he laid bare the hypocrisy of those great Virginians who have become—and were becoming even then—the heroes of our American mythological story. The knights in shining armor. Men who struggled with their consciences and agonized over their unsolvable dilemma. Men who did the best they could with the contradictory circumstances in which they found themselves.

Carter demonstrated that emancipation was possible, and economically feasible, even providing through his Deed of Gift a detailed blueprint for how it could be done gradually, without removal of Blacks from the southern states, and with minimal economic disruption. Moreover, had more large planters followed his lead, it might well have been possible to build an integrated society that did not give rise to Black Codes, the Ku Klux Klan, and Jim Crow.

We'll never know, of course, because not one other large Virginia planter had the courage to follow Carter's lead. Not only that, but most of his peers—and even some of his heirs—made it clear that they thoroughly disapproved of his decision, and turned him into a social outcast instead of a person to be admired and emulated.

And because Carter was neither a writer nor a politician nor a man who sought attention and acclaim, he left no stirring explanations of what he had done or why he had done it. There was not then and is not now anything so inspiring as Patrick Henry's "Give me liberty" or Thomas Jefferson's "All men are created equal" or James Madison's "We the People."

45. Re-thinking American History

We have only Carter's no-frills, functional, nuts-and-bolts Deed of Gift, which begins, "I have for some time past been convinced that to retain [these human beings] in Slavery is contrary to the true Principles of Religion and Justice, and that therefor [sic] it was my duty to manumit them."

So much for Jefferson's "wolf by the ears" analogy. Or even Washington's freeing of his 125 slaves in his own will—but not until after Martha had gotten her lifetime's use of their slave labor; they would be freed only upon her death. (She ended up freeing them before she died for fear that they might kill her in order to gain their freedom, but she did not free the scores of slaves she owned in her own right.)

We know very little about what became of the 452 men, women and children who were once Carter's property. Scattered widely over multiple properties owned and leased out by Carter, some of them were never told they'd been freed. Others were re-enslaved by hook and by crook. But many remained free, as did their children and children's children down to the present day.

Only in recent decades have descendants of both Carter and the slaves he freed organized the Carter Society, about which you can learn more at the Nomini Hall Slave Legacy Project (*http://nominihallslavelegacy.com/*).

Meanwhile, especially in these times of Black Lives Matter, George Floyd, and "dog whistle politics," remember that those Founding Fathers we revere, who enshrined slavery in the Constitution of the United States without ever using the word, could have chosen a different path. Instead, they chose to all-but-obliterate from history the man who took that path.

46

More Fun Facts About American History

(*New Hampshire Gazette*, November 5, 2021)

Lately I've been ruminating on American history, in particular on how little most of my fellow citizens know about it. I recently wrote an essay in the *Gazette* (September 24, 2021) that took note of the missing stanza of our national anthem that condemns the British for offering freedom to American slaves, the missing stanzas of Woody Guthrie's "This Land Is Your Land" that criticize capitalism and the owner class, the overt anti-immigrant racism imbedded in American society, and a number of other fun facts most Americans are oblivious to.

I wrote a whole essay (*Gazette*, October 8, 2021) about a Virginia planter named Robert Carter III, who freed all 452 of his slaves in 1791, and whom few people have ever heard of—including, I admit, even me.

But I keep getting reminded of how little we know about ourselves and our country, so once again I find myself returning to the subject, especially in the midst of a societal breakdown that is based on national mythology, the legitimization of bigotry and intolerance, and staggering ignorance.

Only a few weeks ago, I had lunch with a Wellesley graduate in her 80s and a Princeton graduate in his 50s. These are educated, well-read, and thoughtful people. But they have no grasp of how African Americans consistently end up at the bottom of society. The Princeton grad pointed out that Black Democrats have controlled Philadelphia politics for decades, but crime and poverty have only gotten worse, stating his belief that Black politicians have failed to lead properly, and instead have turned their backs on "their own people."

Neither of these well-meaning and humane people knew that African Americans were denied most of the benefits of Franklin Roosevelt's

46. More Fun Facts About American History

New Deal programs because had they been included, southern Democrats would never have approved these programs. Neither of them knew that the post–World War II GI Bill also excluded most Blacks from its benefits, and for the same reason.

Never mind the illegal discrimination against African Americans—the false arrests (read *Slavery by Another Name* by Douglas A. Blackmon), literacy tests, poll taxes, intimidation, lynching. The "legal" discrimination alone was enough to keep an entire class of Americans at the bottom of the ladder for a century and more after the end of slavery.

And it wasn't just Blacks, though the former slaves had a burden no other class of Americans was forced to carry. How many of you have ever heard of the Chinese Exclusion Act? Or the Supreme Court case *Ozawa v. United States*? Or *Hernandez v. Texas*? Do you realize that Native Americans weren't even considered Americans until 1924?

Here are a few other fun facts about U.S. history:

Did you know that Benjamin Franklin was a loyal British subject who wanted nothing more than to preserve the empire and eventually retire to England right up until the spring of 1774 when Alexander Wedderburn, the Solicitor General of the King's Privy Council, publicly humiliated Franklin before Parliament, in the space of one hour turning Franklin into a flaming revolutionary who subsequently returned to Philadelphia and told all those young men of the Continental Congress, "Screw the Brits, boys, they can't treat Ben Franklin like that!"

Did you know that at the end of the French and Indian War, Virginia Colonial Militia Colonel George Washington applied for a regular commission in the British Army only to be told, "Hey, that militia bit was all well and good, but don't think you have the stuff to be a regular British officer." Why do you think George accepted command of the Continental Army in 1775? "Think I haven't got the right stuff? I'll show you!"

Ever heard of Lydia Maria Child? You might know her as the author of the happy little children's poem that eventually became the song "Over the River and Through the Wood." But I'll bet you didn't know she's also the author of *Hobomok: A Tale of Early Times*, an 1824 novel about a white Puritan woman who marries and has a child with a Native American. It didn't make the bestseller list.

And you just might recognize Julia Ward Howe is the author of the poem that became "The Battle Hymn of the Republic," which calls upon young northern men to enlist in the Union army and thrust the "burnished steel" of their bayonets into the guts of young men from the

What We Can and Can't Afford

south. But you may not know that eight years later, she wrote the first Mother's Day Proclamation, which mentioned neither Hallmark greeting cards nor taking Mom out to dinner, but rather calls for the women of the world to come together to organize and put an end to war.

Not long ago, I spent a morning with 8th graders at a local middle school. At the beginning of the school day, the entire school—via a PA system—recited the Pledge of Allegiance to a piece of colored cloth, and to the republic for which it stands, though I rather doubt that a single one of them could explain what a republic even is. And I'll bet they don't know that very few other countries in the world even have a pledge of allegiance. One that does is the Democratic People's Republic of Korea, more commonly known as North Korea.

I wonder what those kids will ever learn about the republic for which their flag stands, what their teachers know and don't know, and how much their teachers are allowed to teach their students without getting fired. I doubt that any public school in the United States would allow a teacher to draw upon Howard Zinn's *A People's History of the United States* or James Loewen's *Lies My Teacher Told Me*, nor would most private schools (though I was lucky enough to get away with it for 18 years). If you want to learn more fun facts about American history, one of these books would be a great place to start.

47

It's a Big Universe Out There

(*LA Progressive*, November 8, 2021;
New Hampshire Gazette, November 19, 2021)

In December 1985, I made my first postwar trip back to Vietnam. I had gone there in 1967 as an 18-year-old Marine, which had turned out to be a very bad idea and a life-changing experience. Eighteen years later, I wanted to see and experience the country of Vietnam, not the Vietnam War. It turned out to be both a humbling and a healing trip.

Very early on, my interpreter, a young man old enough to remember the war but not old enough to have fought in it, asked me if I had been wounded. When I said I had, and then explained that I'd received a few small shrapnel wounds and a hearing loss, he shrugged and quietly said, "Oh." Clearly, to him, my "wounds" were of no significance, Purple Heart Medal or not.

Later we visited the War Crimes Museum in Ho Chi Minh City. It contains several rooms dealing with the American War, but many more rooms dealing with Pol Pot, the old regime in Saigon, Thailand, the French colonial era, and the millennia-long struggle with China. (An even more elaborate museum in Hanoi also details that long history of resistance to Chinese domination. The American War doesn't even rate a mention in that museum.)

For eighteen years, I had been imagining that the Vietnam War was something that had happened to me. I was the star of the show. But on that trip I came to realize that I was an infinitesimally insignificant part of something much, much larger. Of course, the war was not about me. In fact, the American War itself was hardly a pimple-on-a-pumpkin in the long history of Vietnam. The experience forced me to re-think my entire relationship to Vietnam and to that war.

What We Can and Can't Afford

Fast forward thirty-six years. It's 2021. Donald Trump has been kicked out of the White House, but refuses to concede defeat. Dozens of allegedly responsible politicians at the federal, state, and local level—as well as television and radio talking heads—continue to parrot his claim that the election was stolen by devious and conniving Democrats. Millions of American citizens believe this to be true.

Meanwhile, Senator Joe Munchkin (who lines his pockets and the pockets of his family with fossil fuel money) and Senator Kyrsten Cinemax (God only knows what's going on in her head) are the best allies Moscow Mitch McConnell and his Retrumplican cronies could ever wish for, making their task of obstructing any forward progress the Biden Administration might have made in repairing this grotesquely damaged nation ridiculously easy.

And thus it seems all-but-inevitable that the narrow Democratic majority in the House of Representatives and the even party split in the Senate will both shift in favor of the Republicans in 2022. And that, combined with the number of Republican state legislatures that are passing restrictive voting laws guaranteed to disenfranchise large numbers of poor people and people of color, means that Donald Trump himself—or someone dangerously smarter than him—will be back in the White House in 2024.

Add to that our already radically right-wing Supreme Court, the militarization of our domestic police forces, the lunatic gun laws in this country, a few other odds and ends, and, well, to put it bluntly, we're screwed.

Recently, a friend said to me that things are going to get worse before they get better. But even a cursory study of history makes it clear that things don't always get better. Ask the Egyptians. Or the Romans. And the sun never used to set on the British Empire.

Back in 1776, Edward Gibbon published *The Decline and Fall of the Roman Empire*. Will someone someday write *The Decline and Fall of the American Empire*? Then again, with global warming on the way, we may not last long enough for anyone to write that book.

Indeed, all this angst about the United States of America could be wasted energy in light of the approaching global disaster that seems even less avoidable than a Republican Congress in 2022. What are the odds that the entire human race will manage to change how we live significantly enough to stave off the terminal future that awaits this planet and everything on it? Talk about being screwed.

Ah, but there is a different way of looking at all this, and it harkens

47. It's a Big Universe Out There

back to what I learned in Vietnam in 1985: humility. Putting things in proper perspective.

Not long ago, I watched a program on PBS's *Nova* about the Milky Way. Our galaxy contains 100 thousand million stars. Ours is one star—one teeny, tiny star—in the midst of all that.

And the universe itself, NASA estimates, contains at least 200 billion galaxies. Not stars. Galaxies. That translates into a number of stars, more or less like the one we see in our sky every day, that is the equivalent of something like the number of grains of sand on every beach on Earth. Try wrapping your mind around that number.

New stars are born every minute, and old stars die every minute. This has been going on for something on the order of thirteen and a half billion years. That's 13,500,000,000 years. It will continue to go on for, well, God only knows how much longer, but I'm pretty certain it will be a very long time.

Much longer than Donald Trump or Joe Biden will be here. Much longer than the United States of America will be here. Much longer than Planet Earth will be here. Or even good old Sol, our dearly beloved Sun. We think it's all about us, but it's not. It never was. It never will be. The universe doesn't really care about us. It's doing its own thing.

I find that both humbling and comforting.

48

Do You Believe in Unicorns?

(*LA Progressive*, November 24, 2021;
New Hampshire Gazette, December 3, 2021)

Steve Bannon, the Trump-pardoned *Breitbart* founder, former Trump strategist, and current Trump ally, said in a podcast on January 5, 2021, "Strap on. All hell's going to break loose," and just last week declared, "We are taking over school boards, we're taking over the Republican Party with the precinct committee strategy. Suck on this!"

Number 45 himself defended supporters who chanted "Hang Mike Pence" during the insurrection, saying it was just "common sense" given Pence's refusal to deny certification of the 2020 election.

A teenaged white kid carrying an illegally obtained high-powered assault rifle across state lines to defend the property of people he didn't know and never met was acquitted by a nearly all-white jury of all charges related to his shooting of three men, killing two of them.

Meanwhile, the Wyoming Republican Party voted to no longer recognize Representative Liz Cheney as a member of their party. Elsewhere in the House, the GOP stripped all thirteen Republicans who voted for President Joe Biden's infrastructure bill of their committee assignments, those same thirteen receiving multiple death threats and accusations of treason.

Speaking of the House, Representative Paul Gosar posted an anime video of him killing Alexandria Ocasio-Cortez and attacking President Biden, in response to which the House GOP leadership said nothing.

On the other side of the Capitol, Senator Josh Hawley said that because liberals won't let young men be men, they are retreating into

48. Do You Believe in Unicorns?

idleness and porn and video games, he himself apparently believing boys should be taught that women are objects, homosexuality is a sin, and violence is a solution to everything.

Speaking of violence, a public library in Texas has cancelled "Rainbow Story Time" for children, where books chosen to be read advocate tolerance and acceptance of difference without mentioning gender or sexuality, after receiving a deluge of complaints and threats. Across the nation, hundreds of school board members, public health, and election officials have quit in the face of death threats to them and their families.

Turning to practical matters, who's going to pay for the recently—finally—passed infrastructure bill? Well, it won't be Jeff Bezos, who paid less than one percent (1%) tax on $4,200,000,000 of income. In recent years, the richest 400 American families paid an average tax rate of 8.2 percent. (What was your tax rate last year?) The badly underfunded IRS audits those with incomes of about $20,000 at the same rate as those with incomes of $500,000 to $1,000,000.

Meanwhile, when Uncle Joe signed that infrastructure bill, he proudly announced "that despite the cynics, Democrats and Republicans can come together" in bipartisanship.

The cynics?! Is Biden kidding? Is he stupid? Is he blind? Everything you've just read up to this point took place in one single week. *One week.* This is just one week's worth of news. And it's been going on in one form or another since Barack Obama became president, and with ever increasing fury and vengeance and violence and madness since 2016. Bipartisanship is broken. It is no more. It is beyond repair, certainly in my lifetime and perhaps forever.

The radical right has no interest in bipartisanship. The men and women who stormed the Capitol last January, and the men and women who encouraged them and egged them on, are bound and determined to restore white male supremacy, return women barefoot to the kitchen, put people of color back in their place, make homosexuality a crime again, sanction vigilante violence, and restore unlimited and unquestioned power to police.

Through it all, the Democratic Party—with a few exceptions like AOC and the redoubtable Bernie Sanders—continues to act as if this undemocratic, uncompromising, vicious, hateful, violent radical right is still playing by the rules of civil society and two-party political tradition.

It is time, and long past time, for Democrats to get their heads out of their asses and recognize that American democracy is on its last legs,

What We Can and Can't Afford

that unless Democrats at all levels from the national down to the most local of the local, those of us who are appalled by what's been going on before our very eyes can kiss the future good-bye.

And as for moderate Republicans and so-called Independents, if you think Steve Bannon and Donald Trump have any use for you, you might as well believe in unicorns.

49

You Want to Serve Your Country?

(*LA Progressive*, December 4, 2021;
New Hampshire Gazette, December 17, 2021)

I recently received the following e-mail: "First off, Mr. Ehrhart, thank you for your service. My main question is this: what wisdom do you think you have gained from experiencing the Vietnam War? Do you think that younger generations could learn something from you and your experience?"

I replied,

> Thank you for taking the time to write. What wisdom have I gained from experiencing the Vietnam War? What could younger generations learn from me? I hope I don't sound too cynical, but what I learned was to question *everything* I'm told by those in authority. Donald Trump lied to the American people multiple times a day for four years, and is still doing it with his "stolen election" bullcrap, but he didn't invent lying.
>
> The Vietnam War was created out of lies. The Vietnamese were supposed to hold unification elections in 1956, but the Eisenhower Administration went along with Ngo Dinh Diem in refusing to hold those elections; the excuse was that you couldn't have democratic elections with a communist—Ho Chi Minh—in control of half the country, but the real reason was that Ho Chi Minh would have won a free and fair election easily.
>
> Lyndon Johnson jammed the Gulf of Tonkin Resolution through Congress in the summer of 1964—the legal authorization for everything that happened afterwards—with only two dissenting votes by claiming that North Vietnamese torpedo boats had attacked two US destroyers in international waters without provocation. Johnson knew at the time that the US ships were in North Vietnamese territorial waters operating in support of South Vietnamese commando raids on North Vietnamese facilities, and that the second attack never even happened, but the Johnson Administration lied to the American people and even to Congress.

What We Can and Can't Afford

Consider this: after 9/11, the US first invaded Afghanistan, and then Iraq. But the men who attacked the US on 9/11 were 15 Saudi Arabians, 1 Egyptian, 1 Lebanese, and 2 men from the UAE. Neither Afghanistan nor Iraq had anything to do with 9/11. So why did we invade those two countries?

I could go on at great length. But suffice it to say that our government leaders still continue to lie to us. For 20 years, we were told that the US was making progress in Afghanistan when government documents unearthed by the *Washington Post* make it clear that US officials knew from the very start that we had no chance of ever "winning" in Afghanistan, yet year after year they continued what they knew was a losing effort through the Bush, Obama, and Trump Administrations. Biden's decision to withdraw is the first good decision this country has made about Afghanistan since 1978.

I would say to young people: do not be fooled by the patriotic displays at the beginning of NFL football games and NASCAR races, by the Military Appreciation Nights at NHL hockey games, the apparent reverence for all things and all members of the military. I call it "Crocodile Patriotism." Your government does not care about the military men and women who die doing the government's bidding. Lyndon Johnson knew—and said in a recorded conversation in 1964—that we could not win the Vietnam War ... and then he proceeded to send millions of young Americans to Vietnam, thousands of them coming home dead. Fewer Americans have died in Afghanistan, but every one of them died while their government knew we would never win there.

You need to understand that those a nation sends into war are those the government *and* their fellow citizens have deemed expendable. 'We can get along without you. If you die, we'll be fine. We don't need you.' And all the flag-waving hot-air patriotic blather is simply to disguise this truth. The war in Afghanistan cost the American people $3 trillion dollars. But that money didn't just disappear. It ended up in the pockets of corrupt Afghan politicians and warlords, and it ended up in the bank accounts of American arms manufacturers. It was and is a transfer of wealth from ordinary Americans to the Merchants of Death and their accomplices, to those who already have more wealth than they know what to do with.

You thanked me for my service. Why? Who did I serve? I went halfway around the world to kill, maim, and make miserable people who had never done me or my country any harm, nor ever would or could. Do you really want to thank me for that? What was I fighting for? American freedoms and our way of life? But we lost the Vietnam War, and yet you can still worship at the church of your choice, marry whoever you want, and speak your mind. So what were we really fighting for in Vietnam?

Here is what I would say to young people: you want to serve your country? You won't do it by joining the US military. You want to serve your country? Learn to be critical of what you see and read and hear. Seek out alternative sources of information like *Salon, Counterpunch, Toms Dispatch, The Atlantic, The Nation. LA Progressive* for goodness sake. Even BBC radio and

49. You Want to Serve Your Country?

television news, which is far better than any mainstream US network news source.

Get involved in the politics that impact your life: can you even name your US senators, your US representative, your state senators and representatives, the members of your local government? Become informed. Learn what is being done in your name and with your tax dollars at the local, state, and federal levels. Yes, this takes time and effort, but corruption and deceit and dishonesty and injustice thrive on the ignorance of the people.

You want to serve your country? Get engaged. Become teachers, general practitioner doctors, EMTs, firefighters, nurses. Heck, be the best damned check-out clerk in the grocery store. Be polite to people. Be tolerant. Treat others the way you'd like to be treated. Try always to do the next right thing. That's how you can serve your country.

50

A New Birth of Freedom

(*LA Progressive*, January 2, 2022. Reprinted under the cumbersome title of "Too many have yet to embrace the truth laid out by Abraham Lincoln at Gettysburg" in *Beaver County Times, Bucks County Courier-Times, York Daily Record, The Record Herald, Public Opinion, Ellwood City Ledger, Intelligencer, Tri-County Independent, Evening Sun, Pocono Record, Daily American, Lebanon Daily News* & *Erie Times-News*, January 6, 2022)

This January 1 marks the 159th anniversary of the day Abraham Lincoln's Emancipation Proclamation took effect. At that precise moment, however, not a single slave was set free because its provisions only applied to slaves still under the control of the Confederacy. Lincoln worded it that way in order not to risk losing the support of the four Union Border States where slavery was still legal. Only slaves liberated by the advancing Union armies after January 1 would be freed.

The Battle of Gettysburg, still six months in the future, would change all that, in effect rendering the Emancipation Proclamation obsolete.

My connection to Gettysburg has little to do with the famous Civil War battle, but does go back over ninety years and is very deep. My maternal grandparents, Ottavio and Geneva Conti, are buried in Evergreen Cemetery on the backside of what is now known as Cemetery Hill where Lincoln delivered his eloquent Gettysburg Address in November 1863. Also buried there are my maternal great-grandmother, and my Uncle Eddie and cousin Ruth Elaine, both of whom died in infancy.

My mother's family had been living in Brooklyn, where my mother Evelyn and most of her siblings had been born. But in the late 1920s, when my mother was seven or eight, a doctor recommended for health reasons that my grandmother get out of the city, so my grandparents

50. A New Birth of Freedom

Left: Gravestone of my grandmother Geneva Conti in Evergreen Cemetery, Gettysburg, Pennsylvania (author's photo). *Right:* Gravestone of my grandfather Ottavio Conti in Evergreen Cemetery, Gettysburg, Pennsylvania (author's photo). *Below:* Gravestones of cousin Ruth Elaine Conti (died at birth), Uncle Eddie Conti (died at 30 days), and Great-grandmother Evelyn Dundon in Evergreen Cemetery, Gettysburg, Pennsylvania (author's photo).

bought a gas station and cabin complex—what passed for a "motel" in those days—out near Barlow's Knoll, where heavy fighting had taken place on July 1, 1863.

Meanwhile, my father, John Ehrhart, was growing up not far away in the small crossroads community of Hampton, Pennsylvania. He graduated from York Springs High School and became a student at Gettysburg College. To help pay his way, he worked as a "soda jerk" at the drugstore on the town square where my mother and her girlfriends would drop by after a day at Gettysburg High. You can figure the rest of that story.

They were married in 1943 shortly before my father was ordained as a minister. But various Contis continued to live in or near Gettysburg for many years. In 1963, my pal Larry Rush and I spent a week with my Aunt Bert during the centennial commemoration of the battle. I vividly remember the demonstrations of a gun crew loading and firing a cannon and an infantryman loading and firing a musket. Way cool stuff for a 14-year-old.

Then two of my three brothers ended up going to Gettysburg College as well, graduating respectively in 1967 and 1977. So, I spent a lot of time over many years exploring the Devil's Den and Little Round Top and Culp's Hill, climbing the observation towers, and walking through town looking for bullet holes in old houses.

By the time I was teaching U.S. History at the Haverford School for Boys in this new century, and we'd take the students every year on a field trip to Gettysburg, I could have led the battlefield tour myself. And while all the boys headed to McDonald's and Pizza Hut for lunch, my colleague Kevin Tryon and I would always eat at General Pickett's Buffet: all you could eat for ten bucks.

One of the things we always did on this trip was to take the boys to the spot where Lincoln delivered his famous address. One of us would read it aloud with the boys gathered around. It is one of the most misunderstood speeches in American history. When Lincoln praised those "brave men, living and dead," who "hallowed this ground," he was not referring to the Confederate dead, who were trying to dissolve and withdraw from "a new nation conceived in liberty and dedicated to the proposition that 'all men are created equal.'" There were and are no Confederate soldiers buried in the cemetery he was dedicating that day.

Lincoln was referring only to the Union dead, who were willing to sacrifice their lives to see that this nation would "endure." It was their bravery that hallowed the ground at Gettysburg. Their bravery he was honoring.

Moreover, his short speech signaled quietly but unmistakably that, contrary to earlier assertions, the ultimate goal of this war was not just preserving the Union, but rather putting an end to slavery. If you read it carefully, that is what the Gettysburg Address announces.

Why else would Lincoln talk about "a new birth of freedom"? Who do we think he was talking about? White Americans, northern or southern, didn't need "a new birth of freedom." Those in need of freedom were African Americans. The four million enslaved Americans. Lincoln meant to free the slaves.

I recently visited my grandparents' graves again in the company of the artist Jane Irish and her boyfriend. It is simply a matter of coincidence that I have any connection to Gettysburg, Pennsylvania, and

50. A New Birth of Freedom

the terrible battle that was fought there. But every time I go there, I am reminded that one side in that fight was right, and one side was terribly wrong. And it makes me terribly sad that the wrong side in that struggle still wields far more power and influence in this country than it has any legitimate claim to.

51

This Is Democracy?

(*New Hampshire Gazette*, January 14, 2022)

So here we are at the outset of another new year. A Happy New Year? Well, as Shakespeare's Lady Anne replies to Richard III in Act I, Scene 2, when he asks if he can live in hope, "All men I hope live so." Of course, she's talking to one of the Bard's most villainous characters. And though he eventually gets his in the end, we folks (men and women both) these days can—well—only hope that our future works out so nicely.

I can't help finding myself wondering how much longer our American version of democracy is likely to last. Will it survive the 2022 congressional elections? How about the 2024 presidential election? Let's do a little review:

In 1789, when the U.S. Constitution took effect, each congressional district represented about 30,000 citizens. Today, each district represents an average of 710,000 citizens. Okay, the population has grown to such an extent that if districts were still that small, our House of Representatives would have about 10,000 members. Still, Montana's one member of the House represents 994,000 people while Rhode Island's two members each represent only 527,000 people. This is democracy?

But the Senate is even worse ... or better, depending on your sense of humor. Each Wyoming senator represents 568,000 people while each California senator represents 18,671,000 people. That's 18 & ½ million vs. ½ million. This is democracy?

While we're on the subject of Congress, how about those gerrymandered electoral districts? If you want to have some fun, Google "worst gerrymandered districts" and see what you get. Both parties, of course, have been doing this since Massachusetts governor Elbridge Gerry first did it in 1812. But districts are determined by state legislatures, and Republicans currently control twice as many state legislatures as Democrats.

51. *This Is Democracy?*

Thus, in Texas, for instance, the heavily Democratic city of Austin is divided among six districts, only one of which holds a Democratic majority. On the other hand, the Republican-controlled 2nd District around Houston is shaped like the letter C and is only a block or two wide in several areas.

Only one state has a nonpartisan redistricting process. This is democracy?

Or consider this: because of the Electoral College, an anachronism left over from the days of the 3/5th Clause designed to mollify the southern slave states whose population was much smaller than the northern industrial states, five times the presidential candidate who received the most popular votes lost the election. This happened only three times in the first 211 years of our history. But it has already happened twice in the first 16 years of this century. This is democracy?

Meanwhile, in 2010, the U.S. Supreme Court ruled 5–4 that $$$$$ equals free speech. The more $$$$$ you have, the more free speech you get to buy. If you haven't got any $$$$$, tough luck; get a job. This is democracy?

Speaking of the Supreme Court, the Constitution says that the president gets to appoint justices with the approval of the senate. It doesn't say anything about the president not being allowed to appoint anyone in his last year in office, yet a Republican senate majority leader refused to allow a Democratic president to make an appointment in his last year in office only to turn around four years later and allow a Republican president to appoint one less than a month before the 2020 election. This is democracy?

As for Republicans and Democrats, the U.S. Constitution says not one word about political parties, but if you're not a Republican or a Democrat, good luck getting elected Dog Catcher, let alone President. The last successful creation of a new national political party happened in 1856. That would be one hundred and sixty-six years ago. Even "Independent" Bernie Sanders had to start calling himself a "Progressive Democrat" if he wanted to be a player in the 2016 and 2020 elections. This is democracy?

And of course, all of this is layered on top of a soundly defeated former president who over a year later still insists that his re-election was stolen from him, supported and egged on by Fox News Talking Heads, gun-toting elected representatives like Lauren Boebert and Thomas Massie and Josh Hawley, and something on the order of 74 million of our fellow citizens.

What We Can and Can't Afford

But here we are at the beginning of another New Year. Another one of Shakespeare's plays is titled *All's Well That Ends Well*. Will this New Year end well? We can always hope so. But I'm not making any predictions. Only a resolution, lame as it may sound, to do whatever I can to see that it does. Which probably isn't much, but it beats sitting around waiting for Doomsday.

52

Who Needs Diversity, Equity, or Inclusion?

(*LA Progressive*, January 18, 2022; North Penn *Reporter*, January 20, 2022; *Bucks County Herald*, January 27, 2022; Perkasie *News-Herald*, January 30, 2022)

Back in about 2005, I was teaching at the Haverford School for Boys. One day we were reading Langston Hughes's "I, Too" and Claude McKay's "The Lynching," two strikingly different poems by African American writers of the 1930s.

We were comparing the points of view of these two men with Martin Luther King, Jr., and Malcolm X, when one of the students asked plaintively, "Do we have to read this stuff? I never owned any slaves. Why are you trying to make me feel guilty for what my ancestors did?"

"I'm not trying to make you feel guilty for what your ancestors did," I replied. "I'm trying to encourage you to live your life so that your descendants won't have to feel ashamed of you."

Six months later, at the end of the school year, that same student presented me with a large bowl he had made in ceramics class. Written around the rim of that bowl was my quote. Obviously, what I had said had registered with this young man deeply enough for him to have remembered it and incorporated it into his artwork. I hope he has also gone on to incorporate it into his life.

I was thinking about that this morning when an old friend from the community I grew up in told me that the Pennridge School Board in Bucks County, Pennsylvania, has disbanded its Diversity Equity Inclusion Committee, replacing it with an unwieldy *ad hoc* committee chaired by a school board president who has gone on record that there is no such thing as structural or institutional racism in her community or the nation at large.

What We Can and Can't Afford

I wonder what would happen if I were teaching at Pennridge today, and I tried to teach these two poems by Hughes and McKay.

Indeed, the free exchange of ideas doesn't seem to be much in vogue with the Pennridge School District these days. Just last week, I learned that teachers in the Pennridge system were "encouraged" not to discuss the January 6, 2020, attack on our nation's Capital. Given what I know about the current composition of the board, my guess is that any teacher who wants to keep his or her job will be duly "encouraged" to comply.

Teachers have been instructed instead to reply to student questions by saying, "the investigation is ongoing and as historians we must wait until there is some distance from the event for us to accurately interpret it."

But we all watched live and in real time what was happening on January 6 last year, and it doesn't take a historian to interpret what we were watching. Over 700 people have been charged with criminal behavior, and many of them have already been convicted or pled guilty.

And now nearly a dozen people—so far—have just been indicted for seditious conspiracy. *Sedition*. Look that one up. And you're going to tell me that I don't understand what happened that day? I listened to a soon-to-be ex-president tell his supporters to "fight like hell," and then watched as thousands of those supporters fought like hell to stop the legitimate transfer of presidential power, something that has never before happened in the history of this nation.

I'm reminded of that great Jack Nicholson line in *A Few Good Men*, adapted to the Pennridge School District: "You want the truth, kids? You can't handle the truth!"

And that brings to mind another Pennridge lunacy (it's hard to come up with a better word): armed security guards in the halls of the schools. How much protection will they provide? During the horrendous attack at Marjorie Stoneman Douglas High in Florida in 2018, an armed law enforcement officer hid in his car rather than confronting the gunman. Will our PHS cops be any braver? Let's hope we never find out.

But if we do, let's hope that the two of them—that's all the armed guards they've hired—are in the right building at the right time. There's the high school, of course, but what about the three middle schools? Don't those kids need protection? Look up Rigby Middle School (Idaho) or Washington Middle School (New Mexico) or Cummings K-8 Optional School (Tennessee).

And what about the district's seven elementary schools? Ever heard

52. Who Needs Diversity, Equity, or Inclusion?

of Sandy Hook Elementary? Just how and where are those two armed guards deployed every day? Maybe the Pennridge School District needs to hire a whole platoon of armed security guards. How about the Proud Boys or the Oath Keepers?

Or maybe the answer isn't more guns, but rather saner gun safety policies, better mental health care, and a community determined to teach tolerance, inclusion and diversity.

But don't try that one out in today's Pennridge School District. When a group of students peacefully protested gun violence a few years ago in the wake of the Parkland shootings, joining thousands of other students nationwide, hundreds of them were punished by school administrators with Saturday detention.

This is *my* alma mater. My foster mother. I graduated from Pennridge High School in 1966. I was a varsity trackman, vice president of student council, a member of the Honor Society, and a commencement speaker. I'm on the Pennridge Wall of Fame. My father was pastor of St. Stephen's Church for 29 years, and my mother taught for many years in the Bucks County Intermediate Unit. They're both buried up at the top of Market Street in Perkasie.

But I find myself ashamed of what is happening in the Pennridge School District these days. That it is emblematic of what has been happening all over this country does not make it any less shameful. In the halls and classrooms of Pennridge High School, Bob Hollenbach taught me how to think clearly, John Diehl taught me tolerance and humanity, Wayne "Pud" Helman taught me fair play. I wonder which teachers today's Pennridge students will remember, and what those teachers will be remembered for.

53

Does This Mean War?

(*LA Progressive*, January 31, 2022; *New Hampshire Gazette*, February 11, 2022; *Bucks County Courier Times* & *Daily Intelligencer*, February 20, 2022)

The headlines these days are ominous.
"Russia warns of retaliation if its demands are not met."
"U.S. allies are stepping up to counter Russia's Ukraine threats."
"Blinken: No concessions in response to Russia on Ukraine."
"Will there be a war over Ukraine?"

It's enough to keep you awake at night. Russia may no longer be the Soviet Union, but it's still the original Evil Empire: unrepentantly aggressive, a bully, eager to needle the West at every opportunity, willing to risk war to achieve its selfish aims.

Or so our government and our mainstream media would have us believe. But once again—as Americans have always been so adept at— we ignore the facts in order to present ourselves as the righteously aggrieved.

At the end of World War II, the Soviet Union quickly gobbled up all of eastern Europe, installing sympathetic governments and creating the Warsaw Pact. Proof positive of Communist aggression.

But during that war, the Soviet Union lost 27,000,000 soldiers and civilians—more than half of all casualties suffered by all of the nations involved in that war. I am not for a moment arguing that Joe Stalin was a nice guy, but he was protecting his country from future depredations by a hostile West by making sure that the next time the West attacked Russia, they'd have to kill a lot of other people before they actually got to the Russians.

And then there was the Cuban missile crisis. Imagine the gall of those war-mongering Russians (okay, Soviets) to put nuclear missiles

53. Does This Mean War?

only 90 miles from our very shores. Talk about naked aggression. How much more blatant can you get?

Only years later did we learn that just prior to the Soviet introduction of missiles into Cuba, the U.S. had installed ballistic nuclear missiles in Italy and Turkey. So, the U.S. is not threatening Russia with missiles on or near its borders, but when the Russians reciprocate, they're obviously completely unjustified.

And what did Nikita Khrushchev ask for in return for removing the missiles from Cuba? Simply that the U.S. remove its missiles from Italy and Turkey. And he didn't even demand that we admit we'd put missiles there in the first place. So, the American missiles were quietly removed while the whole dangerous affair was portrayed as a great American victory and proof that we could and would stand up to the Russian bully.

And that brings us to the current crisis. There is a good deal of disagreement as to whether or not the U.S. promised Russia after the break-up of the USSR that NATO would not try to expand to include former members of the Warsaw Pact. But promise or not, it must surely be unsettling to anyone living in Russia that NATO now includes three former Soviet Socialist Republics, all with borders on Russia, and six former Warsaw Pact nations, several of these bordering directly on Russia.

Once again, don't mistake me. I am not saying that Vladimir Putin is a nice guy. But I'd like to know how Americans in general and the U.S. government in particular would respond if Russia signed a military alliance with Canada and Mexico. By way of NATO, we've already done much the same thing to Russia, and now we want to include Ukraine in NATO as well?

Moreover, what purpose does NATO serve these days? NATO stands for the North Atlantic Treaty Organization. Turkey is in the North Atlantic? Albania is in the North Atlantic? And Bulgaria, Romania, Croatia? And then consider that nations like Poland, Hungary, Bulgaria, and Turkey make American democracy look like the Golden Age of Athens.

I have no illusions, and certainly no expectation, that the Biden Administration will muster the courage to choose the sensible and reasonable course of action here: promise Putin that Ukraine will never be part of NATO in return for a Russian promise not to invade Ukraine. After the pummeling Biden got for ending our Forever War in Afghanistan, I expect he feels enormous pressure to demonstrate that he's really a tough leader who won't back down from aggression.

What We Can and Can't Afford

And of course, if we do go to war with Russia, most of you reading this won't actually be doing anything or going anywhere at all. It'll just be that tiny little One Percent of our citizenry who will bear the blood price while the rest of us stand up and remove our hats for the Star-Spangled Banner at basketball games and hockey matches.

But I can tell you one bunch who are going to be really happy to see the U.S. and Russia go to war: that would be the Chinese. I just hope it doesn't go nuclear.

54

Propaganda 101
The Art of Creative Lying

(*New Hampshire Gazette*, February 25, 2022)

Recently, I was stopped dead in my tracks by a news report saying law students at Georgetown University were so upset by a professor criticizing President Biden's determination to appoint a Black woman to the Supreme Court that they demanded "an office they can go to … if they want to cry, if they need to break down." They are demanding a Crying Room.

Seriously?

I dutifully wrote up an irate essay excoriating the "Snowflake" sensibilities of many of my Left Progressive fellow travelers, whose sometimes frivolous and inane demands make it so easy for the Radical Reactionary Right to make the entire Progressive Left appear to be unhinged.

I sent the essay to the alleged editor of the *New Hampshire Gazette*, who is not so alleged as he often self-deprecatingly calls himself.

Steve Fowles' response was: "Yes, a bunch of students at Georgetown Law whimpering 'where's my crying room' is ridiculous. So ridiculous that it smelled to me like a set-up, another one of those ginned-up right wing finger pointing exercises. 'Look at these left-wing idiots. Aren't they ridiculous? By extension, aren't all their positions ridiculous?' The Ur-story seems to have been in the *Washington Examiner*. If there's one thing you can count on from the *Examiner*, it's a Tucker Carlsonesque bias."

I had picked the story up from the website of a local ABC News affiliate, and hadn't questioned it because I figured, "Well, ABC News." But when Fowle raised questions, I started digging deeper. Aside from two local ABC affiliates and an online *Newsweek* article written by a member of the American Enterprise Institute, every reference to the

What We Can and Can't Afford

Georgetown Crying Room appeared on websites run by Fox News or clearly arch-conservative organizations like Breitbart, Conservative News Daily, Trending Politics, and others of that stripe.

When I queried Dr. Harry Haines, Professor of Communication and Media at Montclair State University, he replied, "I usually watch ABC network news, and I have not seen a national story about the Georgetown conflict. Sounds like the ABC story remained local. The story may not have risen to the level of worthiness, aside from the right-wing sources fascinated by the crying room angle. I found a lengthy article in the *Hoya* [Georgetown University's campus newspaper] about the conflict [over Prof. Ilya Shapiro], but it did not mention a crying room."

John Baky, Director Emeritus of Library Services at La Salle University, added, "In the end it is hearsay circumstance. The question was probably asked in a meeting by a student and has simply been 'decorated' by accretion via the Loudmouth Right. One tell-tale sign is that the *Chronicle of Higher Education* has been silent on the story." Baky suspects that the absence of clear coverage in sources such as the *Washington Post* indicates the insignificance of whatever "truth" there might have been in the original story.

So, after some diligent searching by Fowle, Haines, and Baky, augmented by my own belated efforts, it seems very clear that the story of Black student demands for a Crying Room at Georgetown University Law School are at best highly embellished hearsay, at worst a deliberately fabricated lie.

I can hardly express my thanks to Fowle who, like Shakespeare's Hamlet, smelled a rat, and let me know it before I made a fool of myself in print. The really embarrassing part of all this is that I was so ready to believe the story. Why?

Well, the truth is that I have indeed gotten very frustrated and impatient with the "Snowflake Wing" of the Progressive Left with their demands for "Safe Spaces" on college campuses where no one is allowed to say anything that might hurt someone else's feelings, and "Defunding the Police" (the poorest choice of terminology since "Collateral Damage" and "Enhanced Interrogation").

But that is no excuse for failing to check my facts adequately before accepting *any* story at face value, especially a tale that plays so readily into the hands of the Radical Reactionary Right. As Edgar Allan Poe writes in "The System of Dr. Tarr and Prof. Fether": "Believe nothing you hear, and only one-half that you see."

54. Propaganda 101

I'm not quite so willing to be as skeptical as Poe suggests, but I've been forcefully reminded that one should never believe without question everything one hears or reads. It's hard enough these days to separate fact from fiction, truth from lies. For my own part, I hope I never again find myself the unwitting and gullible dupe of people who have no use for truth, honesty, or integrity. I wish the same for each of you.

55

What Is a Bayonet?
Or, Who Wins and Who Loses?

(*LA Progressive*, March 18, 2022; *New Hampshire Gazette*, March 25, 2022)

Lately I have been revisiting one of my favorite writers, Stephen Crane. Most famous for his novel of the American Civil War, *The Red Badge of Courage*, his collected writing—fiction, poetry, and journalism published by the University of Virginia Press—runs to ten full volumes. So enamored of his poetry was I that I still have a slim volume of his poems I "removed" (*stole* would be more accurate) from the Pennridge High School library back in 1965 or 1966. (In my defense, the town I grew up in didn't even have a bookstore, and I wanted to possess those poems.)

The best of his short stories and novellas are enduring masterpieces: *Maggie: A Girl of the Streets*, *The Monster*, "The Blue Hotel," "The Bride Comes to Yellow Sky." And "The Open Boat" is among the greatest short stories ever written. In the years since my own encounter with war, however, I came to believe that *The Red Badge of Courage* is the least of his accomplishments, the least interesting, the most sadly conventional.

In his first battle, the book's young protagonist succumbs to fear and runs from the fight as far and as fast as he can go. But after assorted encounters in rear areas with dead men, wounded men, and a dying friend, Henry rejoins his regiment and fights bravely "with his soiled and disorderly dress, his red and inflamed features surmounted by the dingy rag with its spot of blood, his wildly swinging rifle and banging accouterments[.]" And after the battle, "he felt a quiet manhood, nonassertive but of sturdy and strong blood.... He was a man."

The message of the story, in fact, is about as conventional as it gets.

55. What Is a Bayonet?

Back in the old days, before dashing Marines dueled flaming dragons in electronically generated television recruiting pitches, the poster that caught my eye in front of the U.S. Post Office in Perkasie, Pennsylvania, was a nearly life-sized Marine sergeant in Dress Blues with a caption that said, "THE MARINE CORPS BUILDS MEN."

That's what I wanted to be! So I signed up, only to discover that being a man wasn't all it was cracked up to be, that men who are horribly mangled in battle really do cry for their mothers, that war is neither ennobling nor uplifting, but instead mostly degrading, diminishing, and dehumanizing.

Crane, to his credit, seems to have come to the same conclusion. At the time he wrote his Civil War novel, he had never heard a shot fired in anger. But after experiencing a real war in Greece—including not just the battlefield fighting, but the suffering and terror of civilians—he wrote a very different story called "Death and the Child."

In this story, the young soldier also runs away from battle, though he receives his "red badge of courage" in the form of a mortal bullet wound, and with his dying thoughts, reflects upon the ordinary soldiers who make up all armies, and "who, throughout the world, hold potentates on their thrones, make statesmen illustrious, provide generals with lasting victories, all with ignorance, indifference, or half-witted hatred, moving the world with the strength of their arms and getting their heads knocked together in the name of God, the king, or the Stock Exchange—immortal, dreaming, hopeless asses who surrender their reason to the care of a shining puppet, and persuade some toy to carry their lives in his purse."

It is perhaps the most bitter sentence Crane ever penned, and every word of it is true. One is reminded of the question: what is a bayonet? Answer: a tool with a worker at either end.

Or consider Philip Freneau's poem "The American Soldier":

> Deep in a vale, a stranger now to arms,
> Too poor to shine in courts, too proud to beg,
> He, who once warred on *Saratoga's* plains,
> Sits musing o'er his scars, and wooden leg.
>
> Remembering still the toil of former days,
> To other hands he sees his earnings paid;—
> *They* share the due reward—*he* feeds on praise.
> Lost in the abyss of want, misfortune's shade.
>
> Far, far from domes where splendid tapers glare,
> 'Tis his from dear bought *peace* no wealth to win,

What We Can and Can't Afford

> Removed alike from courtly cringing 'squires,
> The great-man's *Levee*, and the proud man's grin.
>
> Sold are those arms which once on Britons blazed,
> When, flushed with conquest, to the charge they came;
> That power repelled, and *Freedom's* fabrick raised,
> She leaves her soldier—*famine and a name!*

This was written about the American Revolutionary War, but it could surely apply just as well to the Peloponnesian Wars, the Napoleonic Wars, the American War in Vietnam, or [*provide your own favorite war*]. The losers are the soldiers who generation after generation willingly offer themselves up as cannon-fodder, and the civilians who get caught in the middle. The winners are the arms merchants, the defense contractors, the oligarchs (do you really think the only oligarchs are Russian?).

So now we've got another war on our hands. This time it's young Russian soldiers and young Ukrainian soldiers who are killing each other while who-knows-how-many thousands of Ukrainian civilians are suffering and dying. So far, at least, young American soldiers are not yet engaged, though additional U.S. forces have been deployed to Poland, and the public clamor to "do something" to help Ukraine grows louder and ever more shrill with each passing day. Let us all hope this war spreads no farther, and comes to an end as mercifully soon as possible.

But whatever happens, it is highly unlikely that ordinary people, everyday folks like you and me—whatever our nationality—will be among the winners.

56

Going Green, Or
Poetic Justice

(*New Hampshire Gazette*, April 8, 2022)

    I've just purchased a piece of the state of New Jersey. Really. It's ten feet by ten feet and located in a lovely pine forest. Sooner or later—I'm 73 now, so I wouldn't hold out too much hope for "later"—it will become my final resting place when I shuffle off this mortal coil and join the Choir Invisible. My wife will eventually be there with me, too, though she's younger than me and thus has a better shot at "later." But why South Jersey? I've never lived there and have no family connection to the area.
    All my life, I've been completely disgusted with modern burial practices. My parents have both been dead for over three decades, but I could dig them up this afternoon and they'd look just about as good as they did when we planted them, what with having been embalmed, then stuck in a satin-lined casket, and then placed in a concrete vault. Talk about inefficient use of land.
    Indeed, for decades I've provided in my will that I be cremated because at least that way I'm not taking up space that might otherwise be put to good use. But it turns out that cremation isn't great for the environment either because it takes a huge amount of energy to cremate a body, and meanwhile the heat that's produced doesn't get used to warm somebody's house or drive a locomotive or bake a casserole or anything. Talk about inefficient use of energy.
    But very recently, I learned about a cemetery in the pine barrens of South Jersey that does "green burials." I didn't even think that was legal, but it is. And it turns out that there is a whole nationwide network of green burial cemeteries and funeral homes (*https://www.greenburialcouncil.org/*). That's how I've wanted my body disposed of all

What We Can and Can't Afford

of my life. After all, I've been walking around on Planet Earth all these years, sustaining myself by eating the plants and the animals that share this life with me. And what do the plants and the animals get in return?

So as soon as I heard about this cemetery, which has been around since the 17th century by the way, I started digging. Well, not literally, but I started checking around, drove down and looked the place over, and liked what I saw. Now I own a piece of New Jersey.

And I'm working with a funeral director who has done this sort of thing before. So, when the time comes, they'll just wrap me in a shroud, dig a hole, stick me in it, and shovel the dirt back in. Chow down, worms and flowers! Have at me! It's your turn now.

If I sound a bit flippant, the truth is that I find the thought of natural decomposition very comforting. The way it ought to be. The natural order of things.

This is the stuff of poetry: from the Old English "Soul and Body I" to the medieval "A Disputacioun betwyx Þe Body and Wormes" to Edgar Allan Poe's "The Conqueror Worm."

Ehrhart standing by the burial plot where he and his wife will eventually take up residence, Steelmantown Cemetery, New Jersey (author's photo).

56. Going Green, Or

And there's another piece to this that I just can't help enjoying, a delicious irony, a kind of poetic justice that is immensely satisfying. Way back in 1975, when I was living in Philadelphia, I drove over to visit a friend of mine in Maple Shade, New Jersey. And since I was going to visit Kathy, another friend asked me if I would take something over to her and save him a trip.

I had just bought a used MG Midget, but the temporary license had come off in a heavy rainstorm. So, this Maple Shade cop and about six of his buddies in three cars cornered me and rousted me out at gunpoint. I don't think the sheriff and his posse liked long-haired hippie-looking guys in convertibles, but I didn't dare mouth off to this Wyatt Earp Wannabee because if he strip-searched me, I'd be in a lot of trouble since what I was delivering wasn't entirely legal.

So, I just showed him my sworn affidavit attesting that my car was properly registered and tagged, and otherwise kept my mouth shut. There wasn't anything he could actually charge me with or run me in for. But Marshall Dillon actually said to me, "Get out of New Jersey. And don't come back." I almost choked. I had a really hard time biting my tongue on that one. But I also really didn't want to end up in prison, so I didn't say a thing.

But now I find myself, nearly half a century later, about to become a permanent resident of New Jersey, and there's nothing Sergeant Striker of the Maple Shade Police Department can do about it. So, I get to be buried the way I've always wanted to be buried, the worms and the flowers get a free lunch, and Officer Krupke gets to go suck an egg. Sweet.

57

Smedley Darlington Butler
From Consummate Imperialist to Strident Anti-Imperialist

(*VVAW Veteran*, v. 52, #1, Spring 2022; an earlier version of this essay was published in the *New Hampshire Gazette* in 2020; this 2022 version contains significant changes)

A recently published book, *Gangsters of Capitalism: Smedley Butler, the Marines, and the Making and Breaking of America's Empire* by Jonathan Katz, is finally bringing much-needed mainstream attention to one of the most fascinating Americans of the 20th century.

My own connection to Butler goes back to the summer of 1966 when I arrived at U.S. Marine Corps boot camp at Parris Island, South Carolina, at the age of 17. We learned all sorts of things that summer, but one thing we learned was the names of the two Marines who had each won not one, but two Medals of Honor: Dan Daly and Smedley Butler.

Butler would have received three Medals of Honor if the award had been available to officers during the Boxer Rebellion in 1900 China. Every enlisted man on a patrol he led as a teenaged lieutenant received one, but he was instead awarded the Marine Corps Brevet Medal, the highest decoration for bravery then available to commissioned officers.

In the course of his career, he also received the Navy Distinguished Service Medal, the Army Distinguished Service Medal, the French Order of the Black Star, two decorations from the Haitian government, and ten campaign medals.

But our drill instructors didn't tell us about the book Butler wrote called *War Is a Racket*. And they didn't teach us what Butler came to believe about himself:

57. Smedley Darlington Butler

> I spent 33 years and four months in active military service and during that period I spent most of my time as a high class muscle man for Big Business, for Wall Street and the bankers. In short, I was a racketeer, a gangster for capitalism. I helped make Mexico and especially Tampico safe for American oil interests in 1914. I helped make Haiti and Cuba a decent place for the National City Bank boys to collect revenues in. I helped in the raping of half a dozen Central American republics for the benefit of Wall Street. I helped purify Nicaragua for the International Banking House of Brown Brothers in 1902–1912. I brought light to the Dominican Republic for the American sugar interests in 1916. I helped make Honduras right for the American fruit companies in 1903. In China in 1927 I helped see to it that Standard Oil went on its way unmolested. Looking back on it, I might have given Al Capone a few hints. The best he could do was to operate his racket in three districts. I operated on three continents.

I only began to learn the whole story of Smedley Darlington Butler's remarkable life during the Reagan Wars against the peasants of Central America in the 1980s, a part of the world where Butler had spent much of his career in the first 30 years of the 20th century.

Butler, it turns out, was an 1898 graduate of the Haverford School for Boys, then known as the Haverford College Grammar School. And as chance would have it, I was hired in January 2001 to teach English and history at the Haverford School (THS) by then-headmaster and retired 30-year U.S. Army colonel Dr. Joseph T. Cox.

Ten years into my 18-year stay, Cox got an e-mail from a 1969 graduate named Fred Housel who had been a "Lifer" at THS, and who had stumbled by accident upon Butler's story while doing unrelated research. Housel asked Cox, "How could I spend 13 years at Haverford and never have heard a word about Smedley Butler?" Cox's reply was, "You should talk to Bill Ehrhart. He's a big Smedley Butler fan."

The answer to Fred's question was easy: after Butler retired from the Corps in the early 1930s, when he began speaking out against what he saw as unjustifiable foreign interventions and what today we would call "the military-industrial complex," the then rich white Republican Philadelphia Main Line clientele of the Haverford School deemed Butler a traitor to "his class," and wrote him out of the school's history. He simply ceased to be.

Until I arrived, that is. From the first day I began teaching there, I had a large poster of Butler hanging in my classroom. Along with a full-length photograph of Butler, the poster included his famous "racketeer for capitalism" quote, which originally appeared in *Common Sense*, a magazine published by socialists in the tradition of Eugene Debs and

What We Can and Can't Afford

Bill Ehrhart and Fred Housel (THS '69) with painting of Smedley Butler done by Haverford School student Bo Collins (THS '11) (author's photo).

Robert La Follette, in November 1935. Below the poster, I added my own sign identifying him as a Haverford School alumnus.

Housel was not pleased to learn that his alma mater had erased Butler from its institutional conscience, and made a substantial donation to the school in return for resurrecting Butler's connection to the school. My classroom was dedicated to Butler's memory, and now bears a plaque attesting to this. An oil painting of Butler in uniform, painted by a student, now hangs just outside the upper school admissions office. And on the campus, circling one of the trees, is the Smedley Butler Bench, which carries six brass plates reading:

57. Smedley Darlington Butler

The Butler bench on the campus of the Haverford School for Boys (photo courtesy of Michael Gillen).

> *Panel 1*
> Smedley Darlington Butler
> 1881–1940
> The Haverford School Class of 1898
> Husband of Ethel Conway Peters Butler
> Father of Ethel, Smedley, Jr., & Thomas
> Incorruptible Outspoken Patriot
> His was a life of Courage, Respect & Honesty
>
> *Panel 2*
> A native of West Chester, Pennsylvania,
> the son of a Congressman,
> Butler was captain of the Haverford School's
> baseball team and quarterback of the football team.
> Not yet 17, he enlisted in the Marines in 1898
> without waiting for graduation,
> but was nevertheless awarded his diploma.
>
> *Panel 3*
> During a career spanning over 33 years,
> Butler rose from 2nd lieutenant to major general.

What We Can and Can't Afford

He served in the U.S., the Philippines, China,
Panama, Honduras, Nicaragua, Mexico, Haiti,
Cuba, the Dominican Republic and France,
earning not one but two Medals of Honor,
the Marine Corps Brevet Medal,
and both the Army and Navy
Distinguished Service Medals.

Panel 4
From January 1924 through December 1925,
Butler took a leave of absence from the Corps
to serve as Philadelphia's Director of Public Safety.
Charged with enforcing prohibition
and rooting out municipal corruption,
he later said: "Cleaning up Philadelphia
was worse than any battle I was ever in."

Panel 5
After retiring from the Corps in 1931,
Butler became an advocate for veterans
and a critic of American military adventurism.
In 1932, he supported the Great War "Bonus Marchers."
In a 1935 essay he titled *War Is a Racket*,
he described himself as having been
"a muscleman for Big Business,"
"a racketeer," and "a gangster for capitalism."

Panel 6
Nicknamed variously the Maverick Marine,
the Fighting Quaker,
the Fighting Devil of the Devil Dogs,
the Fighting Hell-Devil Marine,
the Stormy Petrel of the Marine Corps,
General Duckboard & Old Gimlet Eye,
Butler himself concluded, "To Hell with War!"

 Butler earned the nickname "Maverick Marine" because he repeatedly found himself in trouble with his superiors in the military and the government; he had no patience with bureaucracy, red tape, or armchair strategists, and always put the welfare of the men under his command before everything else.

 In the Philippines, early in his career, he was nearly cashiered for defying orders and commandeering a Navy tug to deliver food and supplies to his isolated command, largely dismantling the tug in order to build a pier from which to offload his cargo once he'd returned to the outpost where his men were stationed.

57. Smedley Darlington Butler

Awarded a Medal of Honor in Mexico in 1914 that he did not feel he deserved, he was told that he had to accept it and wear it, or face court-martial.

Sent to France in 1918, but denied the combat command he desperately wanted, he was assigned instead to command a transient camp for soldiers coming and going between the States and the trenches on the Western Front. Appalled by the unsanitary living conditions at the camp, and refused permission to obtain adequate supplies to upgrade the camp's facilities, he organized a work party that raided a government warehouse in broad daylight and "liberated" the duckboards, shovels, and tents he needed, thus earning him the nickname "General Duckboard."

Butler was not without his warts and blemishes. He loved the adrenalin rush of combat, the sheer challenge and excitement of it. First as a young lieutenant, and repeatedly throughout his career, he complained in letters to his congressman father that the policies he was enforcing in countries like Nicaragua, Honduras, and Haiti were corrupt and immoral, benefiting only the white wealthy ruling class in America, yet he continued his career in the Corps for more than three decades. He began to speak out only after he'd gotten too old and too far up the hierarchy to be allowed to engage in actual combat.

But once he began to speak out, he would not be silenced. Even while still in the Corps, he publicly criticized Benito Mussolini, calling fascist Italy a "mad-dog nation," and causing an international diplomatic scandal for which Herbert Hoover would have had him court-martialed but for the public outcry in support of Butler.

Later, in 1932, he vocally supported the Great War Bonus Marchers who had fought for their country as young men, but were now, at the height of the Great Depression, unable to support themselves or their families. They had come to Washington to ask that their wartime service bonus, due to be paid in 1945, be paid to them now when they desperately needed it. Visiting their encampment on Anacostia Flats, Butler spoke to the men and their families from the roof of a car, telling them that they had as much right to lobby Congress as any corporation did, and calling their gathering "the greatest display of Americanism in history."

Shortly thereafter, when Army Chief of Staff Douglas MacArthur, aided by Major George Patton and Major Dwight Eisenhower, ordered an attack against the men who MacArthur himself had commanded

What We Can and Can't Afford

in France fifteen years earlier, forcibly driving them and their families out of their encampment with tanks, machine guns, tear gas, and cavalry, Butler was outraged. Already no fan of the arrogant and imperial MacArthur, Butler subsequently declared himself a "Hoover-for-Ex-President-Republican."

Perhaps most amazing of all, Butler was approached by wealthy Republican financiers and industrialists interested in persuading Butler to lead what would have amounted to a *coup d'état* against Franklin Roosevelt and the New Deal, using veterans from the conservative American Legion as a front for the interests of Big Business. It would have been the end of American democracy and the beginning of American fascism.

These men chose Butler because they knew that Butler commanded the loyalty and love of ordinary soldiers and veterans. He had put men before mission all his life, and the rank-and-file knew it, and revered him for it. But these rich un–American Americans utterly misunderstood who Butler was and what he believed in. Instead of joining the conspiracy, Butler informed Congress of the plot, putting an end to it.

Butler, by this time, had become deeply isolationist, insisting that "there are only two things we should fight for. One is the defense of our homes, and the other is the Bill of Rights. War for any other reason is simply a racket." We'll never know how Butler would have responded

Former Marine Corps Sergeant and Haverford School Master Teacher Dr. Bill Ehrhart with Marine Corps Major General Smedley Darlington Butler, Haverford School Class of 1898, Oaklands Cemetery, West Chester, Pennsylvania, April 5th, 2021. "War Is a Racket" (author's photo)

57. Smedley Darlington Butler

to the Japanese attack on Pearl Harbor since Butler died in 1940. We do know that he didn't think we should have military bases outside the continental U.S. in the first place, and that included Hawaii, and we do know that as early as the late 1920s he warned that continued U.S. possession of the Philippines would almost certainly lead to war with Japan.

What Butler would have thought about the state of American democracy in the early 21st century is once again a matter of sheer speculation. But he did come to believe—and he made no secret of it—that the key fault line in American life was economic class. By the very early 1930s, even before the election of FDR, he was openly advocating major public works spending, a federal jobs guarantee, stronger labor unions, higher wages for workers, and a federal old age pension. While never a pacifist, he broke with FDR in the 1936 election because he felt Roosevelt was leading the nation toward war, voting instead for the Socialist Party's Norman Thomas.

We will simply never know, of course, but I fully believe that Butler would feel right at home with Bernie Sanders and Alexandria Ocasio-Cortez, would be livid over the events of January 6, and even more outraged by the response from the Grand Old Party of which he had once been a member. Would that Butler were here today to help put an end to our current drift toward fascism and one-party dictatorship. Were Butler with us now, I wouldn't be surprised if he insisted on becoming a member of Vietnam Veterans Against the War. He would certainly fit right in.

58

In Praise of 21st Century Luddism

(*LA Progressive*, 4/27/22;
New Hampshire Gazette, 5/6/22)

Believe me, I really do understand that those little handheld electronic pocket-sized gadgets that do everything from making phone calls to taking photos and videos to locating your exact position on the planet are the future, and the future is already here, and there's nothing I can do about it.

But you cannot make me like it, nor can you make me own one of those machines. And though I try to be polite when other people pull out their Smartphones and iPhones, it is often a struggle to refrain from grabbing the device and smashing it under my heel.

Recently, a friend of ours came to visit for the weekend. He and his wife live several states away, so we don't see them that often. The first few hours went just fine. But after dinner, the husband began to tell us about a trip they were planning later this spring: they were going to rent a cabin on Prince Edward Island and go ocean kayaking.

But he didn't just tell us about the trip. He whipped out his little phone thing and showed me a tiny map of PEI. Then he showed it to my wife. Then he showed me a photo of the cabin they'll be renting. Then he showed it to my wife. Then he showed me a photo of his 22-foot ocean-going kayak. Then he showed it to my wife. Then he showed me a photo of his 22-foot ocean-going kayak with his wife sitting in it. Then he showed it to my wife. Then he showed me a photo of his 22-foot ocean-going kayak with his wife and himself sitting in it. Then he showed it to my wife. Then he showed me a photo of the bay they'll be paddling in at high tide. Then he showed it to my wife. Then he showed

58. In Praise of 21st Century Luddism

me a photo of the bay they'll be paddling in at low tide. Then he showed it to my wife.

He went on like this for most of the rest of the evening. And each time he introduced a new photo on his tiny screen, he would hold the screen up to my face until I made some suitable verbal acknowledgment that I had absorbed and appreciated the photo. "That's nice." "That's beautiful." "That looks like fun."

The next evening, we went out to dinner. When I mentioned that my wife and I would be visiting the Adirondacks this summer, he gleefully took out his electronic gizmo and called up a map of the Adirondacks and showed us where he'd gone kayaking near where we'd be.

From that moment until we left the restaurant, his little gizmo never left the table except when it was in his hand. He showed us a photo of his son and his son's girlfriend. He showed us a photo of his son and his son's dog. He showed us a photo of his other son and his other son's fiancée. He showed us a photo of him in the new suit his son had helped him pick out for his son's forthcoming wedding. He showed us a photo of the two ties his son had helped him pick out to wear with his new suit.

Ties, for crying in a bucket! Not even novelty ties like the ones with the neon hula dancer that say, "I love my wife, but oh you kid!" Just plain—very plain, in fact—ordinary ties. I'm supposed to get excited about his ties?

Please don't misunderstand me. I've known this man for four decades. I like him. He's intelligent and thoughtful. He's a good guy. But this new technology seems to have taken over his life, giving him the ability to provide in detail an illustrated account of every facet of his life and the belief that everyone else finds it all as fascinating as he does.

I recently retired from teaching high school. One big reason I retired was a rising feeling of helplessness in the face of the mindless assault of technology. Even the best students—and they are relatively rare—could not resist the urge to check in on Facebook or text their girlfriends in the midst of a lesson on Ben Franklin. How does one regulate it? By having the students face away from the teacher so I can see what's on their screens? Talk about cutting off your nose. And I've had students who can send text messages without even taking their phones out of their pockets. Really.

My solution was simply to ban all electronic devices from my classroom. But that didn't sit very well with the administration. Most of my colleagues, by the end of my tenure, had their entire courses posted online. And many of my students struggled to read anything longer than

What We Can and Can't Afford

a screen page or write anything longer than 144 characters. "Words" like UR, OMG, and LOL were beginning to show up regularly in formal academic essays. Really.

Then there was the student lounge just outside my classroom door. As the years passed, it got worse and worse. Long before I finally threw in the towel, it was all too depressingly common to see six or eight kids sitting out there, each one staring at the little screen in front of their faces while saying not one word to the kids on either side of them.

And that's not all. I regularly attend a Twelve Step program, but even in these meetings there are always a few people who sit there monitoring their screens, reading and sending text messages, even though every meeting begins with the admonition, "Please turn off your electronic devices and refrain from using them."

The night I was expected to admire several very ordinary ties, there were four young women seated at the table next to us, each one staring at the little screen in her hands, occasionally pushing the screen into the face of another one of the women. As nearly as I could discern, this passed for conversation.

I am fully aware that doomsayers in every generation, going back to the Roman poet Horace and beyond, have been convinced that the world is going to Hell in a handbasket, and yet we pathetic little humans are still here. And maybe we'll manage to survive the self-absorbed anti-social scourge of handheld technology that allows one to spend one's life in a bubble even when surrounded by other people.

But I still carry a flip-phone, and I never answer it unless it is my wife or my daughter calling. I use e-mail, but don't use any other so-called social media. I read books printed on paper. And at 73, with most of my life already behind me, I'm glad I won't be around to see if all this wonderful technology at our fingertips is really as wonderful as most people seem to think it is.

59

Woe Is Me!

(*New Hampshire Gazette*, 5/20/22)

Lately I have been struggling to find something worth writing about. What is the point? Nothing changes. I've written multiple essays about the madness of our uniquely U.S. gun culture, but Americans keep dying at the wrong end of firearms in record numbers, and in most states it's easier to acquire and carry a firearm than it was ten years ago.

I've written multiple essays about the need for the Democratic Party to get its collective head out of its ass and start functioning effectively to counter the insidious and pervasive evil that has become the Retrumplican Party, yet the Democrats keep bumbling along with the competence of the Keystone Kops while Retrumplicans across the nation take control of state legislatures, town councils, local school boards, and even the levers of elections themselves.

And what am I to write about a Supreme Court whose radical conservative majority was appointed by presidents who failed to win a majority of votes, who are young enough to be around for decades to come, who believe that corporations are people, the 2nd Amendment is more immaculate than the Virgin Mary, women's bodies belong to the State, and conflicts of interest don't apply to them?

How does one explain a citizenry that doesn't seem to blink an eye at a president and a presidency that is so corrupt, so crude, so ignorant, so venal, so beyond the pale as to make Rome's Nero look as benign as Captain Kangaroo, but cannot forgive a president for high gas prices in the midst of an international crisis caused by the ruthless dictator our previous president described as "a strong leader" and a "genius"?

And don't even get me started on global warming. The notion that the human race is collectively capable of altering our behavior soon enough and significantly enough to stave off what the entire scientific community tells us is now all-but-inevitable, leading to a Mad

What We Can and Can't Afford

Max world on the way to complete extinction, is the very definition of "chimerical."

How pathetic is it that the most upbeat essay I've been able to manage lately is one about how I've arranged a "green burial" for myself in the middle of a pine forest? How pathetic is it that I'm glad I won't be having grandchildren because I don't have to worry about the kind of world I'm leaving them? How pathetic is it that I'm glad most of my own life is already behind me and I won't have to be around to see how this Shit Show finally ends?

I actually shared some of this Doom & Gloom recently in an e-mail to our Alleged Editor. And then my wife and I spent a day in rural Adams County, Pennsylvania, with my dear friend and artist Jane Irish, and her partner, the philosopher Crispin Sartwell. It was a magnificent spring day, bright sky, warm enough to eat outside on the porch of their converted old schoolhouse, shade provided by a newly leafing maple tree.

Jane showed us her latest project, a series of paintings that, when fully assembled, will be 30 feet by 30 feet, though each panel can also be displayed as an independent work. She was very excited by what she is doing, and her enthusiasm and joy were infectious. Crispin gave me a copy of his latest book, *Beauty: A Quick Immersion*. He signed it, "To Bill and Anne—Beauty, emerging even from the darkness. Crispin 5-16-22."

As we made the two-hour drive home, I found myself thinking about the e-mail I'd sent our Alleged Editor only the night before. Okay, the world is a pretty screwed up place, and maybe my country and the rest of humanity are headed for a cosmic train wreck.

But I am one small man in a very, very, very big universe that—as I wrote in another essay not all that long ago—doesn't really care about me or humanity or Planet Earth. Whatever gave me the idea that what I think actually matters and what I write can actually change anything?

In the Twelve Step program I belong to, we're told that we can only take care of our own side of the street. What happens on the other side of the street is not in our control. We also recite the Serenity Prayer, which reminds us to accept what we cannot change. This doesn't mean docility or silence because we are also urged to find the courage to change what we can. But it does mean that we need to learn to accept and live with our limitations.

Moreover, if I think my little piece of the world is depressing, I really ought to remember what life is like these days for most people in

59. Woe Is Me!

Ukraine or Guatemala or Yemen. At least I've got food in my belly and a roof over my head, and nobody has shot at me lately.

My daughter and her partner just acquired a beehive. They're going to be beekeepers, and they're very happy about learning this new skill and in the process improving their immediate environment. My artist friend Jane has just landed a wonderful and unsolicited commission to do an installation for a prestigious university. My wife—let's be completely honest here—my wife has stuck with me for 42 years, though God knows she's had more than enough reason more than enough times to show me the door.

So, what have I got to feel sorry for? And who knows? Maybe I just could be wrong about where my country, the human race, and this planet are headed. Wouldn't that be nice?

60

A Farewell to Arms?

(*Hollywood Progressive*, 5/20/22;
New Hampshire Gazette, 6/3/22)

Back in 1990, at the first Conference of U.S. & Vietnamese Veteran-Writers in Hanoi, Le Minh Khue, a novelist who had been a teenager with a young volunteers team assigned to the military engineering command, told me that she had gone off to the war with several books in her knapsack: translations of Ernest Hemingway and Jack London.

"I learned a love of life from Jack London, as well as the courage to transcend death, to keep up hope against any odds," she said. "I cherished the anguish of Hemingway, whose wonderful short stories deal with loneliness, death, and love of life, eternal topics of literature and human thought."

Over the next few days, I would discover that many more of the Vietnamese I had fought against were reading Hemingway and London, Emerson, Thoreau, and Walt Whitman even as I and my country were trying to kill them.

That encounter with Khue occurred over three decades ago, but I was recently—and painfully—reminded of it while reading a new book of poems, *Things You May Find Hidden in My Ear*, by the young Palestinian poet Mosab abu Toha (City Lights, 2022). During the 2014 Israeli assault on Gaza, when Toha was a college student, he recalls:

"The Israelis bombed the administration building of my school, the Islamic University of Gaza. The English Department was destroyed. The many books resting on the shelves of my professors were just lying under the rubble of the building. The first book that I could extract was the *Norton Anthology of American Literature*. Of course, it's very ironic that we in Gaza and Palestine read and appreciate and value American literature, we study it, we just love it. But then all of a sudden, a

60. A Farewell to Arms?

rocket, or a heavy bomb that was paid for and manufactured in America, is killing, not only me, but the books that we read and studied in classes."

It is a dangerous thing to speak supportively in the U.S. about the plight of Palestinians, to question the policies and practices of Israel. The brilliant journalist Gloria Emerson discovered this when she published *Gaza: A Year in the Intifada* way back in 1991. She was followed from reading to book-signing to lecture by radical Zionists who vocally disrupted her presentations, accusing her of anti–Semitism and worse. Gloria was a tough lady, but she said they made her life hell.

Carolyn Karcher, editor and contributor to a 2019 book called *Reclaiming Judaism from Zionism*, says that she has not had to endure "any significant abuse" as a result of her book, but some of her fellow contributors have been subjected to significant abuse in response to their advocacy of Palestinian rights.

Meanwhile, Karcher's collection of essays led me to two books by the Israeli historian Ilan Pappe, *The Ethnic Cleansing of Palestine* (2006) and *The Biggest Prison on Earth* (2017). Pappe, who teaches at the University of Exeter in the UK, is treated like an enemy of the state in Israel. His detractors have accused him of cherry-picking facts, distorting facts, making up facts, blatantly lying, and being a self-hating Jew.

Mosab abu Toha is neither a journalist nor a historian, but simply a young man whose four grandparents were forcibly removed from their homes in 1948, whose parents were born in refugee camps, and who himself was born in a refugee camp called al-Shati in 1992. He is married, and the father of three young children. These poems, written in English—he is fluent in English as well as Arabic—are alternately sweet, bitter-sweet, angry, bewildered, and heart-breaking. Here is "Seven Fingers":

> Whenever she meets new people, she sinks
> her small hands into the pockets of her jeans,
> moves them
> as if she's counting
> some coins. (She's lost seven
> fingers in the war.) Then she
> moves away,
> back hunched,
> tiny as a dwarf.

What We Can and Can't Afford

And here is "Olympic Hopscotch Leap":

> We sit and drink tea
> in the hot night of Ramadan.
> Boys play hide and seek.
> Girls hopscotch around.
> Mothers chat and laugh.
>
> A buzzing sound of drones flying
> above my family and friends
> stops the games, the chatting, and the laughter.
>
> A missile fails,
> only falling into farmland nearby.
> Shrapnel cuts electric wires.
> Dust tops off our tea, like latte foam.
>
> More missiles come flying in,
> on the lookout for anything that moves.
>
> Angels get hold of my infant niece.
> We look around and find only
> her milk bottle.

I am not going to wade into the debate over who is right and who is wrong in that part of the Middle East. The history is long and bitter and multi-layered. Mistreatment of the Jews all over the world and reaching back millennia is a fact. What happened to European Jews between 1932 and 1945 is unspeakably horrendous; it would be unimaginable except that we have evidence in irrefutable abundance.

And it is also true that militant Palestinians have strapped bombs to themselves and suicidally murdered Israeli Jews, have repeatedly fired missiles into civilian areas of Israel, and have sworn the destruction and obliteration of the State of Israel.

But there is something just plain unfair about war where Israeli forces kill 2,251 Palestinian men, women, and children, while Palestinians kill 71 Israelis, 67 of them soldiers. Where one side is armed with drone missiles, F-16 fighter-bombers, and tanks, while the other side is armed mostly with rocks.

Moreover, at least since the first intifada over three decades ago, it has become abundantly clear that massive Israeli retaliation against Palestinian provocations simply does not deter the Palestinians from continuing to resist military occupation and an apartheid system that strips them of freedom, justice, and human dignity.

60. A Farewell to Arms?

As far back as the early 1990s, Gloria Emerson made it clear that the Israelis had only two options: learn to live with the Palestinians or kill them all. That is still true today: learn to live with them, or kill them all. Which is it going to be?

61

The Way Things Are

(*New Hampshire Gazette*, June 17, 2022)

Back in the May 20 issue of the *Gazette*, readers may remember an essay of mine called "Woe Is Me!" I began by cataloguing a litany of disasters and lunacies that leave me feeling hopeless about the future of this country and the planet. But then I spent a wonderful day with some friends of mine reminding me that there are indeed still many good things in this world, and lots to be grateful for.

Which is certainly true. The world is full of sad stories, but none of them are mine. And for some people, life is better now than it ever has been. One example: just yesterday, I marched with my Veterans for Peace chapter in the Philadelphia Gay Pride Parade. And while homophobia still exists, gay people are mostly no longer treated as criminals or mental patients.

But just four days after my essay ran in the *Gazette*, an 18-year-old murdered 19 elementary school children and two teachers, and wounded 17 others, with a military-style assault rifle while heavily armed police stood around with their thumbs up their asses for an hour and a half as the slaughter went on within feet of them. So much for good guys with guns.

And the response to this latest madness is as predictable as the tides. Politicians and pundits who think the 2nd Amendment was chiseled in stone by God's hand will argue that it's not a "gun problem," but only a mental health problem (while slashing funding for public health programs), and the solution is to arm teachers.

Politicians and pundits who advocate more stringent gun controls will once again call for banning assault rifles and instituting universal background checks, limiting the capacity of magazines, and other half-assed measures.

Everyone will fly flags at half-mast for a few days, and offer up

61. The Way Things Are

prayers for the souls of the dead and pleas for divine intervention. And then the discussion will fade away again until the next massacre. And *nothing* will change. Absolutely nothing.

How the hell am I supposed to console myself—or anyone else—by pointing out that there is still a lot of good in the world; that flowers are still beautiful; that I have not (yet) been a victim of the rampant gun violence in this country; that regardless of the Supreme Court or state laws, I will never need an abortion; that my child is far beyond school age, so why should I care about school boards that believe Critical Race Theory isn't just history, period, but rather some colossal lie cooked up by trolls who hate America; that I will be long dead before the full impact of global warming kicks in?

Honestly, I don't know what to do or where to turn or how to move forward. Maybe this is just what happens to old men who know they are nearing the end of their lives. You look back and you realize that nothing much has really changed since you were a young man, that human nature is what it is, and there is really not much difference between the lunacy of the Spanish Inquisition and the lunacy of the National Rifle Association, and you are only a little man in a very big universe with very little power to influence anything, and you can either accept that or not, but you can't change it.

Well, I'm trying to accept it. I'm trying to stuff my ego into the tiny box where it belongs, to remember that I am not nearly as important as I've spent my life believing, to embrace the reality that I can only take care of my side of the street, that my only real option is to choose to do "the next right thing," however small or insignificant that might be, and to keep trying to do the next right thing for as long as I have the power to make the choice.

A few years ago, a friend of mine posted lines from a Leonard Cohen song, "The wilderness is gathering all its children back again," something like that, and challenged his poet-friends to turn it into a poem. I came up with this:

What It Is Worth*
for Doug Rawlings

A team of misfits, yes, I guess
that pretty well describes us,
thinking we could find a home,

---

* from *Wolves in Winter*, Between Shadows Press, 2021.

What We Can and Can't Afford

build a world that we could live in,
one that everyone could live in
peacefully. How we doing so far?
Not so good? As you say, "Ah, well."
Cuchulain couldn't defeat the sea,
but that didn't stop him from trying.
The wilderness may well be calling
her children back; I wouldn't know
about that. I only know we've done
what we can; we can look at ourselves
in the mirror and not be ashamed.
Maybe a little foolish for being
naïve enough to think we could
make a difference, even after
all these years of failing to register
even a blip on this lunatic world.
But I'd rather live with that
than live with knowing I did nothing
to try to fix the mess we're all of us in.

Some days I find myself believing the effort has been worth it, even in failure. Some days, I feel very foolish indeed.

62

Let's Talk About Original Intent

(*LA Progressive*, July 6, 2022; *Bucks County Herald*, July 7, 2022; *New Hampshire Gazette*, July 15, 2022)

In a withering, indeed breathtaking, succession of recent decisions rendered by a U.S. Supreme Court now dominated by justices vetted by the Federalist Society and nominated by presidents who did not win the popular national vote, most of the past 120 years of legal progress and precedent have been obliterated.

The rationale for this assault on common sense and common decency is a doctrine called "Original Intent," which states that only those guarantees intended by the framers of the Constitution in 1787 and set forth in the document ratified two years later are valid. This is also sometimes defined as "strict construction," and is always trumpeted by so-called conservatives as a fundamental tenet.

I say "so-called" because their arguments and interpretations of our Constitution are neither conservative nor historically true. Abortion in this country, for instance, was legal from the nation's founding until well into the 19th century. But for now, let's take a closer look at just one example of the flagrantly lunatic application of original intent and strict construction.

The 2nd Amendment states: "A well regulated Militia, being necessary to the security of a free State, the right of the people to keep and bear Arms, shall not be infringed."

The most common firearm of that day was a smooth-bore muzzle-loading flintlock musket that was over four and a half feet long, weighed over ten pounds, had a muzzle velocity of 785 feet per second, could fire no more than three rounds a minute in the hands of a very skilled person, and was accurate up to fifty yards. Today's AR-15s and their knockoffs are barely three feet long and weigh only seven and a half pounds, are fed by magazines holding 20 or more rounds, have a muzzle velocity of 3300 feet per second, are accurate up to 600 meters, and can fire 60 to 100 bullets a minute, even in the hands of a rank amateur. All you have to do is keep pulling the trigger.

I can't prove this, but I find it extremely hard to believe that George Washington, Benjamin Franklin, John Adams, James Madison, and all those other Founding Fathers had the original intent to allow any American over the age of 18 to possess the ability to murder dozens and scores of men, women, and children.

But I can prove—because the words are right there in the 2nd Amendment itself—that what those men had in mind was "a well regulated Militia." And what did they mean by that?

While regulations varied somewhat from state to state, during the late colonial era and into the 19th century, every able-bodied free male between the ages of 16 and 50 was required to enlist in his state's militia. He was required to provide his own firearm. Local militias were organized into companies of 32 to 68 men. Companies were organized into regiments with regimental commanders appointed by state governors.

Militia companies were required to train six days a year, with regimental musters held periodically. Failure to appear for training could result in fines or corporal punishment. Repeated absentees could be sent to prison.

That is what is meant by a well-regulated militia. That was the original intent of the framers of our Constitution. The right of the people to keep and bear arms shall not be infringed in order for them to participate in a well-regulated militia. It's right there in front of your eyes, in print, on paper, in every copy of the Constitution I've ever read.

Though I sometimes find myself scratching my head, in fact I'm pretty certain that John Roberts, Clarence Thomas, Samuel Alito, Neil Gorsuch, Amy Coney Barrett, and Brett Kavanaugh all read, write, speak, and understand the English language.

The National Rifle Association is not a well-regulated militia. The Proud Boys are not a well-regulated militia. Lauren Boebert, Thomas Massie, and Marjorie Taylor Greene are not a well-regulated militia. Nor were Eric Harris, Dylan Klebold, Adam Lanza, Stephen Paddock, Omar Mateen, Dylann Roof, Nikolas Cruz, Salvador Ramos or any of the other mass murderers whose names we've come to know in the past 25 years.

Clarence Thomas writes in his decision in *New York State Rifle and*

62. Let's Talk About Original Intent

Pistol Association v. Bruen that the 2nd Amendment guarantee of the right to bear arms is "not a second class right." Okay, fine, but where's your "well-regulated militia"? Where is your "strict construction"? Where is the framers' "original intent"?

Even the late-though-hardly-lamented-in-some-quarters-at-least Antonin Scalia, when asked what the difference was between himself and Justice Thomas, replied, "Look, I'm an originalist, but I'm not a nut." Alas, it seems that at least six members of our highest court—from which there is no appeal—bear a remarkable resemblance to a large can of Planter's Mixed Nuts.

63

The New Normal

(*LA Progressive*, August 6, 2022;
New Hampshire Gazette, August 12, 2022;
Peace & Planet News, Spring 2022)

My wife and I recently spent four days in the Adirondack Mountains with old friends of ours. It is a six-hour car trip from our home in Pennsylvania, but thanks to Anne's company, the time passed enjoyably. And it was a great pleasure to spend time with our hosts, the wildlife conservationists Amy Vedder and Bill Weber, whom I've known since our college days over half a century ago.

We hiked in woods up and down hills and around lakes, visited the Adirondack Experience Museum, and reminisced for hours while watching chipmunks, hummingbirds, blue birds, and wild turkeys, and enjoying the view from their hilltop home. Over the entire time, we saw no commercial airplanes and only one single-engine plane far off to the east. The night sky overflowed with stars.

To say the trip was rejuvenating is an understatement. It was the first time Anne and I had gotten away together since the summer before the coronavirus pandemic. I'm told that living with this pandemic is now the New Normal. In fact, over the past few years, I've been hearing that a lot of things in our lives are now the New Normal:

A once Republican party that has morphed into the Retrumplican party. A Supreme Court overwhelmingly dominated by right-wing radical activists. Getting shot to death while shopping at the mall or attending church or dancing at a nightclub or sitting in an elementary school classroom. Hundred-year floods every six months. Hurricane seasons beginning earlier and ending later than ever before. As I type this, there are currently 63 major wildfires burning in the U.S. alone covering 1,640,278 acres of land. Far too many people spend their whole lives inside the Fox News bubble or the MSNBC bubble or the Facebook

63. The New Normal

Anne and Bill Ehrhart, Amy Vedder and Bill Weber at the Adirondack Experience Museum, July 2022 (author's photo).

bubble—I can't even keep up with all these narrow-minded myopic bubbles anymore—and never have to hear a single word that doesn't match their pre-conceived and largely shallow fact-absent beliefs. This is only a partial list.

And all of this, I'm told constantly, is the New Normal. I don't know. Maybe if you were born in 2012, or 2002, or maybe even 1992, all of this might pass as "normal." But it leaves me sad and discouraged as I approach the twilight of my life and try to imagine what things will be like in even twenty years, let alone fifty or sixty years from now.

It becomes ever more difficult to hope for a better future, to imagine that a better future is even possible. Fortunately—or maybe unfortunately, it's hard to tell—I can't just crawl under a rock and wait for my inevitable demise. I have to continue to interact with my wife, my daughter, my friends, the world around me without leaving everyone feeling like they've just had a run-in with Eeyore, the pessimistic, gloomy, depressed, anhedonic, old grey donkey of *Winnie the Pooh* fame.

And that brings me back to the friends Anne and I visited last week.

The New Normal

When they first began their work with mountain gorillas in Rwanda in the early 1980s, there were about 250 of them still alive in the Virunga mountain range (including parts of Congo and Uganda as well as Rwanda), and those were rapidly heading toward extinction. Amy and Bill convinced the Rwandan government that saving the gorillas would be far more beneficial to both the local population and the wider Rwandan business community if they saved the gorillas and allowed careful visits by tourists. In effect, these two then-young people invented eco-tourism, and they built a program so solid that it even survived the Rwandan civil war and genocide a decade later. Today, there are over 600 mountain gorillas in the park and the program is thriving.

Amy and Bill are almost preternaturally low-key about their work, and will tell you—with much truth, no doubt—that they had lots of help along the way. But the mountain gorillas of Rwanda would almost certainly be extinct today if not for these two people.[*]

I have found myself, especially in recent years, thinking of these two friends and trying hard to keep their example alive in my heart. I think of the remarkable impact of Greta Thunberg, a young schoolgirl who decided to stand up and say, "Enough." Or the work that Stacy Abrams did in Georgia to influence (legally) the outcome of the 2020 elections in her state. And only this week, the voters of Kansas—not exactly a left progressive hotbed—resoundingly offered our Supreme Court a clear rebuke over the denial of women's right to control their own bodies.

I don't like this New Normal. It sucks, frankly. I wish passionately that more of my fellow citizens were as uncomfortable and unhappy with it as I am. But as the saying goes, "Where there's life, there's hope" (a saying variously attributed to *Ecclesiastes*, the Roman comic playwright Publius Terentius Afer, or J.R.R. Tolkien, take your pick).

So even if it all ends as badly as I fear it's going to, in the immortal words of Monty Python, "I'm not dead yet." And my wife and I had a really good time in the Adirondacks with Amy and Bill.

---

[*] You can read the story of Vedder and Weber in *In the Kingdom of Gorillas: the Quest to Save Rwanda's Mountain Gorillas*, published by Simon & Schuster.

64

Trumpster Nation

(*LA Progressive*, August 24, 2022; *New Hampshire Gazette*, August 26, 2022; *The Intelligencer*, August 28, 2022; *Bucks County Courier Times*, August 29, 2022)

Recently, I had occasion to drive the length of the Pennsylvania Turnpike all the way to the Ohio border. Western Pennsylvania is beautiful and mountainous. It is also, for the most part, solid Trump Country. Indeed, aside from Philadelphia and its suburban counties, and less dependably Pittsburgh, the entire state is as red as a male cardinal.

I did not see a single billboard supporting Democrat John Fetterman's bid to win a U.S. senate seat. And the only billboard mentioning current Democratic state attorney general Josh Shapiro's run for the governorship was sponsored by his Republican opponent and Trump-endorsed Doug Mastriano, that said, "If You Love Higher Murder Rates, You'll Love Josh Shapiro," and included huge photos of Shapiro and Joe Biden with a big grin giving a thumbs-up.

But my favorite was a highly visible tractor-trailer perched on a hillside along the highway with TRUMP in huge red block letters painted on it. Below that, in smaller black block lettering, were the words GOD, GUNS, FREEDOM, and NO SOCIALISM.

This is not just a Pennsylvania phenomenon. Trumpism has taken hold across the length and breadth of this nation. And as I drove along on my way to Detroit, hours and hundreds of miles away, I had plenty of time to think. Why would anyone imagine that Number 45 has anything to do with "God," this man who holds upside down a Bible he's never read and brags about grabbing women by their genitals?

"Guns" I kind of get, though I don't agree with it. If you're steeped in gun culture, I suppose it's possible to believe that "guns don't kill people," and maybe the guy with that trailer likes to hunt deer (I hope he eats what he kills) or shoot varmints around his farm. But "freedom"?

What We Can and Can't Afford

Does he mean the freedom of #45 to play by his own rules, turn lying into an art form, cheat on everything from his wives to his taxes, thumb his nose at the Constitution, and foment insurrection?

And as for "No Socialism," that one just drives me bugfuck. What does the guy with that trailer think Social Security is? And Medicare? I don't know who that guy is, but I know a lot of Trumpsters who are all on Social Security and Medicare, and don't even know such programs are socialism-in-action.

How does that guy and others like him think they get drinkable water when they turn on their taps? That the crap they flush down the toilet gets treated and disposed of? That their roads get plowed when it snows, and paved when they get too full of potholes? That someone will pick up the phone when they dial 911, and send police or an ambulance if they need help?

All of these things, and a whole lot more, are socialism-in-action. Everyone pays into a common fund, and that money is then used for the common good.

Indeed, the biggest socialist organization in this country is the United States military. Everyone with the same rank gets pretty much the same pay, regardless of their jobs, whether you're a private or a general. Everyone gets free housing, free clothing, free medical care, free dental care, and free food.

We're not talking Communism here. We're not talking Karl Marx or Joseph Stalin and Mao Zedong: "you will work in a steel mill, and you will go to the country and grow rice, and this factory had better produce 500 tractors a month or you will be shot for treason." That's not what socialism is.

I don't suppose that guy with the trailer ever stopped to think about it, but Jesus Christ himself was a socialist. He healed the sick and didn't even charge them for His services. He provided counseling and advice, and fed the multitudes, and all for free. He got really angry with the greedy capitalists who had taken over the temple. He criticized the Pharisees and their "holier-than-thou" elitism, and stood up for the poor and the outcast and the downtrodden.

That's what I found myself thinking about as I wiled away the hours driving to Detroit. What would Jesus think of Donald Trump? Or Mitch McConnell, or Lindsey Graham, or Kevin McCarthy, or even Joe Manchin? Which model of rifle would Jesus buy? Who would Jesus vote for in November 2022?

Don't get me wrong. I don't have a very good opinion of Democrats,

64. Trumpster Nation

either. To a very large degree, the foibles and corruption and incompetence of the Democrats over the past forty years have a lot to do with how we've all ended up in this mess. And I could go on at length about the Democrats' willingness to lock up whistle blowers, and toss around drone missiles like they're handing out American flags at a 4th of July parade, and genuflect to Big $$$$ like they were, well, Republicans.

But I hope the guy who put that trailer out there along the Pennsylvania Turnpike doesn't get the future he's wishing for. He may not like it as much as he thinks he will. And I'm damned sure I won't like it at all.

65

Why I Like to Watch Bike Racing

(*Hollywood Progressive*, September 4, 2022; *Peace & Planet News*, Fall 2022; *New Hampshire Gazette*, September 9, 2022)

For the past week and a half, I've been watching *La Vuelta a Espana*, the Tour of Spain bicycle race. I've watched *Le Tour de France* every July for the past twenty-five years, and since the coronavirus showed up, I've taken to watching *la Vuelta* as well.

I enjoy watching sports in general because you never know how it's going to end until it ends. And I especially like watching bike racing because it is so international with riders from all over Europe, the Americas, Australia, New Zealand, and even the Middle East, Central Asia, and Africa. There are teams sponsored by Bahrain, the United Arab Emirates, and Israel, and the riders themselves are a mix of nationalities. Of the 184 riders representing 23 teams, only three riders in this year's *Vuelta* are from the United States.

One never hears those mindless chants of "USA! USA!" One is not subjected to the mandatory "Ladies and gentlemen, please stand and remove your hats for our national anthem." No one drags a giant American flag across the starting line as if I'm going to forget what country I live in if I don't see the Stars-n-Stripes thirty-seven times a day. And there is never a military flyover with F-16s or A-10s or Apache helicopters (oh, the irony of that name, but don't get me started).

Don't misunderstand me. I am an American citizen. I've never missed voting in an election—general, primary, or special—since the first time I was eligible to vote over half a century ago. I am an honorably discharged U.S. Marine, and I've never felt any need to remove the "USMC" tattooed on my left arm. I pay my taxes. There are many things about my country that I like very much.

65. Why I Like to Watch Bike Racing

But I am not "proud" to be an American because there are a lot of things I don't like about this country, nor should any other thinking person. Our wars of extermination against the original inhabitants of this country, for instance. Or our embrace of slavery as a major source of labor and therefore wealth, and the ongoing and often legalized subordination of those former slaves. Our wars of aggression against Mexico, Spain, the Philippines, much of Central America, and in more recent times Vietnam, Grenada, Panama, and Iraq. Our wars against organized labor in the 19th and 20th centuries. Just to name a few of the things I'm not proud of.

You may want to argue about some or all of the points I've made in the preceding paragraph, but I have history and the facts on my side, not national mythology or myopia. Ask Little Turtle or Black Kettle or Frederick Douglas or Emmet Till or Emilio Aguinaldo or Maurice Bishop or Augusto Sandino or Mother Jones. Critical Race Theory isn't critical race theory; it's just *history*.

And while the United States of America isn't an "evil empire," it isn't very exceptional, either. It is just another empire with aspects to be admired and aspects to be deplored and ashamed of.

Which is why I object to the kind of chauvinistic jingoism I am subjected to every time I tune into an NFL or NHL or MLB or NASCAR event, and even at high school lacrosse matches and middle school spelling bees. No other country on earth postures so ridiculously except maybe North Korea. Nazi Germany used to posture like this. I think Stalin's Soviet Union did, too. Yet another reason I find myself embarrassed to be an American.

Just this morning, I saw a video clip of House Minority Leader Kevin McCarthy claiming that President Joe Biden is "dividing" the nation. This from a man who first criticized Trump for fomenting the January 6 insurrection only to block every subsequent attempt to hold the former president accountable. This from a man who refuses to condemn Trump for insisting that the results of the 2020 election are fraudulent. But Biden is "dividing, demeaning, and disparaging his fellow citizens"?

Never mind the long sweep of American history. How am I *not* supposed to be embarrassed by a country where nearly half the voters elect a vulgar, ignorant, narcissistic "reality show" conman president, nearly re-elect him for a second term, and then refuse to accept the outcome of what was arguably the most transparently honest election in U.S. history?

What We Can and Can't Afford

That's why I like to watch Grand Tour bicycle racing. The flags that fans wave along the bike route range from Denmark to the Netherlands, from Belgium to Wales (coolest flag in the world; it has a dragon on it!), from Slovenia to Italy. I've even learned to recognize the Basque, Breton, and Manx flags by watching bike racing.

And it's all mixed up together, just like the racers themselves: a Swiss flag here, a Slovak flag there, a Union Jack a little farther on. Indeed, bike racing is kind of like a United Nations on wheels. The way the UN is supposed to work. The way the world ought to work. And no one is shouting, "USA! USA!" As if that had anything to do with football or track & field or bicycles or the accident of birth by which I ended up an American instead of an Ethiopian.

Military History of W.D. Ehrhart

W.D. Ehrhart formally enlisted in the Marines on 11 April 1966, while still in high school, beginning active duty on 17 June. He graduated from basic recruit training at the Marine Corps Recruit Depot, Parris Island, South Carolina, as a private first class on 12 August and completed his basic infantry training at Camp Lejeune, North Carolina, on 12 September 1966. (While at Parris Island, he qualified as a rifle sharpshooter on 18 July 1966, subsequently qualifying as a rifle expert on 11 April 1968 and as a pistol sharpshooter on 24 April 1969.)

Assigned to the field of combat intelligence, Ehrhart spent 10 October to 15 December 1966 with Marine Air Group 26, a helicopter unit based at New River Marine Corps Air Facility, North Carolina, meanwhile completing a clerk typist course at Camp Lejeune in November 1966 and graduating first in his class from the Enlisted Basic Amphibious Intelligence School at Little Creek Amphibious Base, Norfolk, Virginia, in December 1966. He also completed a Marine Corps Institute combat intelligence correspondence course in December while at New River.

Before leaving for Vietnam on 9 February 1967, Ehrhart received additional combat training with the 3rd Replacement Company, Staging Battalion, Camp Pendleton, California, in January and February. Upon arrival in Vietnam, he was assigned to the 1st Battalion, 1st Marine Regiment, first as an intelligence assistant, later as assistant intelligence chief. In March 1967, he was temporarily assigned to the Sukiran Army Education Center, Okinawa, where he graduated first in his class from a course in basic Vietnamese terminology before returning to permanent assignment.

While in Vietnam, Ehrhart participated in the following combat operations: Stone, Lafayette, Early, Canyon, Calhoun, Pike, Medina, Lancaster, Kentucky I, Kentucky II, Kentucky III, Con Thien, Newton,

What We Can and Can't Afford

Osceola II, and Hue City. He was promoted to lance corporal on 1 April 1967 and to corporal on 1 July 1967.

Ehrhart was awarded the Purple Heart for wounds received during Operation Hue City, a commendation from the commanding general of the 1st Marine Division, two Presidential Unit Citations, the Navy Combat Action Ribbon, the Vietnam Service Medal with three stars, the Vietnamese Cross of Gallantry Unit Citation with palm, the Civil Action Meritorious Unit Citation, and the Vietnamese Campaign Medal. He completed his Vietnam tour on 28 February 1968.

Ehrhart was next assigned to the 2nd Marine Air Wing Headquarters Group at Cherry Point Marine Corps Air Station, North Carolina, from 30 March to 10 June 1968, where he was promoted to sergeant on 1 April. After a brief assignment with the Headquarters Squadron of Marine Air Group 15 based at Iwakuni Marine Corps Air Station, Japan, he was then reassigned to Marine Aerial Refueler Transport Squadron 152, Futenma Marine Corps Air Facility, Okinawa, from 20 July to 30 October 1968, where he received a commanding officer's meritorious mast.

Ehrhart completed his active duty with Marine Fighter Attack Squadron 122, based alternately at Iwakuni and Cubi Point Naval Air Station, Philippines, from 31 October 1968 to 30 May 1969. While in the Philippines, he completed a field course on jungle environmental survival in February 1969.

On 10 June 1969, Ehrhart was separated from active duty, receiving the Good Conduct Medal. While on inactive reserve, he was promoted to staff sergeant on 1 July 1971. He received an honorable discharge on 10 April 1972.

About the Author

W.D. Ehrhart was born in 1948 and grew up in Perkasie, Pennsylvania. After graduating from Pennridge High School in 1966, he enlisted in the U.S. Marine Corps at age 17, serving three years including 13 months in Vietnam. He has since earned a Bachelor of Arts from Swarthmore College, a Master of Arts from the University of Illinois at Chicago Circle, and a Doctor of Philosophy from the University of Wales at Swansea, UK.

In his 20s and early 30s, he worked a variety of jobs including construction worker, forklift operator, newspaper reporter, magazine writer, merchant seaman, and legal assistant for the Pennsylvania Department of Justice Office of the Special Prosecutor. He has since taught sporadically at three Friends Schools and several colleges, as well as holding an appointment as Visiting Professor of War & Social Consequences at the University of Massachusetts at Boston. He recently retired after 18 years as a Master Teacher of English & History at the Haverford School for Boys.

Over the years, Ehrhart has been awarded a Mary Roberts Rinehart Grant, two Fellowships from the Pennsylvania Arts Council, the President's Medal from Veterans for Peace, a Pew Fellowship in the Arts, and an Excellence in the Arts Award from Vietnam Veterans of America. His writing has appeared in hundreds of publications ranging from the *American Poetry Review, North American Review, Virginia Quarterly Review,* and *Utne Reader* to *USA Today, Reader's Digest,* the *Los Angeles Times,* and the *New York Times.*

Index

Abrams, Stacy 230
Adams, John 110
Adams, Samuel 87
Agnew, Spiro 61, 62, 68
Aguinaldo, Emilio 235
Aldrich, Thomas Bailey 165
Alito, Samuel 123, 226
Amis, Kingsley 6
Anderson, Brooke 76

Baky, John 196
Bannon, Steve 176, 178
Baradar, Abdul Ghani 161
Barrett, Amy Coney 226
Barry, Jan 17, 77, 105–108
Battelle, Richard K. 22, 25, 26, 30
Beanie the Cat 133–134
Behringer, Harriette 5, 8
Bezos, Jeff 171
Biden, Joseph Robinette (Joe) 115, 122, 124, 130, 131, 134, 135, 140, 142–145, 147, 153, 161, 163, 175, 176, 177, 193, 195, 235
Bishop, Maurice 235
Black Kettle 235
Blackburn, Marsha 161
Blackmon, Douglas A. 171
Blunt, Roy 152
Bly, Robert 121
Boebert, Lauren 148, 153, 187, 226
Boehner, John 66
Booker, Cory 115
Braestrup, Peter 26
Braunstein, Larry 116
Breyer, Stephen 123
Brokaw, Tom 5
Brown, Jim 155
Bryant, Anita 9
Bundy, Cliven 148
Burke, Edmund 140
Burns, Ken 166
Bush, George H.W. 41, 54, 128, 143
Bush, George W. 41, 66, 72, 161
Butler, Smedley D. 59, 204–211

Calley, William 57
Captain Kangaroo 215
Carlson, Tucker 138, 161
Carruth, Hayden 6
Carter, Robert III 167–169, 170
Castile, Philando 126
Chao, Elaine 138
Cheney, Dick 66, 161
Cheney, Liz 176
Child, Lydia Maria 171
Churchill, Winston 58
Clark, Laverne Ray 22, 27
Clark, Petula 43
Cleland, John 167
Clinton, Bill 143
Clinton, Hillary 137, 143
Clyde, Andrew 152
Cohen, Leonard 223
Cole, Nat "King" 62
Coleman, Horace 76–77
Collins, Robert "Bo" 206
Columbus (Christopher) 12
Conti, Edward 183
Conti, Evelyn *see* Ehrhart, Evelyn
Conti, Geneva 182, 183
Conti, Ottavio 182, 183
Conti, Ruth Elaine 183
Costello, John 138
Cox, Joseph T. 205
Crane, Stephen 198–199
Cronauer, Adrian 47
Crozier, Brett 116, 118
Cruz, Nikolas 111, 226
Cruz, Ted 138
Cuchulain 224

Davidon, William 39
Debs, Eugene 205
Denton, Jeremiah 150
DeVos, Betsy 138
Dickinson, Emily 167
Dickinson, John 110
Diehl, John 191
Diem, Ngo Dinh 58, 95, 179
DiRienz, John A., Jr. 22, 26

What We Can and Can't Afford

Dole, Sanford 59
Dostoyevsky, Fyodor 74
Douglas, Frederick 235
Douglas, Keith 6
Dundon, Evelyn 183

Eeyore 229
Ehrhart, Anne 201, 217, 228–230
Ehrhart, Evelyn (Conti) 182, 183
Ehrhart, John H. 183
Ehrhart, Leela 122–124, 209
Eisenhower, Dwight 60, 209
Ellsberg, Daniel 57
Emerson, Gloria 13, 219, 221
Emerson, Ralph Waldo 218

Feinstein, Diane 115
Fetterman, John 231
Floyd, George 126, 153, 169
Forsyth, Keith 39
Fowle, Steve 2, 195, 196, 216
Franklin, Benjamin 148, 171, 213, 226
Franklin, H. Bruce 149, 150
Franklin, Robert (Robbie) 1
Freneau, Philip 199–200
Frontera, Joseph 22, 26
Fussell, Paul 3–8, 167

Gaddafi, Muammar 41
Garner Eric 126
Gehlot, Betsy 35
Gerry, Elbridge 174
Gibbon, Edward 174
Gillen, Mike 207
Gingrich, Newt 154
Ginsburg, Ruth Bader 123
Godshall, Kathryn 34
Goodspeed, Tyler 138
Gorsuch, Neil 123, 226
Gosar, Paul 152, 176
Graham, Lindsey 131, 138, 142, 152, 232
Grant, John 4, 7
Gravel, Marcus 82
Graves, Robert 4
Gray, Freddie 126
Gray, J. Glenn 6
Greene, Marjorie Taylor 153, 226
Gregory, Dick 66
Grisham, Stephanie 138
Grosz, Otto L., Jr. 22, 27–28
Gruner, Elliot 149, 150
Guthrie, Woody 165, 170

Hackman, Gene 150
Haines, Harry 196
Hamilton, Alexander 110
Hannity, Sean 138
Harris, Eric 226
Harris, Kamala 115, 130, 131

Hawley, Josh 138, 152, 161, 176–177, 187
Hayden, Tom 66
Heinl, Robert J., Jr. 52, 54, 88
Hellman, Wayne "Pud" 191
Hemingway, Ernest 218
Henry, Patrick 166, 167, 168
Hitler, Adolf 132
Ho Chi Minh 57, 92, 93, 94, 95, 166, 179
Hoffman, Abbie 66
Hoffman, Daniel 3, 8, 16–17
Hollenbach, Robert (Bob) 191
Hoover, Herbert 209
Hoover, J. Edgar 38–39
Horace 214
Housel, Fred 205, 206
Howarth, David 167
Howe, Julia Ward 171–172
Hughes, Langston 126, 189, 190
Hussein, Saddam 41, 54

Ingraham, Laura 138
Irish, Jane 184, 216
Isaacs, Arnold 162

Jackson, Andrew 140
Jefferson, Thomas 167, 168, 169
Jenner, Caitlin 67
Jesus of Nazareth 114, 143, 232
Johnson, Lyndon B. 9, 82, 92, 179, 180
Johnson, Samuel 6, 69
Jones, Lowell E. 22, 26
Joplin, Janis 62

Kaepernick, Colin 70, 71
Kagan, Elena 123
Karcher, Carolyn 219
Kavanaugh, Brett 123, 226
Kehs, Beverly 35
Kehs, Janice 35
Kehs, Judie see Much, Judie
Kehs, Kathryn see Godshall, Kathryn
Kehs, Walter L. ("Casey") 20–35
Kelly, Devin 85
Kelly, John 129
Kennedy, John F. 58, 63, 65
Kerry, John 40, 115
Key, Francis Scott 164
Khan, Ghazala 129
Khan, Khizr 129
Khashoggi, Jamal 142
Khruschchev, Nikita 63, 74, 92, 193
Khue, Le Minh 218
King, Martin Luther, Jr. 57, 62, 165, 189
Kinnell, Galway 121
Kirsten, Lincoln 6
Kissinger, Henry 9
Klebold, Dylan 226
Kyle, Sharon 2

242

20. Index

Laden, Osama bin 162
La Follette, Robert 206
Lanza, Adam 85, 111, 226
La Pierre, Wayne 148
Lazarus, Emma 164
Lembcke, Jerry 51, 78, 149–151
Levy, Andrew 167
Liliuokalani 59
Limbaugh, Rush 66
Lincoln, Abraham 65, 182, 184
Little Turtle 235
Liuzzo, Viola 13
Loewen, James 60, 172
Logan, Doug 153
London, Jack 218
Lyons, Paul 5, 66, 167
Lyons, Chaplain Richard 81–83

MacArthur, Douglas 209, 210
Macron, Emmanuel 114, 136
Madison, James 147, 148, 168, 226
Manchin, Joe 154, 174, 232
Mao Zedong 232
Malcolm X 189
Marciano, John 61
Marcos, Imelda 136
Marshall, John 140
Marx, Karl 232
Massie, Thomas 187, 226
Mastriano, Doug 231
Mateen, Omar 111, 226
Mattis, James 129, 137
McAdoo, Jimmy 13
McCain, John 116, 128
McCarthy, Kevin 152, 156, 161, 232, 235
McConnell, Mitch 131, 138, 142, 152, 156, 174, 232
McFarland, Elizabeth (Liz Hoffman) 17
McGrath, Thomas 119–121
McKay, Claude 126, 189, 190
McKnight, Richard 22, 28
McNamara, Robert Strange 9, 96
Melville, Herman 167
Merkel, Angela 136
Miller, Mrs. (Elva Ruby) 43
Miller, William J. 22, 24, 25, 26, 34
Moffat, Abbott 95
Mother Jones 235
Much, Dave 35
Much, Judie 35
Mulvaney, Mick 138
Mussolini, Benito 132, 209

Nagl, John 40
Negroponte, John 66
Nero 215
Nicholson, Jack 190
Nixon, Richard 9, 57, 149

Norris, Chuck 150
Novick, Lynn 166

Obama, Barack 50, 56, 57, 58, 72, 89, 143, 177
Ocasio-Cortez, Alexandria ("AOC") 176, 177, 211
Ochs, Phil 66
O'Reilly, Bill 66

Paddock, Stephen 85, 111, 226
Pappe, Ilan 219
Paquet, Basil 106
Parks, Rosa 125
Patton, George 209
Pence, Mike 141, 176
Poe, Edgar Allan 196, 197, 202
Pol Pot 173
Polk, James 59
Pompeo Mike 161
Pottinger, Matthew 138
Price, Dick 2
Publius Terentius Afer (Terence) 230
Putin, Vladimir 116, 132, 136, 193

Quayle, Dan 66

Radziminski, Edwin F. 22, 27
Raines, Bonnie 39
Raines, John 39
Ramos, Salvador 226
Rapinoe, Megan 141
Rawlings, Doug 223
Reagan, Ronald 52, 53, 54, 56, 67
Redding, Otis 47
Rice, Tamar 126
Rich, Adrienne 121
Risner, Robinson 150
Roberts, John 123, 226
Robin, Larry 5
Rogovin, Paula 105
Roof, Dylann 226
Roosevelt, Franklin D. 92, 170–171, 211
Roosevelt, Theodore 59
Rosenberg, Issac 6
Ross, Diana 46
Rottmann, Larry 106
Rukeyser, Muriel 121
Rumsfeld, Donald 161
Rush, Larry 183
Rusk, Dean 36
Rustin, Bayard 13, 66
Ryder, Mitch 47

Saint Marie, Buffy 43
Salman, Mohammed bin 142
Sanders, Bernie 67, 113–115, 124, 131, 177, 187, 211

243

What We Can and Can't Afford

Sandino, Augusto 235
Sartwell, Crispin 216
Sassoon, Siegfried 5
Scalia, Antonin 102, 227
Schlafly, Phyllis 9
Schurz, Carl 71, 166
Shakespeare, William 12, 90, 100, 186, 188
Shapiro, Josh 231
Sherman, Roger 110
Sinema, Kyrsten 174
Sirica, John 13
Skywalker, Luke 72
Smith, Bob 73
Sophocles 12
Sotomayor, Sonia 123
Spock, Benjamin 66
Stalin, Joseph 232
Stallone, Sylvester 150
Steele, Danielle 74
Stern, Fred 119
Stockdale, James 150
Strunk, William 3
Summers, Harry, Jr. 36

Taney, Roger 163
Taylor, Beonna 126
Thieu, Nguen Van 157
Thomas, Clarence 123, 226, 227
Thoreau, Henry David 218
Thunberg, Greta 230
Thune, John 152
Till, Emmet 235
Toha, Mosab abu 218–221
Tolkien, J.R.R. 230
Trudeau, Justin 136
Truman, Harry S. 5, 57
Trump, Donald 90, 113, 115, 116–118, 122, 123, 128–132, 133–135, 136–139, 146, 152, 161, 174, 175, 176, 178, 179, 231–233
Trump, Ivanka 137
Trung Sisters 96
Tryon, Kevin 184
Tuberville, Tommy 153
Twain, Mark 71
Tynan, Gene 22, 26, 28, 33, 34

Un, Kim Jong 136
Updike, John 167

Vedder, Amy 228–230
Vindman, Alexander 129
Voltaire (François-Marie Arouet) 167

Wallace, George 9, 64
Washington, George 110, 148, 167, 169, 171, 226
Washington, Martha 169
Weber, Bill 228–230
Wedderburn, Alexander 171
Westmoreland, William 82
White, E.B. 3
Whitman, Walt 60, 218
Wilbur, Gene 150
Wilbur, Tom 149–151
Wilde, Oscar 1
Will, George 41
Winthrop, John 59
Woodham-Smith, Cecil 167

Young, Marilyn 96

Zinn, Howard 172
Zoelick, Robert 66

www.ingramcontent.com/pod-product-compliance
Lightning Source LLC
Chambersburg PA
CBHW032037300426
44117CB00009B/1089